D1619506

Visions of the Real
Modern Houses in the 20th Century I
20世紀のモダン・ハウス：理想の実現 I

Guest Editors: Ken Tadashi Oshima and Toshiko Kinoshita
ゲスト・エディター：ケン・タダシ・オオシマ　木下壽子

Foreward
編集者序文

Before the Dawn

The 20th century can be remembered as a century when industrialization developed at an unprecedented pace. Henry Ford popularized the automobile, ushering in the age of mass production and mass consumption. Patterns of everyday life changed as living environments were adapted to the emerging systems of industrial society. Massive consumption of resources, mass transportation systems, finance, urbanization, internationalization — all of these brought about unprecedented changes in our lifestyles.

As an editor with first-hand knowledge of only a small fragment of the 20th century, I have had few chances to directly experience the historical backgrounds that lie behind the modern houses which appear in books and publications. However, this does not mean that these houses can only be experienced through plans and the black and white photos of the time. Moreover, I learned from guest editor Ken Tadashi Oshima's series of articles on modern houses in the postwar period that many of these houses exist in good condition and are still lived in. This discovery provided the incentive to reexamine the modern house in this special issue.

This two-volume issue is therefore not simply a historical record of 33 modern houses. The houses introduced here were surely shaped by their architect's vision of the future and a variety of perspectives on the age that was to come. The following photos taken over the past three years should provide material for examining, as of the year 2000, the way in which residents have interpreted the vision behind the architect's proposal and turned the architect's ideals into reality. According to the Italian philosopher Benedetto Croce, "All history is contemporary history. History is possible only because we look at the past through the eyes of the present and understand the past in the context of contemporary problems." Based on this premise, the 33 modern houses introduced here should have much to tell us about the present. Through a close examination of these houses, we should find a number of hints to direct our own visions of the future.

At the onset of the 21st century, the age of industrialization is giving way to the age of information. Although we are still without a clear vision of the future, we can sense signs of change. New experiments are being made every day in the practice of architects, and new developments are sure to appear in the house, as the environment of everyday life.

The dawn is near.

(Translated by Thomas Donahue)

Nobuyuki Yoshida,
Publisher/Editor

夜明け前

20世紀は工業化がかつてないスピードで展開した世紀であろう。

フォードが自動車を大衆化させ、大量生産、大量消費社会が始まり、人々の生活はこれら工業社会システムに適応する環境をつぎつぎとつくりだしてきた。膨大な資源消費、大量輸送システム、金融、都市化、国際化など、このような要素が、我々の生活スタイルをかつてないほどに変化させてきた。

20世紀のほんの一部しか知らない編集者は、様々な書物のなかで登場するモダン・ハウスが建てられたこの歴史的な背景を実際の経験のなかで捉えることはできない。しかし、これらの多くが、単に書物のなかでみられる当時のモノクロ写真や図面でしか経験できないものではなく、現在でも生活の場としてそこに存在していることを、本書のゲスト・エディターであるオオシマさんから知らされ、それらをもう一度検証したいと思ったことが、この本をつくるきっかけであった。

それゆえ、本書は単に、I・II巻合わせ33作品のモダン・ハウスを紹介した記録書ではない。ここに紹介される住宅は、建築家が来るべき新しい時代を読み取り、それぞれが抱いた時代へのヴィジョン、それを投影させた住宅であるものと確信する。

2000年の現在、それぞれの住宅に提案した建築家のヴィジョンが住み手にどのように理解され、建築家の理想をどのように現実化してきたのかは、我々がこの3年間で新たに撮った写真から読み取ることができるであろう。

そしてイタリアの哲学者クローチェが言うように「すべての歴史は現代史である。もともと歴史というのは現在の目を通して、現在の問題に照らし合わせて過去をみるところにより成り立つ」のであるならば、我々はここに紹介する33のモダン・ハウスを検証することで、現在を検証し、さらに我々のこれからのヴィジョンを見つめるヒントを発見することが可能なのではないだろうか。

21世紀を目前とした我々は、工業化社会から情報化社会へと変化してゆくなかで、いまだ明確なヴィジョンを示すに至っていない。しかし、このような変化の兆しを察知した新たな試みが、建築家たちにより、日々、行われているであろうし、それはおそらく人々の生活の場である住宅のなかで展開しているのであろう。

夜明けは近い。

Architecture and Urbanism
March 2000 Special Issue
Visions of the Real:
Modern Houses in the 20th Century I

建築と都市
2000年3月臨時増刊号
20世紀のモダン・ハウス：理想の実現 I

Volume I: 1900-1949

Contents

Volume II: 1950-1975

Front cover:
Tugendhat House by Mies van der Rohe.
Back cover:
Dammann House by Arne Korsmo.
p. 2: Une Petite Maison by Le Corbusier.
Photographs by Shinkenchiku-sha.

I 巻: 1900-1949

目次

II 巻 1950-1975

表紙：ミース・ファン・デル・ローエ、
　　　トゥーゲントハット邸
裏表紙：アルネ・コルスモ、ダマン邸
扉裏：ル・コルビュジエ、小さな家―母の家
撮影：新建築社写真部

Introduction
Towards a Vision of the Real
Ken Tadashi Oshima

The primordial instinct of every human being is to assure himself of a shelter. The various classes of workers in society to-day no longer have dwellings adapted to their needs; neither the artisan nor the intellectual.[1]

Le Corbusier, *Vers une Architecture*, 1923

A study of the single-family house — man's most intimate environment — enables one to understand better than anything else whether a man really knows how to build.[2]

Sigfried Giedion, 1951

These statements, by master architect Le Corbusier and modern movement proponent/ historian Sigfried Giedion, underscore a fundamental challenge to twentieth-century architects — namely, how to create living spaces suited to the dwelling needs of a rapidly modernizing world. Despite the critical social importance of the modern house, architectural media have often promoted houses as pure formal objects isolated from their particular context — the context of design process, and of the relations between architect, client, and society so crucial to their creation. For example, the Museum of Modern Art's 1932 exhibition catalogue, *Modern Architecture* (for a show better publicized since through Henry Russell Hitchcock and Philip Johnson's *The International Style*), featured Mies van der Rohe's landmark Tugendhat house (1930) as an abstract white box, not an inhabited space, on its cover. For Mies himself, however, form was not a goal, but resulted from the resolution of building problems, a resolution that could "only be understood as a living process." In the Tugendhat house, as in his other residential designs, Mies grappled with a wide variety of forces in tension. His exploration of new building materials like steel and glass did not preclude his use of vernacular prototypes. In addition, the design of living space, furniture, and light fixtures as a *total work of art*, or *Gesamtkunstwerk*, did not impede the creation of a hygenic living space bathed in sunlight. Finally, while Mies designed the Tugendhat house as a private residence for the Tugendhats, its widely published photographs also revealed the project to public gaze.

Visions of the Real examines architects' attempts to resolve the complex social, technical, and artistic problems of house design in the twentieth century. This two-volume special issue explores visions of domesticity throughout the architects' extended design process: from drawings, to built reality, to realized inhabitation, and then through the building's evolution over time. This collection presents original drawings and historical photographs together with new photographs that show how the initial vision has endured — to evaluate, as Giedion demanded, how well these architects knew how to build.

In this special edition, some familiar modern masterworks are featured, but some of the boundaries of the established canon are also questioned. For example, lesser-known works like the early Petite Maison (1923) and the later Maison Curutchet in Argentina (1949) illustrate the extent and development of Le Corbusier's smaller residences. As Bruno Reichlin notes, this development can also be traced through a "Stories of Windows." The ubiquitously published Villa Savoye (1929–31) appears not simply as an iconic masterwork, but also reflecting the vicissitudes of time, in Arthur Rüegg's essay on the complicated story of color in its preservation. Amancio Williams' House over the Brook (1945) in Argentina, although an important building, has remained relatively unknown until recently, remote as it is from centers of architectural journalism. Finally, the fall of the Iron Curtain in 1989 has led to the renovation of houses such as the Tugendhat house in the Czech Republic and Konstantin Melnikov's own house in Russia (1929), enabling them to be properly photographed in color.

Notes:
1. Le Corbusier, *Vers une Architecture* (trans. as *Towards a New Architecture*, New York: Praeger Publishers, 1970, p. 269).
2. Sigfried Giedion, "The Humanization of Urban Life (1951, 1952)," in *Architecture You and Me: Diary of a Development* (Cambridge, MA: Harvard University Press, 1958), p. 125.

理想の実現をめざして

ケン・タダシ・オオシマ

木下壽子訳

自らのシェルターを確保する本能は、すべての人間に根本的に備わっている。職人、知識階級の別なく、今日、社会のあらゆる階層の労働者たちは、もはや彼らの要求に応じた住宅をもっていない。

ル・コルビュジエ、『建築をめざして』[1] (1923)

人間が建物を建てる術を本当に知っているかどうかを理解するには、戸建て住宅 —人間にとって最も身近な環境— の研究がなによりの近道である。

ジークフリート・ギーディオン[2] (1951)

Above: Tugendhat house, Brno, Mies van der Rohe, 1930. Below: Villa Savoye, Poissy, Le Corbusier, 1929–31.

上：トゥーゲントハット邸、ブルノ、ミース・ファン・デル・ローエ、1930年。下：サヴォア邸、ポアジー、コルビュジエ、1929～31年。

原註

1-ル・コルビュジエ、『建築をめざして』（吉阪隆正 訳、鹿島出版会、1972年）。

2-ジークフリート・ギーディオン、『現代建築の発展』（生田勉、樋口清 訳、みすず書房、1961年）。

訳註1-ここではタイトルの「Visions of the Real」を「理想の実現」と訳したが、ヴィジョンには、理想像という意味以外に先見の明、未来像、見解といった意味がある。したがって、文中では「vision」という単語をあえて訳さず、「ヴィジョン」としている。

近代建築の巨匠、ル・コルビュジエと、歴史家で近代建築運動の弁護者であったジークフリート・ギーディオンによる上記の声明は、20世紀において建築家が挑んだ課題の本質が何であったかを端的に示唆している。それはすなわち、急激に近代化する世界を前にして、新たに発生した居住に関わる要求に応じた住空間をいかにつくりだすか、という課題であった。このように近代において「住宅」は社会的にきわめて重要な問題であったにもかかわらず、建築メディアは、しばしばモダン・ハウスを、設計プロセス、建築家と施主の関係、そのデザインを成立させた社会的背景といった、個々の住宅に固有の文脈から切り離された純粋なオブジェとして推奨してきた。たとえば、ニューヨーク近代美術館（MoMA）で1932年に行われた「近代建築」展（展覧会と同時に出版された『インターナショナル・スタイル』と題する出版物を通してより広く知られている）の展覧会カタログの表紙のなかで、ミース・ファン・デル・ローエの記念碑的な作品であるトゥーゲントハット邸(1930)は、住空間というよりも抽象的な白い箱として扱われている。しかしミースにとって形態は最終的な目的ではなく、建築的問題、すなわち「生きたプロセスとしてのみ理解しうる」問題の解決によって得られた結果にすぎなかった。ミースは自らが手がけた他の住宅建築と同様に、トゥーゲントハット邸のデザインにおいても様々な対立し合う要素を巧みに取り扱った。彼は、鉄やガラスといった新しい材料を探求することによって、ヴァナキュラー(訳註 2)な先例に倣うことをやめはしなかった。また、総合芸術としての居住空間、家具、そして照明器具のトータルなデザインが、太陽の光に満ちた衛生的な住空間を生み出すことを妨げはしなかった。さらにミースは、この邸宅をトゥーゲントハット家のプライヴェートな住宅としてデザインしたが、その一方で、出版物にこの住宅の写真が繰り返し紹介された結果、それはパブリックな関心を集めることとなったのである。

『20世紀のモダン・ハウス：理想の実現』では、20世紀において、いかに建築家たちが住宅デザインの複雑な社会的、技術的、そして芸術的問題を解決しようと試みたかを考察する。この二巻からなる臨時増刊号において我々は、建築図面、その建物の実態、現実の住生活、さらには時間の経過とともにその住宅が経験した変化に至るまで、デザイン・プロセスを幅広く考察することによって住生活にたいして抱かれたヴィジョンを考察することを試みた。また、建築家の当初のヴィジョンがいかに持続したかを示す上で、オリジナル図面と当時の写真を、新たに撮り下ろされた写真とともに紹介している。それは、ギーディオンが問うように、20世紀の建築家たちが建物を建てる術をどの程度心得ていたかを評価することにもなるだろう。

本号では、すでによく知られているモダン・ハウスの名作もいくつか登場するが、同時に西欧を中心とした既存の規範的枠組みを問い直している。たとえばル・コルビュジエの住宅として、ここではすでに頻繁に出版物を通して紹介されてきたサヴォア邸ではなく、彼の小規模な住宅の広がりと展開を説明するために、初期の作品である「小さな家」(1923)と後期の作品であるアルゼンチンの「クルチェット邸」(1949)を取り上げた。ブルーノ・ライヒリンが彼のエッセイのなかでも述べているように、この展開は「窓の物語」にも見出すことができるだろう。サヴォア邸については、この住宅の修復の際に明らかになった複雑な「色」の問題を考察したアルトゥール・リュエッグのエッセイのなかで、単にイコン的な名作としてではなく、時間の推移を反映するものとして取り上げられている。アルゼンチンにあるアマンシオ・ウィリアムズの「小川に架かる家」(1945)は、きわめて重要な建物であるにもかかわらず、地理的に建築ジャーナリズムの中心から遠く離れていたため最近

The current reality of these architects' visions is inevitably complex. While photographs typically show self-contained, carefully-framed design perfection, many of the new images depict the result of painstaking restorations, like those of Richard Neutra's Desert house (1946) and the Maison Curutchet. Many of the houses are still inhabited as originally designed, but some are preserved as museums and have only been brought to their current pristine state after a long period of decay and neglect. Wolf Tegethoff's essay on the history of the Tugendhat house since its completion examines such a complex story. Further, a dialogue with Kenneth Frampton underscores the need for an ongoing reevaluation of the nature of the modern house. The buildings published here each remain visionary in their own way, transcending the time of their making and their specific function, and continuing to provide inspiration for the twenty-first century.

Old versus New: Vernacular Sources and Modern Materials

The modern house is defined very broadly in *Visions of the Real* as innovative dwellings responsive to contemporary needs for living that were realized in the twentieth century. But the roots of the modern house lie in the nineteenth century, first planted by ideals of domestic reform, which demanded the rational re-design of the plan, structure, and furnishings of the bourgeois home. These reforms can be seen in Hvitträsk (1903), the first house featured in this volume, which embodies the idea of the house as a total work of art embracing vernacular prototypes. Hvitträsk, like other twentieth-century houses, owes a great debt to the nineteenth-century theorization of the English house. As articulated in German architect Hermann Muthesius's (1861–1927) influential book, *Das Englische Haus* (1904), this theorization sprang from the reformist ideologies of John Ruskin (1819–1900) and William Morris (1834–1896), who wished to mitigate the harmful effects of the Industrial Revolution. For Morris, "the core of the life of communities should not be factories but houses." These were not elite palaces, but small, detached houses. Although humble in scale, these nineteenth-century English dwellings were complete environments, and for Morris included "giving dignity of form to the objects of daily use," through the complete design of the interior. Thus, to counter the disjunctions of nineteenth-century life produced by the alienation associated with the division of labor, Morris created a residential *Gesamtkunstwerk*. This idea of the house, as a design unified at all scales, was to become one of the most pressing themes of the modern dwelling.

Above: The Red House, Kent, Philip Webb, 1859.

上：赤い家、ケント、フィリップ・ウェ
ッブ、1859年。

The principles that Morris envisioned are saliently expressed in Morris's own Red House, built by his associate Philip Webb in 1859. Like Hvitträsk, this red brick house, which broke away from the cold grip of classicism to draw from vernacular masonry techniques, expressed Morris's concern for structural integrity, and his desire to integrate the dwelling with its site and local culture. The Red House, like the buildings of C.F.A. Voysey and Baillee Scott, achieved these aims through a simple, practical design using local materials and sensitive site layout, and reflecting a deep respect for traditional building methods. These early examples of the modern house were thus not abstract artistic creations; they used vernacular architecture as a prototype. As Muthesius noted, the vernacular house "possessed everything that had been sought and desired: simplicity of feeling, structural suitability, natural forms instead of adaptations from the architecture of the past, rational and practical design, rooms of agreeable shape, color and the harmonious effect that had in former times resulted spontaneously from an organic development based on local conditions."[3]

In contrast to domestic reform based on vernacular precedents, another vision of the modern house sought to rethink the idea of the home through the optimal use of modern materials. Building on the rationalism of Prussian architect Karl Friedrich Schinkel, Viennese architect Otto Wagner articulated this notion in his book, *Moderne Architektur* (1896). Here he asserted that building must be based on three principle themes: "simplicity in the accommodation of modern needs," avoidance of "the artistic and ethical ruin of eclecticism," and "a new style based on present technologies and methods of construction."[4] Wagner designed his own rationalized neoclassical villas as the ideal location for the

3. Hermann Muthesius, *The English House*, [trans. of 1904 German text] (New York: Rizzoli, 1979), p. 15–16.
4. Otto Wagner, *Modern Architecture* (Santa Monica, CA: Getty Center Texts, 1988), p. 29.

まで比較的知名度が低かったが、近年ようやく正当な評価がなされるようになった。さらに1989年の冷戦の終結は、チェコ共和国のトゥーゲントハット邸や、ロシアのコンスタンティン・メルニコフ自邸(1929)といった重要な近代建築の修復を促し、近年、新たにカラーでの撮影が可能となった。

こうした建築家たちのヴィジョンが示す現状は、必然的にきわめて複雑である。写真はその性質上、独立し、注意深く縁取りされたデザインの完璧さを伝えているが、新しい画像の多くは、たとえばリチャード・ノイトラのカウフマン・デザート・ハウス(1946)やル・コルビュジエのクルチェット邸の場合、困難な修復事業の結果だけを映し出している。ここで紹介する住宅の多くは、現在も当初デザインされた通りに住まわれているが、なかには長い間放置された後に現在の良好な状態に修復され、博物館として保存されているものもある。ヴォルフ・テゲトフは、トゥーゲントハット邸完成後の歴史について記したエッセイのなかで、このような複雑な背景について考察している。さらにケネス・フランプトンは、筆者との対話のなかで、モダン・ハウスの本質についてさらに再評価を進める必要性を強調している。ここで取り上げた住宅は、それぞれ固有のヴィジョンを維持しつつ、建てられた時代や特定の機能を超越し、今後も21世紀に向けてインスピレーションを提供しつづけるであろう。

新旧の対立：ヴァナキュラーな伝統と近代の材料

この号ではモダン・ハウスを大まかに、20世紀に建てられた、住生活の現代的要求に応じた革新的な住宅と定義している。しかしモダン・ハウスのルーツは、中産階級の住宅の平面計画、構造、家具類を合理的にデザインし直すことを要求した、19世紀の住生活改革の理想にある。本号の最初に登場する「ヴィトラスク」(1903)は、ヴァナキュラーな先例を取り入れ、「総合芸術」としての住宅という思想を具体化した住宅であり、こうした19世紀の改革を反映している。他の20世紀の住宅と同様に、「ヴィトラスク」は19世紀の英国住宅の理論化に多くを負っている。こうした理論化は、ドイツ人建築家、ヘルマン・ムテジウス(1861-1927)の名著、『The English House（英国の住宅）』(1904)のなかで指摘されているように、産業革命が社会に与える有害な影響を軽減しようとしたジョン・ラスキン(1819-1900)およびウィリアム・モリス(1834-1896)の改革主義イデオロギーから生まれたものであった。モリスにとって「コミュニティにおける生活の中心は、工場ではなく住宅であるべき」であり、それはエリートの大邸宅ではなく、小規模な１戸建てを意味した。これら19世紀の英国の住宅は、規模的には慎ましいものであったが、人間のための完結した環境であり、さらにモリスは、インテリアをすべて総合的にデザインすることによって「日用品の形態に威厳を与える」ことを目指した。19世紀に労働の分業がもたらした生活の解体に抵抗して、モリスは住宅の「総合芸術」を創出した。あらゆるスケールの要素が一体化したデザインというこの住宅にたいする考えは、近代における住宅建築の最も差し迫ったテーマとなったのである。

モリスが思い描いた原理は、彼の仲間のフィリップ・ウェッブが設計し、1859年に建てられたモリスの「赤い家」にきわめて明確に表現されている。「ヴィトラスク」のように、ヴァナキュラーな建設技術を用いることで古典主義建築の冷たさを打ち破ったこの赤い煉瓦の家には、構造的な誠実さにたいする考慮と、住宅を敷地および地域の文化に溶け込ませるというモリスの考えが表現されている。C・F・A・ヴォイジーやベイリー・スコットの住宅と同様に、伝統的な建設技術に深い敬意を払い、身近な材料、注意深い敷地のレイアウトに根差した簡素で実用的なデザインとすることで、「赤い家」はこの考えを実現したのである。このように、モダン・ハウスの初期の例は、抽象的で芸術的な作品ではなかった。これらの住宅は、ヴァナキュラーな建築を手本としたのである。ムテジウスが述べているように、伝統的な民家は「我々が求め、願ったもの、すなわち過去の時代において、地域の条件にもとづいた有機的な発展から自然発生的に生まれたシンプルな感覚、構造的適切さ、過去の建築の模倣ではない自然な形態、合理的で実用的なデザイン、妥当な形の部屋、色彩と調和的な趣きを有する」ものであった。[3]

ヴァナキュラーな先例にもとづいた住生活の改革とは対照的に、モダン・ハウスには、近代的な材料を最も適切な方法で使用することによって住宅の概念を再考しようとするもう一つのヴィジョンが存在した。ウィーンの建築家、オットー・ワグナーは、ドイツ人建築家、カール・フリードリッヒ・シンケルの合理主義をさらに推し進め、自著『近代建築』のなかでこの概念について説明している。このなかで彼は、建物は三つの本質的な主題、すなわち、「簡潔さをもって近代の要求に対応する」「折衷主義の芸術的・道徳的堕落」の回避、「現

Above: Villa Wagner II, Vienna, Otto Wagner, 1912–13.

上：ヴィラ・ワグナー II、ウィーン、オットー・ワグナー、1912～13年。

3-英文参照。

訳註2-ヴァナキュラー（vernacular）とは、その土地固有のという意味。建築・デザインの分野でいえば、その土地固有の民家、民芸、建築材料、構法などを意味する。

cultivation of a private aesthetic life, but also incorporated steel and glass into their structure. While houses at the turn of the century were formally distant from the more abstract dwellings that would appear in the following decades, the fundamental ideals of domestic reform based on vernacular prototypes and the domestication of modern materials would prove to be ongoing issues throughout the century.

Hygiene and Art

Based on these principles—the domestication of industrial society and the use of modern materials—the houses featured in this volume result from visions of both a hygienic architecture, and of a total work of art. The architect stood in a unique position, creating spaces based on hygiene, as the specialized universal science of promoting health, and on art, as a synthetic individual creative activity that does *not* rely on science. In Hvitträsk, for example, not only did Eliel Saarinen design rugs, lamps, and furniture to harmonize with the house, but he also took great care to increase natural light and ventilation, particularly in the children's room, to make it hygienic.

At the beginning of the twentieth century, in particular, architects sought to maximize natural light and ventilation to reduce the risk of infectious diseases such as tuberculosis. Such concerns would in fact continue to be a driving force for many subsequent decades—from Le Corbusier's "Citrohan" house (1921), which provided for "all hygienic needs," to the call from the Czechoslovakian architectural magazine *Stavba* for the modern interior to promote, first and foremost, "hygiene." Nevertheless, as seen in Hvitträsk, the rise of the modern house at the turn of the century marks the increase of both quantitative and qualitative domestic standards.

At the very core of the modern house, the concern for hygiene manifested itself through innovations in plumbing. As Adolf Loos pointed out in his essay, "The Plumbers" (1898), hygiene is the modern project's supreme act, and "increasing water usage is one of the most pressing tasks of culture."[5] Consequently, more than embracing a formal style, the modern house could be defined in material terms as a dwelling with running water, water closets, lighting, and improvements for washing, ironing, and cooking. In this light, it did not simply break from all past traditions but was part of a constant development where, at least for Loos, change was only permissible if it improved upon the past.

Concern for the health of household occupants would continue to inform residential design both implicitly and explicitly. Both Rudolf Schindler and Richard Neutra's residential designs for Doctor Phillip Lovell in the arid climate of Southern California became known as "health" houses. In addition, the program for a doctor's house and hygienic clinic proved particularly appropriate for the modern house, as illustrated in Pierre Chareau's Maison de Verre (1932) and in the Maison Curutchet. Light and air were both physically and aesthetically essential to the life of the house and its occupants—a fact that would remain valid all the way to Richard Meier's Douglas house (1973).

The design of houses as total works of art, developing parallel to the specialized scientific pursuit of the hygienic house, evolved throughout the twentieth century. As the "equipment" for the modern house, furniture could be both hygienic and artistic. But more than individual objects in the house, furniture was designed to be in harmony with architecture. Its specific form, however, varied greatly. Frank Lloyd Wright, Mies van der Rohe, and Paul Rudolph all designed furniture to match their architectural designs, yet in different materials—wood, chrome, and Plexiglas, respectively. Conversely, Walter Gropius designed his 1937 house in Lincoln, Massachusetts to fit his furniture collection, designed by Marcel Breuer at the Bauhaus. In the 1950s architect Kiyosi Seike adapted the *Gesamtkunstwerk* aspect of the traditional Japanese house, in which *tatami* mats harmonize with both building structure and living patterns, to create a modern movable variation of the *tatami* mat to fit his minimal dwelling. Pieces such as those by Seike and Breuer, unlike custom-designed objects, were intended to be efficient, mass-produced prototypes for use in any dwelling. In the case of Breuer and Alvar Aalto, their mass-produced furniture designs would

Above: Bathroom of Tugendhat house, Mies van der Rohe, 1930. Below: Toilet of Rietveld Schröder house, Utrecht, Gerrit Thomas Rietveld, 1924.

上：トゥーゲントハット邸の浴室、ミース・ファン・デル・ローエ、1930年。
下：リートフェルト・シュレーダー邸の洗面所、ユトレヒト、ヘリット・T・リートフェルト、1924年。

5. Adolf Loos, "Plumbers," trans. by Harry F. Mallgrave in *Plumbing: sounding modern architecture*. New York: Princeton University Press, 1997, p. 19.

在の技術と建設手法にもとづいた新しいスタイル」にもとづかねばならないと主張した。[4] ワグナーは合理化された新古典主義様式の自邸を、私的な芸術的生活を送る理想的な場所としてデザインしたが、同時にその構造に鉄とガラスを組み入れた。これら世紀の変わり目に建てられた住宅は、その数十年後に現われる、より抽象的なデザインの住宅とは一見、形態的にはかけ離れているようにみえるが、ヴァナキュラーな手本にもとづいた住生活改革の基本的な理想と、近代的な材料を家庭内で身近なものとして使用する試みは、20世紀を通して継続するヴィジョンとなった。

衛生と芸術

工業化社会を住生活に受け入れ、近代的な材料を使用するという原則にもとづいて、ここで取り上げた住宅は、衛生的な住宅、そして「総合芸術」としての住宅という二つのヴィジョンから生み出された。建築家たちは、居住者の健康を向上させることを目指した専門化された普遍的な科学にもとづいた衛生的な空間をつくり、科学に頼らず総合的な個人の創造活動として芸術的な空間をつくるという興味深い立場にあった。たとえば「ヴィトラスク」において、エリエル・サーリネンは住宅と調和した敷物、ランプ、家具をデザインしただけでなく、衛生面の質を向上させるために、とりわけ子ども部屋において、自然採光や換気に気を配った。20世紀初頭は結核に代表される感染症にかかることを避けるために、建築家たちが最大限の自然採光と換気を求めた時期であった。このような配慮は、「あらゆる衛生上の要求」に応えたル・コルビュジエの「シトロアン」住宅(1921)から、近代の内部空間はなによりもまず「衛生」を要求すべきであることを主張した旧チェコスロヴァキアの建築雑誌『Stavba』に至るまで、何十年もの間、住宅を設計する上での推進力となった。「ヴィトラスク」をみてもわかるように、世紀の変わり目のモダン・ハウスの興隆は、住生活の量的、質的水準を向上させたのである。

モダン・ハウスの本質的な部分において、衛生への配慮は配管技術の革新をもたらした。アドルフ・ロースが「The Plumbers（配管工）」(1898)と題するエッセイのなかで指摘しているように、衛生の追求は近代プロジェクトの究極的な行為であり、「使用水量増加への対応は、最も緊急の文化的課題」[5] であった。したがって、形態としての様式を越えて、モダン・ハウスは、物理的には水道、水洗便所、照明のある住宅であり、洗濯、アイロン、調理の改良がなされた住宅と定義することができるだろう。この視点からみるならば、モダン・ハウスは過去の伝統を打ち破って突如出現したのではなく、継続的な発展の延長線上にあるのであり、少なくともロースにとっては、過去のものが改善された場合のみ変化は許されるものであった。

居住者の健康への配慮は、間接的あるいは直接的に住宅デザインの基礎となった。ルドルフ・シンドラーとリチャード・ノイトラがそれぞれ、乾燥した南カリフォルニアで医師のフィリップ・ロヴェルのためにデザインした住宅は、「健康」住宅として知られるようになった。またピエール・シャロウのガラスの家(1932)やル・コルビュジエのクルチェット邸(1949)からは、モダン・ハウスが医師の住宅と衛生的な診療所の計画にとりわけふさわしいことがわかる。太陽の光と空気が、身体的にも美的にも住宅と居住者の生命にとって本質的なものであるという事実は、1973年に建てられたリチャード・マイヤーのダグラス邸に至るまで変わっていない。

衛生的な住宅という科学的な追求と平行して、総合芸術としての住宅デザインも20世紀を通して継続的に発展した。モダン・ハウスの「装置」として、家具は衛生的かつ芸術的になりえたし、また家のなかの独立したオブジェである以上に、家具は建築と調和するようにデザインされた。しかしながら、結果的に生み出された形態は実に様々である。フランク・ロイド・ライト、ミース・ファン・デル・ローエ、そしてポール・ルドルフは、木、クロムめっきを施した金属、プレクシグラスという異なる材料で、建築と調和する家具をデザインした。一方、ウォルター・グロピウスは、家に合った家具を特別にデザインするかわりに、彼が所有するバウハウス家具（マルセル・ブロイヤーがデザインしたもの）のコレクションが収まるように、マサチューセッツ州リンカーンの自邸(1937)を設計した。また清家清は、畳が建物の構造および生活パターンと調和するという伝統的な日本家屋の総合芸術的な側面に注目し、1950年代に、彼のミニマルな自邸に合った近代的な可動式畳をデザインした。清家やブロイヤーの家具は、特別あつらえの家具とは異なり、どのような住宅でも使用しうる効率的で量産可能なプロトタイプとして考えられた。実際、ブロイヤーとアアルトがデザインした量産家具は、彼らがデザインした住宅よりも遥かに多くの人々に使われたのである。

しかしながら、建築家の支配的な権力を否定したアドルフ・ロースのような建築家たちは、ゆきすぎた総合芸

Above: Douglas House, Richard Meier, Harbor Springs, Michigan, 1973.

上：ダグラス邸、ミシガン州、リチャード・マイヤー、1973年。

4-オットー・ヴァーグナー、『近代建築－学生に与える建築手引き』(樋口清、佐久間博 訳、中央公論美術出版、1985年)。
5-英文参照。

in fact be used by far more people than their residential designs.

The *Gesamtkunstwerk* idea carried to an extreme, however, was highly criticized by architects such as Loos, who adamantly rejected the overbearing hand of the architect. Loos attacked the all-encompassing notion of total design in his fable "The Story of a Poor Rich Man," in which a wealthy businessman commissioned an architect to design his house, its furnishings, and even the clothes of its occupants. In Loos's residential designs, such as the Villa Scheu (1912), built-in benches harmonized with the overall interior space. But Loos ultimately intended his houses to be filled with his clients' choice of furnishings — including in this case a traditional overstuffed leather sofa. As Loos asserted in his 1910 essay, "*Architektur*," the "house satisfies a requirement, it must serve [the residents'] comfort, it must be cozy, look comfortable."[6]

An alternate strategy, to produce a more egalitarian *Gesamtkunstwerk*, derived from the use of industrial mass-produced objects offering the benefit of lower cost. Within Le Corbusier's quest for a "synthesis of the arts," mass-produced objects typified the "decorative arts of today." They provided appropriate furnishing for the dwelling, as attested by the appliances and plumbing fixtures in the Petite Maison, designed for his parents. Bauhaus-founder Walter Gropius pursued his quest to unify art and science in his own home through the incorporation of standard industrial fittings like inexpensive door handles. While radical in its time, their use was both economical and in keeping with Gropius's overall design sense. The notion of the house as a total work of art expanded from an emphasis on interior space to the design of outside space as well. Frank Lloyd Wright took great pains to unify the interior geometric composition of furniture, lights, and even heating ducts in his early domestic projects. Ultimately, though, the unity of its horizontal composition with the Midwestern plain would provide a name for this early work. The Prairie House, a building type which Wright had begun to develop at the end of the nineteenth century, and which found its apotheosis in the Robie house (1910), freed domestic space from the rigid box composed of separate rooms. Rather, interior rooms flowed together as one space under low, cantilevered roofs hovering parallel to the ground. Likewise, the interior harmonized with its surroundings, using "light-screens" instead of walls within an "organic architecture" unified from the scale of the chair, to the house, to the overall landscape.

The seemingly infinite spatial conception and the geometrical composition of the Robie house subsequently proved influential around the world. The German *Wasmuth* publication of Wright's work in 1910 strongly influenced the Dutch *de Stijl* group in their abstract geometric paintings, as well as Gerrit Rietveld's free-flowing planar composition in his house design for Mrs. Schröder-Schrader (1924). Like Wright, Rietveld broke from the notion of a solid box, in his case using movable doors and windows to create free-flowing space centrifugally expanding from the central stair to the exterior landscape. Transcending strictly abstract composition, Rietveld's swinging and sliding doors transform the space, changing a living area to a private bathroom space, or creating a free flow of air and view to the outside. Rietveld's composition of primary colors, planes, and lines could be further seen on both a macro and micro scale: from the composition of eaves and balconies, to his red and blue chair, all the way to a yellow and blue drawer for combs.

Austrian-born American architect Richard Neutra was strongly influenced both by Wright's ideals and the way they were worked out by other architects around the world. He not only worked for Wright himself, but had once also spent a night in the Rietveld Schröder house. Neutra created his own organic *Gesamtkunstwerk* in the Desert house, designed for Edgar Kaufmann Jr. (owner of Wright's Fallingwater) in Palm Springs, California. Neutra designed built-in shelves and desks to create micro-spaces integral with the composition of the house as a whole; he also made interior space flow effortlessly through floor-to-ceiling openings to the extremes of the arid mountain background. While much larger in scale than Rietveld's precedent, Neutra's house also used louvers that could be opened to provide ventilation or shading in the extreme desert climate, creating a comfortable house for its inhabitants. The examples of Rietveld and Neutra therefore illustrate that total design did not simply mean an endless unity of patterns, but rather the design of the overall human environment, both inside and out.

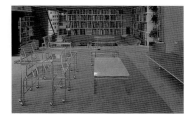

Top to bottom: Furniture design by Frank Lloyd Wright, Mies van der Rohe, Paul Rudolph.

家具のデザイン：上から、フランク・ロイド・ライト、ミース・ファン・デル・ローエ、ポール・ルドルフ。

6. Adolf Loos, "Architecture" (1910), in *The Architecture of Adolf Loos*, trans. Wilfried Wang and Rosamund Diamond (London: Arts Council of Great Britain, 1985), p. 107–108.

Top to bottom: Furniture design by Marcel Breuer, and Alvar Aalto.

家具のデザイン：上から、マルセル・ブロイヤー、アルヴァ・アアルト。

6-アドルフ・ロース、「建築について」(1910年)、『装飾と罪悪－建築・文化論集』（伊藤哲夫 訳, 中央公論美術出版, 1987年）に収録。

術のあり方を厳しく批判した。ロースは、裕福なビジネスマンがこのような建築家に、住宅、家具、そして住む人の衣服までもデザインしてもらうという内容の「The Story of a Poor Rich Man（哀れな金持ちの男の話）」と題する物語を書いて、総合芸術の網羅的な概念を攻撃した。ショイ邸(1912)に代表されるロースの住宅デザインにおいては、造り付けの長椅子が内部空間と調和している。しかしロースは、最終的にはその住宅が伝統的な革張りのソファといった施主が所有する家具や調度品で満たされることを想定していた。1910年に書かれた「建築」と題するエッセイのなかでロースが主張しているように、「住宅は要求を満たす。住宅は（居住者に）快適さを提供し、居心地よくあらねばならず、また快適そうにみえなければならない」。6

かわって、量産された低価格の工業製品を使用するという、より平等主義的な総合芸術をつくりだす方法が生み出された。ル・コルビュジエは「芸術の統合」というテーマを探求したが、彼にとっては量産品が「今日の装飾芸術」を象徴していた。彼が両親のために建てた「小さな家」(1923)で使われた電気機器や衛生設備が証明しているように、量産品は住宅の適切な設備となりえた。バウハウスの創設者であるウォルター・グロピウスは、自邸のデザインにおいて、安価なドア・ハンドルなどの標準的な工業製品を取り入れることによって、芸術と科学を統合するという課題を追求した。当時としては急進的であったが、標準的な工業製品を採用することは経済的であり、また全体としてグロピウスのデザイン感覚と合っていた。

「総合芸術」としての住宅という概念は、内部空間を中心とした考え方から、外部空間のデザインへと発展していった。フランク・ロイド・ライトは初期の住宅プロジェクトにおいて、家具、照明、さらには暖房用のダクトのデザインに至るまでを幾何学的構成として一体化することに全力を尽くした。これら初期の住宅は、最終的には米国中西部の草原と一体化したその水平性を強調した構成から、「プレーリー・ハウス（草原住宅）」と名づけられた。ライトが19世紀末から使い始めた、ロビー邸(1910)に代表されるこの「プレーリー・ハウス」というビルディング・タイプは、いくつもの部屋から構成される箱としての家という硬直した概念から住宅を解放した。地面と平行して宙に浮いた低い片持ち屋根の下で、内部の部屋が一つの空間として融合している。同様に、椅子のような小さなスケールのものから、家全体、さらにはランドスケープをも一体化した「有機的建築」においては、壁のかわりに「軽いスクリーン」を用いることで内部空間が周囲と調和した。

ロビー邸の発展性のある空間概念は、やがて世界的に影響を与えたことが明らかになった。1910年にドイツのヴァスムート社から出版されたライトの作品集は、デ・スティル派の抽象的な幾何学的絵画ならびに、ヘリット・リートフェルトがシュレーダー夫人のために設計した住宅(1924)の自由自在な平面構成に強い影響を与えた。ライトと同じく、リートフェルトは、可動式のドアと窓を用いることで箱としての家という硬直した概念から脱し、中心にある階段から外部のランドスケープへと広がる自由自在な空間をつくりだした。リヴィング・エリアを私的な浴室に変え、あるいは自然な換気と外部の眺めをもたらすなど、リートフェルトの引き戸および前後に開く自在ドアは、厳密な抽象的構成を超えて空間を変貌させた。リートフェルトの基本的な色彩、平面、および線の構成は、軒やバルコニーの構成から赤と青の椅子、さらには櫛を入れる黄色と青の引き出しまで、マクロ、ミクロ両方のスケールで展開されている。

オーストリア生まれの米国人建築家、リチャード・ノイトラは、ライトの理想と、世界各地の建築家たちによるその理想の具現化に強い影響を受けた。彼はライトの下で働き、またリートフェルトのシュレーダー邸で一夜を過ごした経験をもっていた。ノイトラは、自らの有機的な総合芸術を、エドガー・カウフマン・Jr.（「落水荘」のオーナー）のために設計したカリフォルニア州パーム・スプリングスのカウフマン・デザート・ハウスで実現した。ノイトラは、全体としてデザート・ハウスの構成と一体化したミクロ空間をつくりだすために、造り付けの棚と机をデザインした。さらに彼は、床から天井まである開口部を通して、周囲に広がる乾燥した山々に向かって、内部空間が自然と流れる出るように計画した。先に建てられたリートフェルトの住宅よりもスケールはかなり大きいが、ノイトラの住宅においても、砂漠の究極的な気候のなかで換気や日影をもたらし、居住者にとって健康的な住宅をつくりだすためにルーヴァーが用いられた。リートフェルトとノイトラの住宅は、総合的なデザインが、単にパターンを無限に繰り返すことではなく、内部および外部における人間環境全体のデザインを意味することを示唆している。

さらに身体芸術という視点からみれば、居住者の動きが総合芸術としての住宅を完成させると考えることができよう。トゥーゲントハット邸の素晴らしさは、一つに、玄関から湾曲した階段を降りて居住空間に至るという予期せぬ移動体験（プロムナード）から生まれている。また有機的な曲線を描くハンス・シャロウンのシュミンク邸(1933)の論理は、敷地の眺めを建築に調和的に取り入れることから生まれている。アマンシオ・ウィリアムズの「小川に架かる家」に入ると、小川の上にいるというだけでなく、木々のなかに浮いているように

Moreover, the movement of the houses' occupants could be seen to complete the house as a total work of art, in a choreographical sense. One of the most spectacular aspects of Mies van der Rohe's Tugendhat house derives from its unexpected promenade, from the entrance down into the living space via a curving stair. The logic of Hans Scharoun's organically curvilinear Schminke house (1933) in fact derives from an orchestration of views of the site in which stairs turn at critical points. Entering Williams' House over the Brook not only elevates one over the stream below, but also suspends one high up in the trees. In the Maison Curutchet, the promenade along a ramp leads the occupant to the elevated living space opening out to a wooded park beyond, encouraging a healthy life, with light and air creating a true "synthesis of the arts."

Publicizing the Private

As revolutionary as some of these architectural ideas may be, the true test of any house is how livable it is. Unfortunately, without traveling great distances to visit these houses, the only way to know them is through their representation in photographs, plans, sketches and other documents. These filter our perception of the architecture. Indeed, the changing nature of architectural journalism has had a significant impact on the way we see and understand the modern house.

While many modern houses remain physically closed to the public, many have been opened to public gaze through published photographs in the mass media. Le Corbusier spread his architectural ideas through *L'Esprit Nouveau* publications, including *Vers une Architecture* (1923) and *Un Maison, Une Palais* (1928). Many journals were devoted exclusively to residential architecture, including the early numbers of the Japanese journal *Shinkenchiku*. Photographs of modern houses were central to the Museum of Modern Art's *International Style* exhibition. F.R.S. Yorke's *The Modern House* (1934) further illustrated examples from Europe and America of the residential building type, defined by "plan," "wall and window," and "roof."

Throughout these early publications, black and white photographs portrayed powerful abstract images of the modern house. The photographs were often closely cropped, eliminating context, and emphasizing architecture as isolated form isolated from everyday life. Black and white photographs, by their very nature, transformed color to shades of gray to portray a monochromatic modern architecture. This abstraction produced powerful iconic images of modern houses, which created an "international" vision of the modern house through their worldwide reproduction. These idealized images, which could make virtually any building look good on the printed page, often eliminated the human subject and the primary aspect of living.

Today, however, one can look beyond these abstract images to find further richness and complexity in the past. The idealized visions of the modern house were far from universally uniform, but existed as a complex constellation of distinct variations. Recent advances in color photography and printing technology, as well as lower-priced airfares, have made it possible to re-photograph these houses and capture tactile, material qualities along with their dynamic interaction with the sun, sky and verdure of their sites. While the twentieth century witnessed radical changes in technology, seen most notably in the effect of kitchen appliances, televisions, and telephones, the house still fundamentally serves as shelter to provide space to eat, converse, and sleep. Some historic photos, like those of the Gropius house, show owners living in their houses, and new photographs have been taken to allow the reader to imagine life in these buildings.

A critical examination of the publication of the private realm, rather than obscuring the essential nature of the home, *can* therefore serve as an invaluable means for the architect to see the extended design process in order to actually design for living.

感じられる。クルチェット邸では、斜路にそったプロムナードが居住者を木々が生い茂った公園に向かって開かれた上層階の居住空間へと導き、真の「芸術的統合」をつくりだしている太陽と空気にあふれた健康的な生活を提供している。

プライヴェートの公開

建築家たちのアイディアがいかに革命的であったとしても、その住宅の真価は住みやすさによって問われる。これらの住宅を訪ねて世界各地を旅することが無理ならば、それについて知るには、写真、図面、スケッチ、その他の資料から読み取るしかない。しかしながら、これらの資料は、我々の建築にたいする理解に多かれ少なかれフィルターをかけることになる。実際、20世紀における建築ジャーナリズムの本質の変化は、我々のモダン・ハウスを見る目、あるいは理解する方法に重大な影響を与えた。

Above: Shinkenchiku, cover, volume 11, January, 1935.

上：『新建築』誌、1935年1月号表紙。

多くのモダン・ハウスは、いまだプライヴェートな領域として一般には開かれていないが、マスメディアに写真が掲載されるというかたちで公開されたものも多い。ル・コルビュジエは「建築をめざして」や「住宅と宮殿」(1928) といったエッセイが掲載された『レスプリ・ヌーヴォー』誌を通して、彼の建築思想を広めた。初期の『新建築』誌をはじめ、世界の多くの雑誌はもっぱら住宅建築を取り上げた。モダン・ハウスの写真は、1932年にニューヨーク近代美術館で行われたインターナショナル・スタイルの展覧会において中心的な役割を果たし、また、F·R·S·ヨークが著した『The Modern House (ザ・モダン・ハウス)』(1934)には、「平面」「壁と窓」「屋根」という分類で分析された、ヨーロッパおよび米国の住宅建築の例が多数紹介された。

これら初期の出版物を通して、モノクロ写真はモダン・ハウスの力強い抽象的なイメージを描き出した。その多くは対象を接写し、建物がたつ特定の文脈を削除し、独立した形態としての建築を強調した。モノクロ写真はその性質上、白と黒以外の色はすべて灰色の影となるため、結果的にモダン・ハウスを単色のものとして伝えた。この抽象化が、モダン・ハウスの力強いイコン的イメージを生み出し、世界各地で複製された建物を通して、モダン・ハウスの「インターナショナル」なヴィジョンをつくりだしたのである。このような理想化されたイメージは、実際にはひどい建物でも印刷された誌面上では素晴らしく見せかけることができ、しばしば、そこに住む人間や生活の最も基本的な側面が削除された。

しかしながら、今日、抽象的なイメージを超えてこれらの住宅をみることが可能になり、過去におけるその豊かさと複雑さが少しずつ明らかになってきた。モダン・ハウスの理想像は、各国一律からはほど遠く、別個のヴァリエーションの複雑な集合体として存在してきたのである。近年におけるカラー写真、印刷技術の進歩は、航空券の価格の低下と相俟って、これらの住宅を改めて撮り直し、建物の実体的な材質感、さらにはその敷地の太陽、空、自然環境との力強い相互作用を捉えることを可能にした。20世紀は技術の急激な変化を経験し、その影響は台所用電気製品、テレビ、そして電話に最も顕著に表れているが、住宅そのものは、今も基本的には食べ、会話し、寝るための空間を提供するシェルターとして機能することに変わりはない。ここで紹介している歴史的な写真（たとえばグロピウス邸の当時の写真）と新たに撮り下ろされた写真から、読者はこれらの建物での生活を想像することが可能となるだろう。かつてのように住宅の本質を曖昧にするのではなく、プライヴェートな領域の出版について批評的に検証することは、したがって、デザイン・プロセスを幅広く理解することを可能にし、それは建築家が実際に生活空間をデザインする上でのきわめて重要な作業となるだろう。

新たな伝統の成長

今日においても、建築家は、急激に近代化する環境に適合した住空間をつくりだすという、ル・コルビュジエやギーディオンが指摘した課題に直面している。この情報化の時代において、世界は社会的、政治的、技術的に変化しつづけており、建築家は住宅設計のみならず、より一般的な意味において、新しいものと古いもの、科学と芸術、パブリックとプライヴェートといった問題に取り組まねばならない。歴史的な視野でみることによって、モダン・ハウスを単なる抽象的なオブジェではなく、「新たな伝統」（ギーディオンの発展性を秘めた著書『空間・時間・建築』の副題）ともいうべき継続的なデザイン・プロセスの一部とみなすことが可能になる。5回にわたるこの著書の再版(1941−67)の度に、章を付け足し改訂を加えることによってギーディオンが

The Growth of a New Tradition

Architects today continue to face Le Corbusier and Giedion's challenge to create livable spaces suitable to a rapidly modernizing world. As the social, political, and technical aspects of the world continue to change in the information age, architects must still resolve old and new, science and art, public and private, both in house design and in a more general sense. Through historical perspective, one can now see the modern house not simply as an abstract object, but as part of a cumulative ongoing design process that can be seen as *"the growth of a new tradition"* — the subtitle to Giedion's seminal text on modern architecture, *Space, Time, and Architecture*. Just as Giedion himself expanded his presentation of the modern movement by adding chapters and revisions to his book in its five subsequent editions (1941–1967), the following houses can be seen to expand our understanding of the modern house.

Architects in the twentieth century, working within the larger project of modernization to liberate the human being, have thus sought to realize this vision through innovative design at many scales and from many perspectives. Examples such as the Petite Maison illustrate the fact that modern houses in the twentieth century were actually outdoor spaces as much as indoor ones. Homes by architects such as Melnikov, Asplund (1937), Gropius, and Aalto (1953) were their own experimental living spaces. Their relatively modest budgets also proved that good design and efficiency can in fact raise living standards. Other houses such as the Robie house, the Rietveld Schröder house and the Fisher house (1967) were inspired by the mutual participation of client and architect to produce appropriate living spaces that would become portraits of their owners as much as their architects. Many of these individual houses, such as the Melnikov house and the Sert house (1957) were designed as prototypical standard dwellings to be infinitely repeated as the basis for a larger urban strategy; they address the need to shelter the "various classes of workers in society to-day." Loos's stepped-roof Scheu house informed the design of his 1923 Inzersdorferstrasse housing scheme in Vienna, and Petite Maison, as a basic unit, would continue to inform Le Corbusier's residential designs both small and large, and other architectural themes in general.

The wide scope of the houses included here underscores the fact that there is no single ideal modern house. These homes also could not be duplicated easily. Many were archetypal ideal solutions for enlightened, often affluent clients, not easily reproducible, prototypical solutions. For example, while the Maison de Verre's standardized modular construction system would seem possible to mass produce, the project took four years to build and was never duplicated, even by Chareau himself. But an understanding of the fundamental concepts of the modern house in its many possible incarnations, and of the specific, tangible realities of diverse twentieth-century contexts, can continue to inform the design of both single houses and housing today. While these two volumes do not cover the last quarter of the twentieth century, a more objective re-examination of this period will be possible in the years to come.

The following houses, which have stood the test of time, are to be understood in all of their guises, through the dialectic between ideal vision and real experience as living space. Many of these houses remain as radical and contemporary today as they were when first completed. They thereby provide lessons for dwelling in the twenty-first century. As Marcel Breuer noted,

Architecture is not the materialization of a mood. Its objective is general usefulness, including its visual impact. It should not be a self-portrait of the architect or the client, though containing personal elements of both. It should serve generations and while man comes and goes, building and idea endure. I love to think of the most luxurious house I have built as an experiment to find solutions applicable for general use.[7]

7. Marcel Breuer, *Sun and Shadow, the Philosophy of an Architect* (New York: Dodd, Mead, 1955), p. 11.

Thus the challenge for architects of the past, present, and future remains toward a vision of the real — to build living spaces that give new dimensions and meaning to everyday life.

モダン・ムーヴメントにたいする理解を発展させたように、ここで紹介する住宅は、我々のモダン・ハウスにたいする理解をより深めてくれるにちがいない。

20世紀の建築家たちは、人間を解放することを目指した、より大規模な近代プロジェクトのなかで活動し、様々なスケールや視点で革新的なデザインを生み出すことによって、このヴィジョンを実現しようとした。メルニコフ、アスプルンド、グロピウス、アアルトといった建築家が設計した住宅は、彼ら自身の実験的な住空間であった。また彼らの建設資金が比較的限られていたことは、結果的に、よいデザインと効率のよさが実際に生活水準を高めることを証明した。ロビー邸、リートフェルト・シュレーダー邸、そしてフィッシャー邸(1967)といった住宅は、施主と建築家、相互の関与によって、建築家だけでなく施主の「肖像画」でもある好ましい居住空間を生み出した。メルニコフ邸やセルト邸(1957)といった個人住宅は、より大規模な都市の戦略を念頭におきつつ、再生可能なプロトタイプ的標準住宅としてデザインされた。そしてそれは「今日の社会における、あらゆる階層の労働者」に見合ったシェルターを供給するという課題にも取り組んでいる。ロースが設計した階段状の陸屋根をもつショイ邸は、1923年につくられたウィーンのインザドルファシュトラッセ・ハウジング計画の、またル・コルビュジエの「小さな家」は、その後彼が手がけた大小規模の住宅および建築的テーマ一般の基礎となった。

ここで紹介する住宅を広い視野から眺めれば、一つの理想的なモダン・ハウスなど存在しないという事実が明らかになる。これらの住宅はまた、容易に複製できるものではない。その多くは、教養があり、またしばしば裕福な施主のためのアーキタイプ（原型）として考え出された理想的な解答であり、簡単に再生できるプロトタイプ（基本形）としての解答ではなかった。たとえばガラスの家の標準化されたモデュールにもとづく建設システムは、量産に適用可能であることを示唆しているが、このプロジェクトの建設には４年が費やされ、シャロウ自身ですら、このシステムをふたたび用いることはなかった。しかし、実際に建てられた建物からモダン・ハウスの根本的な概念を理解し、さらに20世紀という複雑な文脈のリアリティを理解することによって、これらの住宅は引きつづき今日の戸建て住宅およびハウジング・デザインの参考となるであろう。二巻からなるこの臨時増刊号では1975年以降の住宅を扱っていないが、この時期にたいするより客観的な再評価はいずれ可能となるだろう。

時の試練に耐えたこれらの住宅は、理想的なヴィジョンと実現された住空間のリアルな経験の弁証法を通して理解される。その多くは、今日においても建設された当時と同じ斬新さと同時代性を維持し、21世紀の住宅に様々な教訓を与えている。マルセル・ブロイヤーは次のように述べている。

「建築は雰囲気を形にすることではない。建築の目的は、視覚的インパクトをも含んだ一般的な有用性にある。それは建築家、クライアント双方の個性を含むものではあっても、どちらか一方の肖像画であってはならない。人間は入れかわっても、建築は何世代にもわたって使われるべきで、建物とその理念は継続する。私は一般的用途に応用しうる解決策を見出すための実験として建てた、この贅沢な住宅について考えるのが好きでならない」。[7]

このように、過去、現在、そして未来の建築家にとっての挑戦は、ヴィジョンの実現にほかならない。我々の日常生活に、新たな広がりと意味をもたらす居住空間をつくりだすことを目指して。

Hvitträsk
Luomo, Finland 1903
Eliel Saarinen with Armas Lindgren, Herman Gesellius

ヴィトラスク
フィンランド、ルオモ 1903
エリエル・サーリネン（アーマス・リンドグレン、ヘルマン・ゲゼリウスと共同）

Hvitträsk, a monumental example of National Romantic expression in Finland, was built between 1901–1903 as an atelier and home for the three architects Eliel Saarinen, Armas Lindgren, and Herman Gesellius. These three young professionals established their office in 1896, designing the Finnish Pavilion for the 1900 Paris Exposition. Soon after, they purchased 16 hectares of beautiful lakeside land on a forested ridge at Luomo, some 30 km away from Helsinki, where they began to build Hvitträsk.

At Hvitträsk, the three partners designed their family living quarters around a central courtyard. The main building, located on the western side of the courtyard, contained Saarinen's residence to the south, Lindgren's residence with its pointed tower to the north, and a central atelier originally provided with separate access from the courtyard. Gesellius, still a bachelor at the time of planning, lived in the small dwelling across the courtyard. The picturesque watercolor elevation that Saarinen painted around 1907 shows the two wings, with their own independent identities, in harmony with the whole. However, the partnership fell apart soon after completion, when Lindgren resigned and left Hvitträsk at the beginning of 1905. Gesellius died in 1916. Saarinen subsequently owned all of Hvitträsk and together with his second wife Loja (Gesellius's younger sister), who was blessed with artistic talent, worked further on the design of the interior and garden. Saarinen's assistant Frans Nyberg recollected that "enthrallment with the pursuit of art unusually gripped the entire [Saarinen] family" and for son Eero, who was still a child at the time, "shadow and perspective constructions obviously aroused his mathematical aptitudes." In 1922 the north wing with its medieval-style tower burned down. It was redesigned by Eero Saarinen in 1936 in the form in which it stands today. The portion of the complex closest to the original design is Saarinen's own residence, whose interiors are pictured here, and which is currently open to the public as a museum.

The design of Hvitträsk marks the birth of an indigenous modern expression in Finland. It reflects foreign influences entering Finland through architectural journals and the international exchange of architects, as well as indigenous Finnish elements. Most apparent is the influence of the English Arts and Crafts Movement. The Finnish architects' vision resonates clearly with William Morris's medievalist ideas, based here on leaving the city to pursue architecture in a beautiful natural setting as "a total work of art." Further, their adherence to vernacular materials like stone, logs, and brick, and to traditional craftsmanship draws from the same tradition. The influence of H.H. Richardson in America, of perhaps Viennese Secession, and of C.R. Macintosh in Glasgow can also be seen in the design. However, the flowing spatial composition is uniquely Saarinen's and the overall impression comes from residential Finnish vernacular.

In 1922, Saarinen received second prize in the Chicago Tribune competition. He emigrated to America the following year. However, he returned to Hvitträsk every summer until the year before he died in 1950. Clearly, for Saarinen, Hvitträsk was an ideal place to live and work. (TK)

ヴィトラスクは、19世紀末から20世紀初頭にかけてフィンランドで活躍した三人の建築家、エリエル・サーリネン、アーマス・リンドグレン、ハーマン・ゲゼリウスの住居および設計事務所として1901〜03年に建設された、フィンランドにおけるナショナル・ロマンティシズムの記念碑的な建築である。1896年に設計事務所を設立し、1900年のパリ万国博フィンランド館の設計などを通して若くして成功を収めた三人は、1901年、ヘルシンキから約30km離れたルオモの美しい湖畔に16haの敷地を購入しヴィトラスクの建設に着手した。

ヴィトラスクにおいて、三人の建築家はそれぞれの自邸をデザインした。中庭を挟んで西側にあるメインの建物は、尖塔を頂いた北棟をリンドグレンが、南棟をサーリネンがそれぞれの家族の住居として設計した。またその中間に事務所を設け、これが両棟をつないだ。1907年頃に、サーリネンが描いた水彩の西側立面図からは、二つの棟がそれぞれに個性を有しながらも全体として調和のとれた、当時のピクチャレスクな姿をうかがうことができる。当時まだ独身であったゲゼリウスは、中庭を挟んで東側にある、現在はレストランとなっている建物に居を構えた。しかし、1905年にリンドグレンがパートナーシップを解消してヴィトラスクを去り、1916年にゲゼリウスが死亡した後は、サーリネンの家族がヴィトラスク全体を所有し、芸術家としての才能に恵まれた2度目の妻（ゲゼリウスの妹）とともに、インテリアや庭園を完成させていった。サーリネンのアシスタントだったフランス・ニューバーグは、サーリネン一家の生活が芸術活動とつねに一体であり、当時まだ幼かった息子のエーロも事務所に出入りして「陰影と透視図の立体構成が彼の数学的才能を目覚めさせた」と回想している。中世風の尖塔が特徴的だった北棟は1922年の火事で焼失し、1936年にエーロ・サーリネンの設計にもとづいて現在の建物に建て替えられた。したがって、現在、最もオリジナルに近い状態で残っているのは、今回写真で紹介されているサーリネンの住居部分である。

ヴィトラスクは、当時盛んになりつつあった建築家たちの国際的な交流や建築雑誌などの出版物を通してもたらされた海外からの影響と、フィンランド固有の土着的要素が混ざり合い、きわめて独自の表現を生み出している。最も顕著なのは、英国のアーツ・アンド・クラフツ運動の影響であろう。都会を離れてフィンランド特有の美しい自然に囲まれ、日々の生活とデザインが一体となった環境で総合芸術としての建築を目指した彼らのヴィジョンは、アーツ・アンド・クラフツ運動の指導者であったウィリアム・モリスの中世主義に根ざした思想と共鳴している。また、ヴィトラスクに見られる、石、丸太、煉瓦といったヴァナキュラーな材料や伝統的なクラフトマンシップへのこだわりも、その流れを汲んでいる。さらには、米国のH・H・リチャードソンの影響、あるいはウィーンのゼツェッションやグラスゴーのC・R・マッキントッシュの影響もデザインの随所に見出せる。しかし、流れるような空間構成はサーリネン独自のものであり、全体として想起されるのは紛れもなくフィンランドのヴァナキュラーな住宅建築である。

1922年にシカゴ・トリビューンの設計競技で2位に入選したサーリネンは、翌年、ヴィトラスクを去って米国に移住する。しかしその後も、死の前年まで、彼は毎年かかさず夏をヴィトラスクで過ごしたという。サーリネンにとって理想的な創作活動と生活の場であったヴィトラスクは、修復されて当時の姿を取り戻し、現在はミュージアムとして一般に公開されている。 (TK)

*Above: View of main building from
the east with entry to Saarinen's
residence.*

上：東側からみたメインの建物。左手に
サーリネンの住居への入口がみえる。

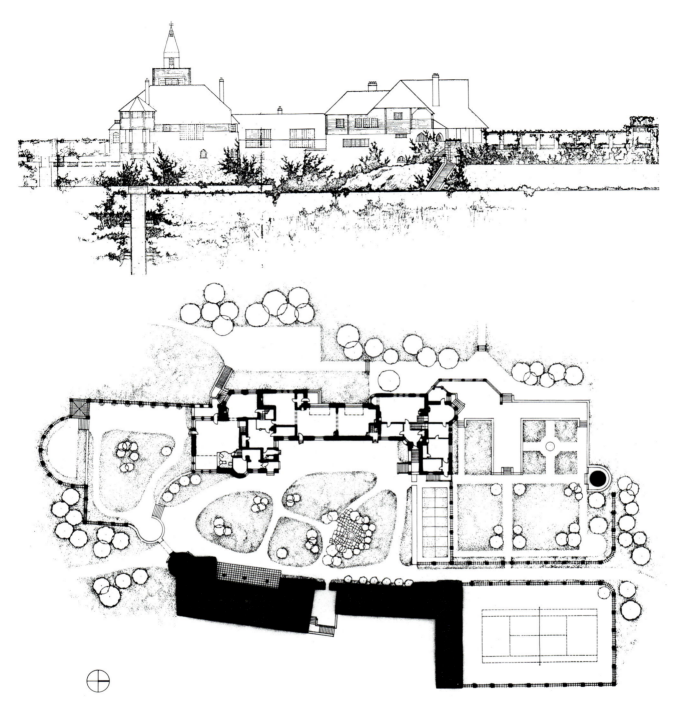

Above: Lake side elevation. Middle: Site plan. Left: Gesellius' house opposite the main building across the courtyard.

上：西側の湖側立面図。中：配置図。左：中庭を隔ててメインの建物と対面するゲゼリウスの住居。

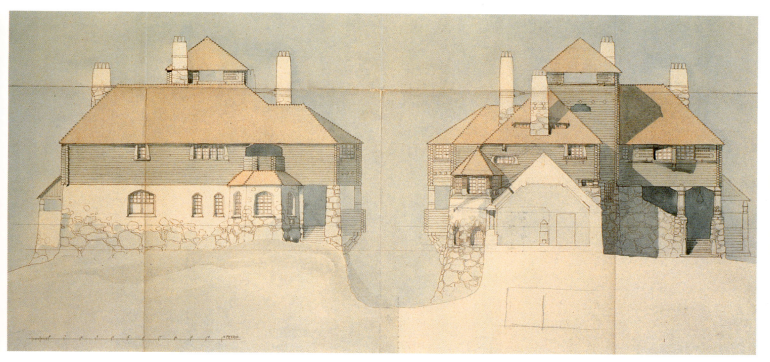

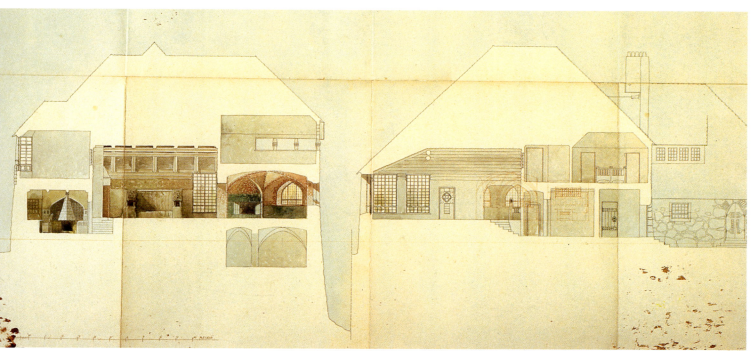

Above: North and south gables of the north wing; sectional drawing of the studio. Ink and wash drawing by Eliel Saarinen (?), c. 1902. Below: Sections through the south wing. Ink and wash drawing by Armas Lindgren (?), c. 1902.

上：北棟の北側立面図と南側立面図、および中央のスタジオ断面図。インクと水彩による図面。サーリネンによるものか、1902年頃。下：南棟断面図。インクと水彩による図面。リンドグレンによるものか、1902年頃。

pp. 22–23: View of the lake side
facade from the south. Above: Door
to the studio from the courtyard.
Opposite: View of.the south wing of
the main building (Saarinen's
residence).

22〜23頁：湖側のファサード。南側から
みる。上：中庭に面した、スタジオへの
扉。右頁：南棟（サーリネンの住居）を
みる。

Above: The studio in the early 1910's. From right, Eliel Saarinen, Pipsan Saarinen, and Frans Nyberg. Opposite: The studio in 1999.

上：1910年代のスタジオ。右から、エリエル・サーリネン、娘のピプサン・サーリネン、フランス・ニューバーグ。右頁：現在のスタジオ。

p. 28–29: Living room. Dining room is seen in the back to the left. Furniture and chandelier were designed by the Saarinens; tapestry by Akseli Gallen-Kallela. Above: Living room. Opposite: Fireplace in the dining room. Living room is seen on the left.

28〜29頁：居間。左手奥に食堂がみえる。家具、シャンデリアなどはサーリネン夫妻のデザイン。タペストリーは、アクセリ・ガレン-カレラ作。上：居間。右頁：食堂の隅の炉辺。左手に居間がみえる。

Above: Ground-floor library adjacent to studio. Below: Children's room on the 2nd floor where Eero Saarinen played.

上：1階の書斎。スタジオにつづいている。
下：子ども室。エーロ・サーリネンはこ
こで遊んだ。

Above: Furniture in the children's room. Ryiji *rug in the middle by Eliel Saarinen.*

上：子ども室の家具。中央のライジー・ラグ（敷物）もエリエル・サーリネンのデザインである。

Robie House
Chicago, Illinois, USA 1910
Frank Lloyd Wright

ロビー邸
米国、イリノイ州、シカゴ　1910
フランク・ロイド・ライト

The long horizontal profile of this house, built for bicycle manufacturer Frederick C. Robie on a narrow corner lot adjoining the University of Chicago, has come to epitomize Frank Lloyd Wright's Prairie Style. Low-hipped cantilevered roofs, horizontally-raked brickwork, and limestone sills all emphasize the horizontality of the building on the site. The elongated volume of the second floor, with prow-like forms at either end, seems to float above the site like a steamship on the ocean. Inside, Wright reduced the number of separate rooms, joining discrete functions in one space to create "a sense of unity." In Wright's powerful geometric composition, he sought to "to eliminate the room as a box and the house as another by making all walls enclosing screens." The whole house formed an "organic architecture" such that all furnishings, heating, lighting, and even plumbing were constituent parts of the overall design.

In the Robie house, Wright sought to create a natural space for living. He used out-swinging casement windows to create free openings to the outside, not traditional double-hung windows, referred to by the architect as "guillotines." Wright designed the leaded windows not simply as geometrical ornaments, but also to provide ventilation, light, and views out. Overhangs and setbacks provided shade during summer months and interior privacy from the street. At the center of the house, the fireplace provided both structural support and warmth for living spaces on all three floors.

In the years following its completion, this revolutionary house has been both celebrated as a work of great power and condemned. The publication of the Robie House in the *Wasmuth* volumes in 1910 was profoundly influential in Europe for *de Stijl* architects such as J. J. P. Oud, who lauded Wright's "plastic exuberance, sensuous abundance." The publication also inspired architects such as Rudolph Schindler and Richard Neutra to emigrate to America to work for Wright. At home, neighbors considered the house a monstrosity, Wright mad, and Robie a fool. The house resolutely embodied the type of home its client sought and Robie's son considered it "the most ideal place in the world." But Robie was forced to sell the house after less than two years, as a result of growing debt and divorce from his wife.

The Robie house, designed early in Wright's long career, was one of his favorite residential designs. He proclaimed it "the cornerstone of modern architecture" in 1957 in response to plans to raze it. Through the efforts of Wright himself and his foundation, the house has survived destruction. In the year 2007, it will be fully restored and will continue to stand as a testimony to Wright's creative energy and innovation.   (KTO)

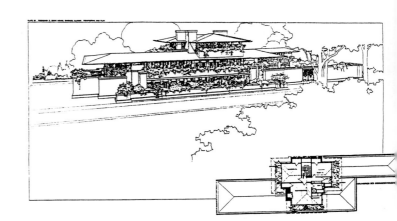

Right: Perspective and plan as published in Wasmuth, *1910.*
Opposite: Detail of leaded window at the east end of the dining room.

右：透視図および平面図。1910年にヴァスムート社から出版された作品集に掲載された。右頁：食堂の東端の窓のステンド・グラスのディテール。

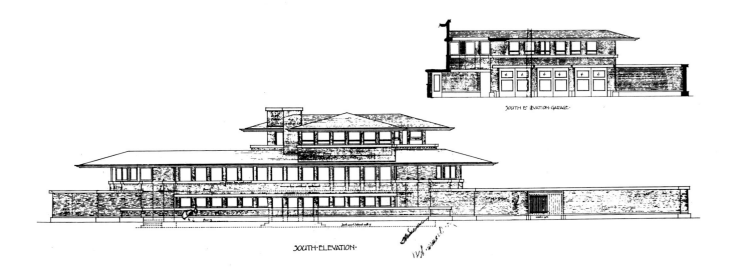

SOUTH ELEVATION GARAGE.

SOUTH·ELEVATION·

この住宅は、自転車製造業を営むフレデリック・C・ロビーのためにシカゴ大学に隣接する細長い角地に建てられた。その特徴的な水平に長く伸びた輪郭は、ライトの「プレーリー・スタイル」の理想形となった。低い寄棟の片持ち屋根、水平の溝が特徴的な煉瓦の積み方、そして石灰岩の土台のすべてが敷地の水平性を強調している。2階の居室の先端が船首のような形をしている水平に伸びたこの建物は、海洋における蒸気船のように草原の上に浮かんでいる。内部空間において、ライトは「統一感」を生み出すために個室の数を減らし、一つの空間としてまとめた。ライトは力強い幾何学的構成のなかで、「すべての壁をスクリーンとすることによって、箱としての部屋、さらにもう一つの箱としての家を消し去る」ことを目指した。ここでは、すべての家具、暖房設備、照明、そして衛生設備さえも全体を構成する要素の一部であり、家全体が「有機的建築」を形成している。

ロビー邸において、ライトは自然な生活空間を創造しようとした。ライトが「ギロチン」と呼んだ一般的な上げ下げ窓を使うかわりに、彼は外開き窓を用いて、より自然に外部に開かれた開口をつくりだした。ライトは鉛枠を用いた窓を単なる幾何学的な装飾としてではなく、換気をおこない、日の光と外の景色を取り込むためにデザインした。張り出しとセットバックは、夏に日陰をもたらすと同時に、通りからのプライヴァシーを確保している。この住宅の中央に設けられた暖炉は、構造体であると同時に、三つの階すべての暖房装置として機能している。

完成後、この革命的な住宅は、その計り知れない影響力のために賞賛と非難を受けた。ロビー邸がドイツのヴァスムート社から出版されたライトの作品集のなかで紹介されると、J・J・P・オウトをはじめとするヨーロッパのデ・スティル派の建築家たちに大きな影響を与えた。彼らは、ライトの「生き生きとした造形力、感覚的豊かさ」を賞賛した。またこの本は、ルドルフ・シンドラーやリチャード・ノイトラといった建築家がライトのもとで働くために米国に移民するきっかけともなった。しかし自国の米国では、隣人がこの家を奇怪なもの、ライトを狂人、ロビーを愚か者とみなした。ロビー邸は施主が探し求めた住宅像を断固たる決意で実現したものであり、ロビー氏の息子はこの家を「世界で最も理想的な場所」と考えた。しかし2年もたたないうちに、負債の増加と妻との離婚が原因となり、ロビー氏はこの家を手放すことを余儀なくされた。長期にわたるライトの設計活動の初期にデザインされたロビー邸は、ライトが最も気に入っていた住宅デザインの一つであった。1951年にこの住宅の取り壊しが計画された際、彼はこの住宅は「近代建築の第一歩」であると述べた。ライト自身と彼の財団の努力によって、この住宅は取り壊しを免れた。2007年に完成する修復を経て、ライトの創造的エネルギーと革新的業績の証人としてロビー邸は今後も存在しつづけるであろう。　　　　　　　（KTO）

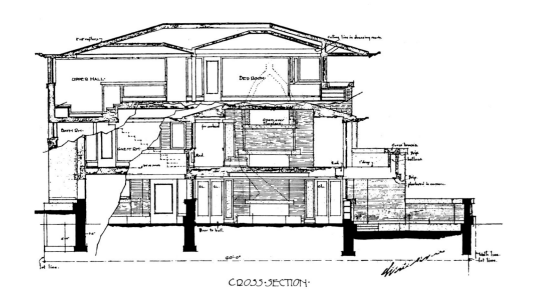

CROSS·SECTION·

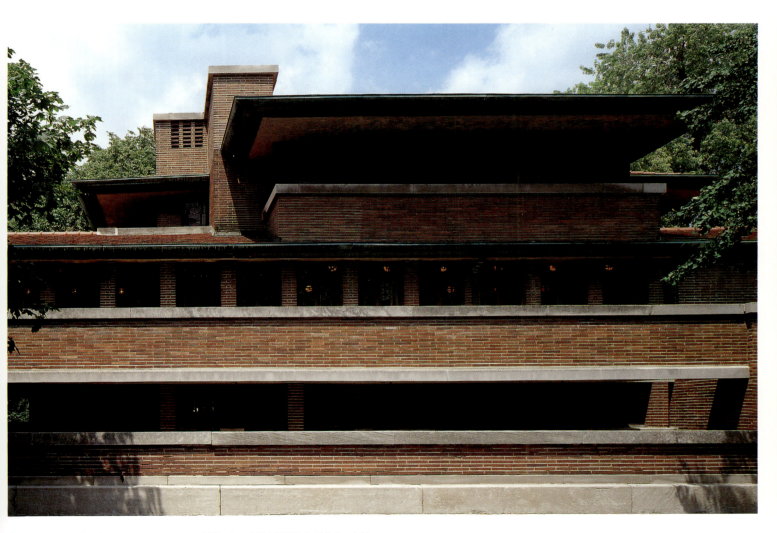

Opposite, top: South
elevation/south elevation of
garage. Bottom: Cross section.
Above: South facade emphasizes
horizontal lines. pp. 38–39:
General view from the southwest.

左頁、上：南側立面図および車庫の南側
立面図。左頁、下：短辺方向断面図。
上：水平方向のラインを強調した南側フ
ァサード。38〜39頁：南西からみた全景。

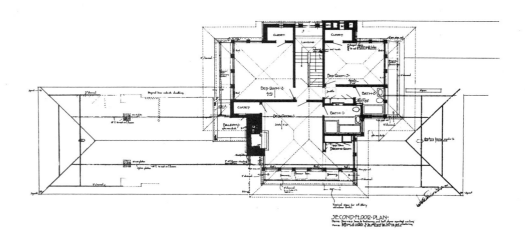

SECOND·FLOOR·PLAN·

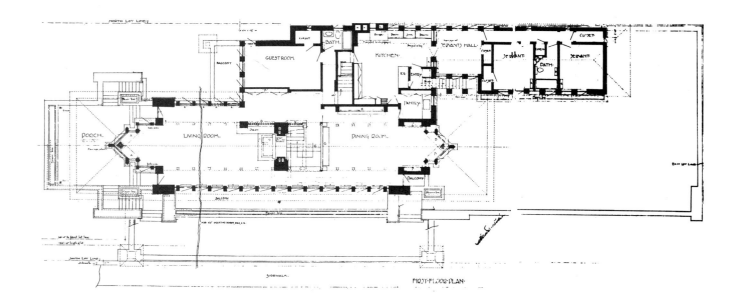

FIRST·FLOOR·PLAN·

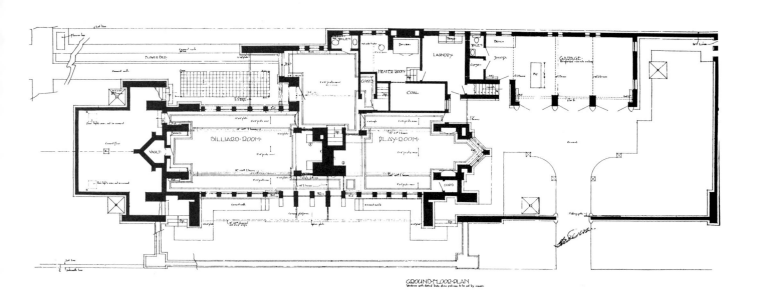

GROUND·FLOOR·PLAN·

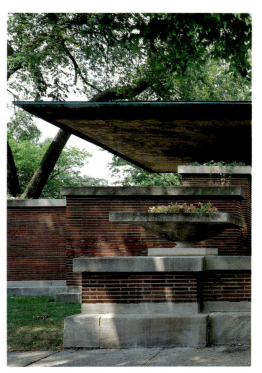

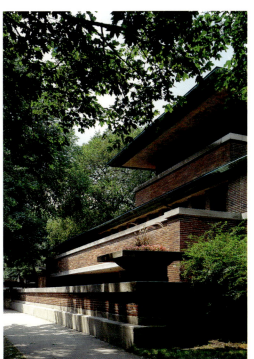

Opposite, to bottom: 2nd floor plan,
1st floor plan, ground floor plan.
This page, clockwise from left top:
Entry from the north; view of the
cantilevered roof on the west; view
of the south facade from the east;
view of the south facade from the
west.

左頁、上から：3階平面図、2階平面図、1
階平面図。左上から、時計回りに：北側
の入口。西端の屋根の張り出し。南側の
ファサードを東からみる。南側のファサ
ードを西からみる。

*Above: East end of the dining
room. Opposite: View of the living
room.*

上：食堂の東端。右頁：居間をみる。

Above: Living room. View toward
the fireplace.

上：居間。暖炉側をみる。

Above: View of the leaded windows opening to the porch on the south side of the living and dining rooms.

上：居間・食堂南側のポーチに開く鉛枠のガラス戸をみる。

Scheu House
Vienna, Austria 1912
Adolf Loos

ショイ邸
オーストリア、ウィーン　1912
アドルフ・ロース

One of the first modern houses in Europe to use its flat roofs as terraces, the Scheu House radically challenged the conventional image of the house in this affluent suburb of Vienna. Loos himself later noted, "Years ago I built this house for Dr. Gustav Scheu in Hietzing, Vienna. It aroused general disapproval. It was thought that this type of building would have been fine in Algiers, but not in Vienna. I had not even thought of the East when I built this house. I just thought that it would be pleasant to be able to step out onto a large common terrace from the bedrooms located on the [second level]. In Vienna just as much as in Algiers. So this terrace, repeated on the [third level] (a rented apartment) represented something unusual, abnormal even. One person went to the Municipal Council to ask if this type of building was permitted by the law."* In order to appease the authorities, Loos promised to grow plants over the plain facade and to produce a house design for the adjacent site.

While the stepped form of the Scheu house broke from neoclassical convention and current taste, it was neither unprecedented nor irrational. Such a form could be found in hillside dwellings in the Mediterranean as well as in ancient ziggurats. Although the Scheu House's street facade broke from the frontal symmetry of its neighbors, it maintained a basically symmetrical massing along an east/west axis such that all terraces face east. Loos sited the volume on the extreme northwest corner of the lot to maximize garden space to the south and create a buffer between the street and garden. While the smooth, unornamented, white plaster exterior seems to epitomize modern abstract form, the house was actually built using traditional masonry construction.

Just as seemingly incompatible ideas of avant-garde and vernacular design simultaneously inform Loos' house, a dialectical disjunction remains — between exterior and interior, private and public, diurnal and nocturnal, and service and served. As the architect noted, "The house should be discreet on the outside; its entire richness should be disclosed on the inside." The entry thus serves as a ritual transitional space for the initial withdrawal from the city, for the removal of street clothes and washing up before entrance to the living spaces. An early elaboration of Loos's *Raumplan* concept, interior spaces were further divided by floor: the basement for service, the 1st level for daily activities such as living, dining, and music, the 2nd level for bedrooms, and the 3rd level as a rental unit or service quarter. The interior, with its comfortable rusticity, contrasts dramatically with the severe monumentality of the exterior. Since Loos considered the house a conservative entity rather than a work of art, he used the comfortable elements of English Arts and Crafts interiors: exposed oak-veneered beams on the ceiling, abstracted stile-and-rail paneling, and built-in furniture which allowed the owner to add his own comfortable leather seats to the ensemble. Wood surfaces were lightly stained to bring out the natural character of the grain and add visual interest to the interior, replacing moldings or ornament with particular stylistic associations. Loos believed a room should adapt to the people who live in it — "like a violin adapts to the music." Furthermore, he designed bedrooms clad in white-painted wood to create a marked contrast with the darker wood interiors below, as a balance between day and night spaces. In the years following its completion, portions of the terraces and the entry stair were enclosed, but these additions were removed in 1970s renovations. While some of the service and sleeping spaces have been slightly modified, the main living spaces correspond to Loos's original design. (KTO)

Note:
* Adolf Loos, "Das Grand-Hotel Babylon," in *Die Neue Wirschaft*, Jahrg. I 20 December 1923.

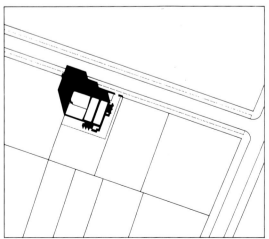

Opposite left: Perspective view of
Scheu house and proposed scheme
for adjacent site by Adolf Loos.
Opposite right: Site plan. Above:
View from Larochegasse street on
the north side.

左頁、左：ショイ邸と隣地のためのプロ
ポーザル。アドルフ・ロースによる透視
図。左頁、右：配置図。上：北側のラロ
フェ通りからみる。

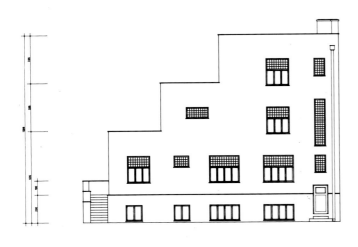

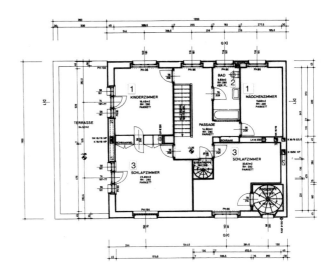

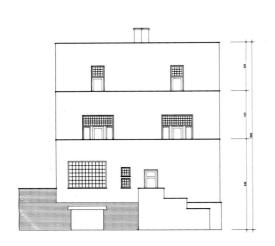

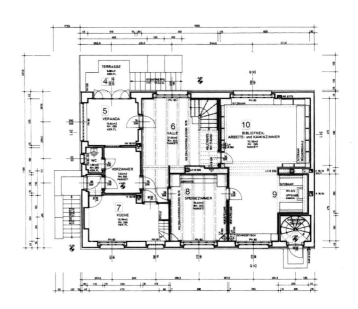

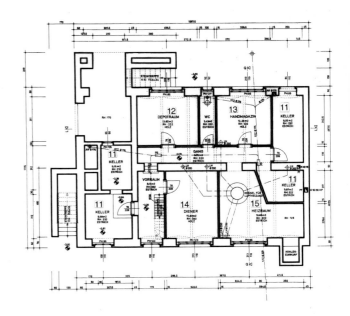

Opposite left column, top to bottom: North elevation, east elevation, south elevation. Opposite right column, top to bottom: 2nd floor, 1st floor plan (main entry from eastern stair). These drawings and site plan were drawn at the time of reconstruction Scheu house, 1980–1982. Above: Street facade. Legend: 1) Child's room, 2) Bathroom, 3) Bedroom, 4) Terrace, 5) Veranda, 6) Hall, 7) Kitchen, 8) Dining room, 9) Hearth, 10) Library, 11) Cellar, 12) Storage, 13) Closet, 14) Maid's room, 15) Heating room

左頁、左、上から：北側立面図。東側立面図、南側立面図。左頁、右、上から：2階、1階、地階平面図。東側の階段がメイン・エントランスとなる。

これらの図面、および配置図はショイ邸の1980〜1982年の修復の際描かれた。上：通り側のファサード。

凡例：1）子ども室、2）浴室、3）寝室、4）テラス、5）ヴェランダ、6）広間、7）台所、8）食堂、9）炉辺、10）ライブラリー、11）食品庫、12）倉庫、13）物置、14）使用人室、15）暖房機室

陸屋根を屋外テラスとして利用したヨーロッパで最初のモダン・ハウスの一つであるショイ邸は、ウィーン郊外の裕福な住宅地の伝統的な住宅のイメージにたいする挑戦であった。アドルフ・ロースは、後に次のように書き留めている。「ずいぶん昔、ウィーンのヒートツィングに、医師のグスタフ・ショイ氏のためにこの家を建てた。それは周囲の人々の非難を巻き起こした。この種の建物はアルジェでは問題ないが、ウィーンでは受け入れられないと考えられたのだ。この住宅を建てた時、私は東方のことなど考えもしなかった。私はただ、2階のベッドルームから大きなテラスに出ることができれば気持ちがよいと考えただけなのだ。アルジェ同様、ウィーンにおいても。したがってこのテラスは3階（賃貸アパート）においても繰り返され、見慣れないもの、あるいは異質とさえいえるものを表現した。ある人物は、この種の建物が法律的に許されているのかどうか確認すべく市議会に赴いた」[1] 当局への譲歩として、ロースは簡素なファサードにプランターを設けて植物を植え、さらに隣接する敷地の住宅もあわせてデザインすることを約束した。

ショイ邸の階段状の形態は、新古典主義の伝統や当時の趣味からは逸脱するものであったが、先例のない新奇なものでも非合理的なものでもなかった。このような形態は地中海の丘に建てられた民家や古代のジグラットに見出すことができる。道路側の左右非対称のファサードは、近隣の左右対称のファサードからは逸脱しているが、東西軸にそって左右対称のヴォリュームになっており、そのためすべてのテラスが東に面している。庭の広さを最大限に確保し、通りと庭の間に盾を設けるために、ロースは敷地の北西の角にヴォリュームを置いた。さらに、なめらかで装飾のない白いプラスター仕上げの外観は近代の抽象的な形態の典型のようにみえるが、この建物は伝統的な石造技術を用いて建てられている。

一見ちぐはぐな、この前衛的なデザインとヴァナキュラーなデザインの共存は、同時に、ロースの住宅における内部と外部、プライヴェートとパブリック、日中と夜間、サーヴィスする側とサーヴィスされる側の間の弁証法的な命題を示唆している。ロースが記しているように、「住宅は外部から分離すべきである。すべての豊かさは、内部に表わされるべき」なのだ。たとえば入口は、外出用の衣服を脱ぎ、手や顔を洗うことによって、居室に入る前に外界とパブリックな生活から離れる清めの空間としてしつらえられている。内部空間はさらに階によって分節されており、ロースが「ラウムプラン」の概念（空間における平面の分節）を展開し始めていることがみてとれる。すなわち、地下はサーヴィス、1階は日々の生活、食堂、音楽のための空間、2階は寝室、3階は賃貸アパート（サーヴィス空間）に分割されている。内部空間の心地よい田舎っぽい雰囲気は、外観の厳格なモニュメンタリティと劇的な対比をなしている。住宅は芸術作品ではなく本質的に保守的なものだと考えた彼は、心地よい英国のアーツ・アンド・クラフツ的なインテリア・デザインを用いた。オークで覆われた天井の露出した梁、縦框の羽目板、心地よい皮製の椅子といった居住者自身の家具を許容する造り付けの家具などにその影響がうかがえる。流行を追ったモールディングや装飾のかわりに、木目の自然な性質を引き出し、インテリアを視覚的に興味深いものとするために薄く木に着色が施された。ロースは、「ヴァイオリンが音楽に合わせるように」、部屋は住む人に合わせるべきであると信じた。さらに彼は、下階のうす暗い木のインテリアと明確な対比をつくりだすために、日中と夜間の空間の精神的バランスを考慮し、ベッドルームには白く塗られた木を用いた。

一時的にテラスの一部と入口の階段が覆われた時期があったが、その後、1970年代に行われた修復によって取り除かれた。サーヴィス空間と寝室には若干の変更が加えられたが、現在のオーナーによって丁重に維持されている1階の居室は、ロースのオリジナルのデザイン思想を現在に伝えている。　　　　（KTO）

Opposite: South facade from the garden. Above: View of the terrace to the garden on the south side.

左頁：南側のファサード。庭からみる。
上：南側の庭へのヴェランダ前テラス。

pp. 52–53: Library on the upper
ground level looking toward the
south. Above: View of the study
area. Middle: View of inglenook
study. Below: North-south section
and east-west section. Opposite:
Hall with main staircase.

52～53頁：1階のライブラリー南側。上：
書斎。中：書斎の炉辺。下：南北断面図、
東西断面図。右頁：主階段のあるホール。

Manifestoes of the Modern House

モダン・ハウスのマニフェスト
マニフェスト：主義あるいは意思の公的な宣言、とりわけ政治的なもの

木下壽子訳

The modern house, has undergone constant redefinition throughout the 20th century. For many architects such textual definitions, often promoted widely through increasingly available books and journals, became powerfully influential manifestoes for new forms and social change. Accompanying drawings and models also sparked the imaginations of readers worldwide. The following collection of excerpts from influential texts provide a cross-section of this discourse, illuminating the dwelling's potential to effect change both in its historical context in the 20th century and future context in the 21st century.

(KTO)

モダン・ハウスは、20世紀を通して様々な定義がなされてきた。多くの建築家にとって、こうした文章化された定義は、新しい形態と社会的変化にたいして大きな影響力をもつマニフェストとなり、ますます身近になった本や雑誌を通してしばしば広く推奨された。付随するドローイングや模型もまた、世界中の読者のイマジネーションを刺激した。以下に編集した重要な文献からの引用は、このようなディスコースの断面を示すものであり、それは、20世紀の歴史的文脈および21世紀の未来的文脈において変化をもたらすであろう住居の可能性を照らし出している。

(KTO)

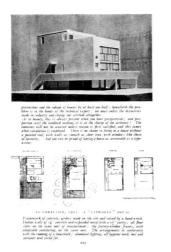

Above left: From Towards a New Architecture, *Le Corbusier, Praeger Publishers, New York-Washington. 1970 (4th printing), pp. 222–223. Above middle: From "Building," G. no.2 (September 1923). Above right: Poster for the Werkbund exhibition*

"The Dwelling," Stuttgart, 1927. Die Baumeister, Ludwig Mies van der Rohe, and Werner Gräff.

左上：『建築をめざして』より。中上：『G』誌No.2、1923年9月号より。右上：工作連盟展示会「The Dwelling（住）」のポスター、1927年。建築家ルードヴィッヒ・ミース・ファン・デル・ローエ、ヴェルナー・グレッフ。

1902
Hermann Muthesius
Excerpt from *Style-Architecture and Building-Art: Transformations in the Nineteenth Century and its Present Condition*

Thus there is a coincidence here of certain sanitary and aesthetic concerns. And the combination of the two appears everywhere in modern designs as we now begin to see, for example, in our dwellings. Here, reforms are taking place — we recognize them most fully in the contemporary English house — that strive to increase the amount of light and air, to design strictly functional rooms, to avoid all useless appendages in the decoration, to eliminate heavy, unmovable household furnishings, and to strive for an overall sense of brightness and impression of cleanliness. These reforms follow the same tendency as our clothing, the closer dwelling that envelops us.

1910
Adolf Loos
Architectur

The house has to please everyone, contrary to the work of art which does not. The work is a private matter for the artist. The house is not. The work of art is brought into the world without there being a need for it. The house satisfies a requirement. The work of art is responsible to none; the house is responsible to everyone. The work of art wants to draw people out of their state of comfort. The house has to serve comfort. The work of art is revolutionary; the house is conservative. The work of art shows people new directions and thinks of the future. The house thinks of the present. Man loves everything that satisfies his comfort. He hates everything that wants to draw him out of his acquired and secured position and that disturbs him. Thus he loves the house and hates art. Does it follow that the house has nothing in common with art and is architecture not to be included amongst the arts? That is so. Only a very small part of architecture belongs to art: the tomb and the monument. Everything else that fulfills a function is to be excluded from the domain of art.

1914
Paul Scheerbart
Glassarchitektur

In order to raise our culture to a higher level, we are forced, whether we like it or not, to change our architecture. And this will be possible only if we free the rooms in which we live of their enclosed character. This, however, we can only do by introducing a glass architecture which admits the light of the sun, of the moon, and of the stars, not only through a few windows, but through as many walls as feasible, these to consist entirely of glass — of colored glass.

ヘルマン・ムテジウス

『Style-Architecture and Building-Art: Transformation in the Nineteenth Century and its Present Condition（様式建築と建設芸術：19世紀における変容とその現状）』

このように、いくつかの衛生上の問題と美の問題はここでは一致する。そして衛生と美の組み合わせは、現在明らかになりつつあるように、近代デザインのあらゆる部分、たとえば我々の住宅に見出すことができる。住宅においては、採光と換気の量を増やし、真に機能的な部屋をデザインし、装飾におけるあらゆる無用の付加物を取り除き、重く動かし難い家庭の家具類を排除し、そして全体的に明るさと清潔感をもたらすべく努力する改革 ―なかでも現代の英国の住宅に最も完全なかたちで見出せる― が行われている。これらの改革は、我々を包み込んでいる、より身近な住処である衣類と同じ傾向に向かって進んでいる。

アドルフ・ロース
『建築について』伊藤哲夫訳　参照

住宅はすべての人たちに気に入られなければならない。このことは、誰にも気に入られる必要のない芸術作品と相違する点である。芸術作品とは芸術家の個人的なものである。ところが住宅は違う。芸術作品は、それにたいする必要性が何らなくともつくられ、世に送り出される。ところが住宅は必要を満たすのだ。芸術作品は誰にも責任を負わないが、住宅は一人一人に責任を負う。また芸術作品は人を快適な状態から引き離そうとするが、住宅は快適さを提供しなければならない。芸術作品は革新的であり、住宅は保守的である。芸術作品は人に新しい道を指し示し、未来を考えさせる。ところが住宅は現在を考えるのである。人間は自分が快適さを得るのに役立つことならなんでも好きだ。そして自分をそうした快適、安全な状態から引き離そうとするもの、邪魔しようとするものならなんでも憎む。このようにみてくると、人は住宅を愛し、芸術を恨むといってよいだろう。かくして、住宅と芸術はなんら関係がないのではないか、そして建築を芸術の一ジャンルに加えることはないのではないか。事実、そのとおりなのだ。芸術に加わるのは、ごく一部の建築でしかない。それは墓碑と記念碑だ。機能を満たすその他の建築はすべて、芸術の領域から閉め出されねばならない。

パウル・シェーアバルト
『Glassarchitektur（ガラス建築）』

我々の文化レヴェルをより高めるには、好むと好まざるとにかかわらず、我々は建築を変えることを強いられている。そしてそれは、我々が住んでいる閉鎖的な部屋を解放することによってのみ可能である。これは、しかしながら、いくつかの窓からだけでなく、可能な限りの壁を通して太陽、月、星の光を入れることができる、もっぱらガラス、それも色ガラスで構成されたガラス建築を取り入れることによってのみ可能となる。

1923
Le Corbusier
"THE MANUAL OF THE DWELLING"
Published in *Vers une Architeture*

Demand a bathroom looking south, one of the largest rooms in the house or flat, the old drawing-room for instance. One wall to be entirely glazed, opening if possible on to a balcony for sun baths; the most up-to-date fittings with a shower-bath and gymnastic appliances.

An adjoining room to be a dressing-room in which you can dress and undress. Never undress in your bedroom. It is not a clean thing to do and makes the room horribly untidy. In this room demand fitments for your linen and clothing, not more than 5 feet in height, with drawers, hangers, etc.

Demand one really large living room instead of a number of small ones.

Demand bare walls in your bedroom, your living room and your dining-room. Built-in fittings to take the place of much of the furniture, which is expensive to buy, takes up too much room and needs looking after.

If you can, put the kitchen at the top of the house to avoid smells.

Demand concealed or diffused lighting.

Demand a vacuum cleaner.

Buy only practical furniture and never buy decorative "pieces." If you want to see bad taste, go into the houses of the rich. Put only a few pictures on your walls and none but good ones.

Keep your odds and ends in drawers or cabinets.

The gramophone or the pianola or wireless will give you exact interpretations of first-rate music, and you will avoid catching cold in the concert hall, and the frenzy of the virtuoso.

Demand ventilating panes to the windows in every room.

Teach your children that a house is only habitable when it is full of light and air, and when the floors and walls are clear. To keep your floors in order eliminate heavy furniture and thick carpets.

Demand a separate garage to your dwelling.

Demand that the maid's room should not be an attic. Do not park your servants under the roof.

Take a flat which is one size smaller than what your parents accustomed you to. Bear in mind economy in your actions, your household management and in your thoughts.

ル・コルビュジエ
「住宅の手引き」
『建築をめざして』に掲載

たとえば昔の応接間のような、家あるいはフラットのなかで最も大きな部屋で、かつ南向きのバスルームを要求しなさい。壁の一面は全面的にガラス張りで、できれば日光浴のためのバルコニーとつながっていること。シャワー・バスと運動器具のある最新の設備を。

それにつながる部屋は、衣服を着たり脱いだりする更衣室に。バスルームで脱衣してはいけない。それは清潔なことではないし、部屋をひどく取り散らかすことになる。更衣室には、5フィート（1.5m）以下の高さで、引き出しとハンガーなどがついた、肌着と衣服のための造り付けの家具を要求しなさい。

いくつもの小さな部屋のかわりに、一つの十分に広いリヴィング・ルームを要求しなさい。

ベッドルーム、リヴィング・ルーム、ダイニング・ルームには、飾りのない剥き出しの壁を要求しなさい。造り付けの家具が、高価で、場所を取り、手入れに手間がかかる家具にとってかわるだろう。

できるならば、匂いを避けるために、キッチンに最上階に設けなさい。

間接照明あるいは拡散照明を要求しなさい。

電気掃除機を要求しなさい。

実用的な家具だけを買い、装飾的な「品々」は買ってはならない。悪趣味なものをみたければ、金持ちの家に入ってみなさい。壁にはほんの少しだけ、それも良いものだけを掛けなさい。

あなたのがらくたは、引き出しかキャビネットにしまっておきなさい。

蓄音機、ピアノラ、あるいはラジオは、第一級の音楽の正確な演奏を提供してくれるであろうから、コンサート・ホールで風邪を引いたり、名演奏家の熱狂を避けることができよう。

どの部屋にも、換気用のガラス窓を要求しなさい。

子どもたちには、住宅は十分な日光と空気で満たされ、床と壁がすっきりしている場合のみ住みうるのだと教えなさい。床の秩序を保つためには、重い家具と分厚いカーペットを排除しなさい。

独立したガレージをあなたの住宅のために要求しなさい。

メイドの部屋は屋根裏に配置しないよう要求しなさい。使用人を屋根の下におかないように。

あなたの両親の世代が馴染んでいるフラットよりも、一回りサイズの小さなものを選びなさい。あなたの行動、家政、思考における経済性を心がけるように。

1923
Le Corbusier
MASS-PRODUCTION HOUSE
Published in *Vers une Architecture*

"Citrohan" (not to say Citroën). That is to say, a house like a motor-car, conceived and carried out like an omnibus or a ship's cabin. The actual need of the dwelling can be formulated and demand their solution. We must fight against the old-world house, which made a bad use of space. We must look upon the house as a machine for living in or as a tool. When a man starts any particular industry he buys the necessary equipment of tools; when he sets up house he rents, in actual fact, a ridiculous dwelling. Till now a house has consisted of an incoherent grouping of a number of large rooms; in these rooms the space has been both cramped and wasted. To-day, happily, we are not rich enough to carry on these customs, and as it is difficult to get people to look at the problem under its true aspect (machines for living in), it is nearly impossible to build in our towns, with disastrous results. Windows and doors must have their sizes readjusted; railway carriages and saloon-cars have shown that man can pass through smaller openings, and that these can be worked out to the last square inch; it is criminal to make W.C.'s 36 feet square. As the price of building has quadrupled itself, we must reduce the old architectural pretensions and the cubage of houses by at least one-half; henceforth the problem is in the hands of the technical expert: we must enlist the discoveries made in industry and change our attitude altogether.

As to beauty, this is always present when you have *proportion*; and proportion costs the landlord nothing, it is at the charge of the architect! The emotions will not be aroused unless reason is first satisfied, and this comes when calculation is employed. There is no shame in living in a house without a pointed roof, with walls as smooth as sheet iron, with windows like those of factories. And one *can* be proud of having a house as serviceable as a typewriter.

ル・コルビュジエ
「量産住宅」
『建築をめざして』に掲載

シトロアン（シトロエンではなく）。これはいわば、自動車のような住宅で、バスや船のキャビンのように構想され、製作されたものである。住居に実際のところ必要とされているものは体系化することができ、解決策が求められている。我々は、空間を無駄に使っている旧世界の家と闘わなければならない。我々は住むための機械、あるいは道具として住宅をみなければならない。人はどのようなものであれ、ある特定の工業を始めるとき、必要な道具設備を購入する。彼が世帯をもつとき、実際のところ、馬鹿げた住居を借りる。今までの住宅は支離滅裂な数々の大きな部屋の集まりからできている。こうした部屋では、空間は窮屈であり、同時に無駄に使われてきた。今日、幸いなことに、このような慣習をつづけられるほど我々は裕福ではなく、また人々に正しい見方（住むための機械）で問題を直視させることは困難であるから、我々の町に建てることはほとんど不可能であり、このような悲惨な結果となる。窓とドアはサイズを新たに調整しなければならない。鉄道車両とリムジンは、人間がより小さな開口でも通り抜けられることを証明し、最後の1平方インチ（6.45㎡）まで計算される。36平方フィート（3.34㎡）のトイレをつくるのは犯罪だ。建設費が4倍に跳ね上がるからであり、我々はかつての建築的要求を減らさねばならず、住宅の容積を少なくとも半分にすべきである。これからは、問題は専門技術者の手中にある。工業が発見したものに積極的に参加し、我々の態度を全面的に改めよう。

美は、常に優れたプロポーションのなかに存在する。そしてプロポーションは家主には一文の負担もかからず、それは建築家にゆだねられている！　感情は、まず理由が説明されなければ目覚めることはなく、それは計算がなされている場合にのみ可能である。尖塔屋根ではなく、鉄板のように滑らかな壁をもち、工場のような窓のついた家に住むことは恥ではない。タイプライターのように便利な家をもつことは誇ることべきことなのだ。

1923
Mies van der Rohe
"Building"
Published in *G*, no. 2 (September 1923)

We know no forms, only building problems.
Form is not the goal but the result of our work.
There is no form in and for itself.
The truly formal is conditional, fused with the task, yes,
the most elementary expression of its solution.
Form as goal is formalism; and that we reject. Nor do we strive
for a style.
Even the will to style is formalism.
We have other worries.
It is our specific concern to liberate building activity [*Bauerei*]
from aesthetic speculators and make building activity [*Bauen*]
again what alone it should be, namely BAUEN.
There have been repeated attempts to introduce ferroconcrete
as a building material for apartment building construction.
Mostly, however, ineptly. The advantages of this material have
not been exploited nor its disadvantages avoided. One believes
one has acknowledged the material sufficiently if one rounds
off the corners of the house and of the individual rooms. The
round corners are totally irrelevant for concrete and not even
all that easy to execute. It will not do of course simply to
translate a brick house into ferroconcrete. I see the main
advantage of ferroconcrete in the possibility of considerable
savings in material. In order to realize this in an apartment
building, one must concentrate the supports and
reinforcements in a few building locations. The disadvantage of
ferroconcrete, as I see it, lies in its low insulating property and
its poor sound absorption. This makes it necessary to provide
sound absorption. This makes it necessary to provide
additional insulation against exterior temperatures. The
simplest way to remove the disadvantage of sound transfer
seems to be to exclude everything that causes noise; here I
have in mind rubber floors, sliding windows and doors, and
similar installations: but then also spatial generosity in the
ground plan.— Ferroconcrete demands the most precise
planning before its execution; here the architect still has
everything to learn from the shipbuilding engineer. With brick
construction it is possible, even if not particularly advisable, to
let the heating and installation crews loose on the house as
soon as the roof is up; they will in the briefest time transform
the house into a ruin. With ferroconcrete such a procedure is
impossible. Here only disciplined work will achieve the desired
result.

ミース・ファン・デル・ローエ
「Building（ビルディング）」
『G』誌 No.2 1923年9月号に掲載

我々は形態を知らない、知っているのは建設の問題のみである。
形態は目標ではなく、我々の仕事の結果である。
形態は、それ自体のなかに、あるいはそれ自体のためにあるのではない。
真に形態があるというのは、制約的で、課せられた課題と融合した、そう、その解決策の最も本質的な表現である。
目的としての形態は形式主義であり、我々はそれを拒否する。また、様式も求めない。
様式をつくろうと欲する気持ちすらも、形式主義である。
我々には他の心配事がある。
それは、美的な思索から建設活動[Bauerei]を解放し、建設活動[Bauen]をふたたびそのあるべき状態、すなわち建設活動[BAUEN]に戻すという関心事である。
共同住宅の建築材料として鉄筋コンクリートを取り入れようとする試みが幾度となく繰り返されている。しかしながらほとんどの場合、そのやり方は不適当だ。この材料の利点は活かされず、欠点も除去されていない。住宅と各部屋の角を落とせばこの材料を十分に承知したと信じている人がいる。丸い角はコンクリートとまったく無関係であり、決して簡単に施工できるものではない。それはもちろん、単に煉瓦の家を鉄筋コンクリートに翻訳したものではない。私は、鉄筋コンクリートの主な利点は、材料を少なからず節約できる可能性だと考えている。これを共同住宅で実現するには、支柱と建物の数ヵ所における補強に集中しなければならない。鉄筋コンクリートの欠点は、私のみるところ、断熱性の低さと吸音性の悪さである。そのため、吸音処置を施す必要がある。また、外気にたいする断熱材を加える必要もある。音の伝達という欠点をなくす最も簡単な方法は、音を出すものを除去することであろう。つまり私は、ゴム製の床、引き違いの窓および戸、そのほか同じような設備を考えている。しかし同時に、ある程度の平面の広さも必要である。鉄筋コンクリートは、施工に入る前のきわめて正確な計画が要求される。建築家は、造船技術から大いに学ぶ必要がある。煉瓦構造では、特にすすめはしないが、屋根が取りつけられた直後に暖房と設備の作業員に任せてしまうことはできるけれども、彼らはすぐさま家を廃墟にしてしまうだろう。鉄筋コンクリートではこのような手順は不可能である。秩序だった作業のみが望ましい結果を生むであろう。

1923
Van Doesburg
"16 points of a Plastic Architecture"

The new architecture is *anti-cubic*, that is to say, it does not
try to freeze the different functional space cells in one closed
cube. Rather, it throws the functional space cells (as well as the
overhanging planes, balcony volumes, etc.) centrifugally from
the core of the cube. And through this means, *height, width,
depth, and time* (i.e. an imaginary four-dimensional entity)
approaches a totally new plastic expression in open spaces. In
this way architecture acquires a more or less floating aspect
that, so to speak, works against the gravitational forces of
nature.

ファン・ドゥースブルフ
「16 points of a Plastic Architecture（造形的建築の16のポイント）」

新しい建築は反立方体であり、それはつまり、異なる機能的空間の小室を一つの閉じた立方体に押し込めようとしないということだ。それよりも、機能的空間の小室を（張り出した水平面、バルコニーのヴォリュームなども同様に）立方体の中心から外に放り出す。そしてこのような方法によって、高さ、幅、奥行き、そして時間（すなわち幻想的な四次元の存在）は、オープン・スペースにおけるまったく新しい造形的な表現に近づく。その結果、建築は、いわば自然の重力に対抗して浮遊しているような外観を獲得する。

1924
Van Doesburg and Van Esteren
"Towards a Collective Construction"

We must realize that life and art are no longer separate
domains. That is why the 'idea' of 'art' as an illusion separate
from real life must disappear. The word 'Art' no longer means
anything to us. In its place we demand the construction of our
environment in accordance with creative laws based upon a
fixed principle. These laws, following those of economics,
mathematics, technique, sanitation, etc., are leading to a new
plastic unity.

1931
Walter Gropius
"The Small House of To-Day"
Published in *Architectural Forum*, March 1931.

In addition to adequate food and heat, the proper health and
growth of human beings absolutely depends upon *ample
sunlight, fresh air, and facility to get outdoor exercise.*
Undoubtedly these three cardinal demands on a good dwelling
are better met by a one family house than by the forbidding
upper floor quarters of crowded tenement houses.....
According to the new view about a dwelling to come up to
present day requirements, the dwelling house should no longer
resemble something like a fortress, like a monument with wall
of medieval thickness and an expensive front intended for
show representation. Instead it is to be of light construction,
full of bright daylight and sunshine, alterable, time-saving,
economical and useful in the last degree to its occupants whose
life functions it is intended to serve. Man and the various
functions of his life at home — living, sleeping, eating, cooking,
bathing, washing — are reinstated as the basis determining the
type and appointments of the house, the biologic principle is
paramount. The *value* of the *house as a place to live in* is
placed foremost and is measured by the degree of success the
builder attains in reducing the onerous features of everyday life
to a minimum and enabling the occupants to lead an easy and
practical life meeting every requirement — in fact, a "beautiful"
life at home — at the least possible cost of space, material, and
building expense.....
The modern creative spirit, which is slowly developing, goes
down again to the bottom of things: To create a house which
will serve its purpose well, its essential nature is first
investigated. The research into "functions" and nature of a
house is subject to mechanical, static, optical, and acoustic
limitations as well as to the laws of proportion on which the
"beautiful" effect depends. Proportion is a matter of the realm
of spirit; construction and materials are its bearers, with the
aid of which it reveals the genius of its creator. It is determined
by the particular functions of a given house, and through it the
latter is imbued with the "tension," a spiritual life of its own,
as it were, beyond the utility value of the house.

ファン・ドゥースブルフ＆ファン・エーステレン
『Towards a Collective Construction（共同建設をめざして）』

芸術と生活がもはや異なる領域に属すものではないということを我々は認識しなければならない。現実的生活から切り離された幻想としての「芸術」の「アイディア」が消滅しなければならないのはそのためである。「芸術」という言葉はもはや何も意味しない。かわりに、確固とした原理にもとづいた創造の法にしたがった環境の建設を要求しなければならない。経済、数学、技術、公衆衛生などにしたがったこれらの法は、新たな造形的なまとまりへと導いていく。

ウォルター・グロピウス
「The Small House of To-Day（今日の小住宅）」
『アーキテクチュラル・フォーラム』誌1931年3月号掲載

望ましい健康と人間の成長は、十分な食べ物と暖かさに加えて、十分な日光、新鮮な空気、そして屋外運動のしやすさに絶対的に左右される。よい住宅に要求されるこれら三つの基本的要求は、まちがいなく、密度の高いアパートの近づき難い上階の居室よりも、1戸建て住宅のほうがより満足に満たされる。
今日の要求にかなった住宅にたいする新しい見方にしたがえば、住宅はもはや城塞のようなもの、つまり中世的な厚い壁とこれ見よがしの高価な正面デザインをもった記念碑のようなものであるべきではない。かわりに、軽い構造体で、明るい日光と日照が得られ、可変性があり、時間の節約ができ、経済的で、居住者の生活が意図した通りに機能するよう限りなく実用的であるべきだ。人間と、家での生活における様々な機能—生活、就寝、食事、料理、入浴、洗濯—が住宅のタイプと設備を確定する基礎として復帰し、生物学的な原理が何にも増して重要となる。「住むための場としての住宅」の「価値」は、最小限のコスト、材料、建設費で、日常生活の厄介な部分を最小限に抑え、居住者があらゆる要求に見合った容易で実用的な生活を送れるようにする —すなわち、家での「美しい」生活— という点において、建設者がどれくらい成功するかにかかっており、またそれによって測られる。
ゆっくりと発展しつつある近代の創造精神は、ふたたび事物の根底にまでたち戻る。目的をきちんと果たす住宅をつくるには、その本質的な性質がまず研究されねばならない。住宅の「機能」と性質の探求は、「美しさ」の効果の拠り所であるプロポーションの法則同様、機械的、静的、視覚的、聴覚的な限界の問題である。プロポーションは精神の領域の問題であり、構造と材料は製作者の能力によってそれに従属させられる。それは、ある住宅の特定の機能によって決定され、そのなかで後者は「緊張」、いわば住宅の実用的な価値を超えたそれ自体の精神的生活を鼓吹される。

Une Petite Maison
Corseaux-Verey, Switzerland 1923
Le Corbusier

小さな家 — 母の家
スイス、コルソ-ヴヴェー　1923
ル・コルビュジエ

By 1923, Le Corbusier was already a leading voice for the modern movement. In that year he designed this "small house" for his parents on the banks of Lake Léman. Le Corbusier's ideas about the modern house, which have left an indelible mark on twentieth century architecture, are clearly expressed in this tiny house with a total floor area of only 60 m².

In order to create an ideal environment for his elderly parents to live peacefully, "after a life of hard work," Le Corbusier established requirements for the house and site before purchase. The site must face south with hills behind, open onto a lake view, and include a view of the Alps reflected in the lake. The house itself was to be "a machine for living." As Le Corbusier himself specified, "dimensions precisely adapted to individual functions permit maximum exploitation of space. The arrangement is practical and spatially economical." Based on these specifications, he determined that a minimal dwelling with 54 m² of livable floor area [60 m² including circulation] would be optimal for his elderly parents.

This house was completed in 1924, and consists of a long, slender, single-level structure running east to west 16 m long, 4 m wide, and 2.5 m high. The free plan, realized through reinforced concrete-block construction, resulted in a plan based on efficient circulation; the free facade made a continuous 11 m-long window possible. Main living spaces and bath face this elongated horizontal window in the south facade, which Le Corbusier called "the chief attraction of the house." Sunlight fills the rooms through this window throughout the day, providing a sense of time passing and emphasizing the ever-changing appearance of the lake and Alps. In order to use the space efficiently, Le Corbusier did not partition it. The sole exception is a foldable sliding panel door closing off the eastern side of the main room as a guestroom. The furniture and light fixtures are simple, economical, and extremely functional. Further, as an economical means of insulation, Le Corbusier put earth on the roof and created a "roof garden," thereby providing the sought-after elements, "sun, space, and greenness."

In contrast to the expansive interior view of the horizontal window, Le Corbusier also built an exterior stone wall to consciously "[block] off the exterior view . . . for the ever-present and overpowering scenery on all sides has a tiring effect in the long run." Ten meters of garden were enclosed by a stone wall on the south side, creating a "verdant room." Within the south wall, he cut out a square opening which from afar resembles a landscape painting. But closer to the window, from the bench by the built-in table, the beautiful view opens up once again.

Le Corbusier's nature-loving father George-Edouard Jeanneret-Gris spent one year here fascinated by the scenery, and his musician mother Marie Charlotte Amélie spent 36 years living in this house until her death at the age of 101. Today, Petite Maison is open to the public, managed by the local government, and owned by the Fondation Le Corbusier.   (TK)

pp. 62-63: Evening view of Lake Léman through the horizontal window from the main living space. Opposite top: Roof garden looking east. Opposite bottom: East facade. Above: Street view from the north.

62〜63頁：メインの居室から水平連続窓を通して眺めるレマン湖の夕景。左頁、上：土の盛られた屋上庭園。東側をみる。左頁、下：東側のファサード。上：北側の通り側全景。

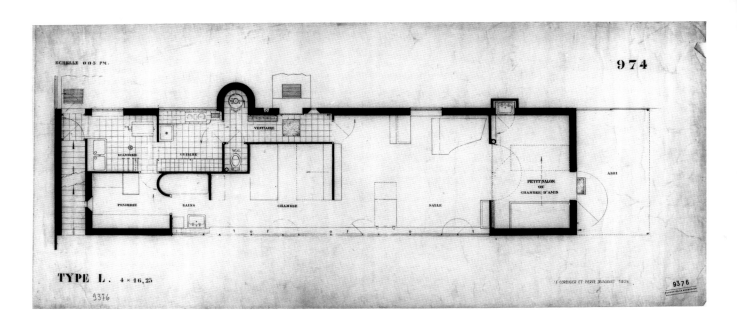

レマン湖の辺に1923年に建てられたこの「小さな家」は、当時すでにモダン・ムーヴメントの指導的建築家として世界的な名声を得ていたル・コルビュジエが彼の両親のために設計した住宅である。延床面積わずか60㎡のこの住宅には、20世紀の建築に大きな足跡を残したル・コルビュジエの住宅にたいするヴィジョンが余すところなく表現されている。

年老いた両親が「長年にわたる多忙な生活を終えて」安らかな日々を過ごすための理想的な環境を獲得するため、ル・コルビュジエは、敷地を購入する以前に、まずは敷地と住宅の条件を設定した。敷地については、南に面していること、山並みを背に湖が南に向かって広がっていること、湖とそこに映るアルプスの山々が西から東にかけて見渡せることが条件であった。住宅については、それが「住むための機械」であるということ、すなわち、「最小限の実用性が得られるように、適切な寸法をもつ簡明な機能に分かつこと。さらに空間が有効に活用できるように、それらを効果的に組織すること。各機能には許される限り最小の面積を充てること」が条件だった。その結果、老夫婦の生活に必要な最小限の床面積は54㎡と計算され、通路なども含めた最終的な延床面積は60㎡となった。

1924年に完成したこの住宅は、高さ2.5m、奥行き4m、長さ16mの東西に細長い平屋である。鉄筋コンクリート・ブロック造によってもたらされた自由な平面は、最も無駄のない動線にもとづいた平面計画を可能にし、自由なファサードは、長さ11mの連続窓を可能にした。主要な居室と浴室は、南面ファサード

に取り付けられたこの水平連続窓に面している。コルビュジエが「この家の主役」と呼んだ水平連続窓はこの住宅の最大の特徴であり、そこからは十分な太陽の光が居室に流れ込み、時間の流れや天候によって刻々と変化する湖とアルプスの山々を間近に感じることができた。部屋と部屋を仕切る扉はない。東端の空間のみが、スライド式の折りたたみパネルによって、来客時にゲスト・ルームとして使えるよう考慮されている。家具や照明器具は、経済性を重視した簡素なものだが、優れて機能的である。また、経済的な断熱方法として屋根には土が盛られ、「屋上庭園」がつくられた。こうして、ル・コルビュジエのいう「太陽、空間、緑」が獲得された。

連続窓の開放的な眺めとは対照的に、「四方八方にひろがる景色というものは圧倒的で、焦点を欠き、長い間にはかえって退屈なものになってしまう」と考えたル・コルビュジエは、視界を限定するために一辺10mほどの庭を壁で囲み「緑あふれる居間」と呼んだ。庭の南側に設けられた石積みの塀に開けられた正方形の「窓」は景色を絵画のように切り取る。しかし、窓に近づき、造り付けのテーブルの側に置かれたベンチに腰掛けて外を眺めると、ふたたびそこには比類なく美しい風景が広がっている。

自然をこよなく愛した父のジョルジュ・ジャンヌレは1年間、音楽家であった母のマリーは101歳で亡くなるまで36年間をこの家で過ごした。現在コルビュジエ財団が所有するこの「小さな家」は、地元の自治体が管理し、一般に公開されている。

(TK)

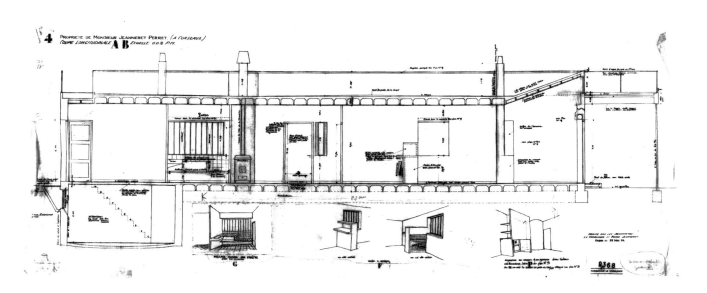

*Opposite top: Floor plan. Opposite
bottom: Section. Above: Main
entrance with corrugated
aluminum siding added later.*

左頁、上：平面図。左頁、下：断面図。
上：メイン・エントランス。耐候性アル
ミニウムの外壁は後に加えられた。

Above: Terrace on the east end.　　　　上：東端のテラス。

Above: View of the lake framed by a column, eaves and wall edge from the terrace. pp. 70–71: Lake side facade with 11-m-long horizontal window.

上：柱、軒、壁のエッジで枠どられた湖をみる。70～71頁：全長11mの水平連続窓のある湖側のファサード。

Opposite: Guest room on the east side of the house. Above: Bathroom. Below: Kitchen.　　　　左頁：東端の客室。上：浴室。下：台所。

pp. 74–75: Foldable sliding
partitions resembling Japanese
shoji screens between the main
living space and the guest room.

74〜75頁：客室とメインの居室を区切る日
本の障子に似た可動の折り畳み間仕切り。

Above: View of the main living space from the guest room.

上：客室からメインの居室をみる。

Above: View toward the east guest room of the main living space.
Left: View from Le Corbusier's mother's bedroom

上：メインの居室。東側の客室方向をみる。左：母の寝室からみる。

Above: Le Corbusier's room.
Opposite: Pierced opening in the
stone wall at the edge of the lake
that frames one's perception of the
landscape.

上：ル・コルビュジエの部屋。右頁：湖
の縁につくられた石壁に穿たれた開口。
時とともに移ろう湖の風景を切り取る。

Stories of Windows
Bruno Rechilin

窓の物語
ブルーノ・ライヒリン
中田雅章訳

Above: Une Petite Maison. View from Lake Léman.

上：小さな家。レマン湖上からみる。

In *Précisions sur un état l'architecture et de l'urbanisme,* Le Corbusier suggests that architecture can also be told as a story of windows. This is not surprising, given the breadth of functional attributes ascribed to this architectural element. The most humble function of the window is to admit light and air into a room. It establishes a physical, psychological and symbolic threshold between the interior and the exterior. It determines the structural pattern and planning module of the building. Its design requires an analytical appraisal of functional requirements and a synthetic understanding of technical solutions. Apertures in buildings play a key role in the definition of the physical and cultural experience of space. At the height of Purism, Le Corbusier put forward his own interpretation of the window in a number of canonical buildings that have since become landmarks of the Modern Movement.

The image and built reality of an innovation
Thirty years after the completion of the *petite maison* at Corseaux, Le Corbusier re-examined the spatial and figurative role of the strip window. The 10.75 meter window along the south front of the building facing the lake was, according to Le Corbusier, "the sole actor of the facade," "the house's primary actor."[1] He noted that this particular window was, in its day, a considerable structural innovation. The strip window, Le Corbusier noted, comes in two basic types. The first type (as in the La Roche-Jeanneret houses) runs from impost to impost, and is flush with the structure.[2] The second type (as in the Villa Stein de Monzie) steps back from the surface of the facade and aligns with the imposts.

The strip window of the *petite maison* is, in effect, a hybrid that creates a visual illusion. The image of the facade suggests the presence of a bold structural gesture, a mighty beam leaping across a distance of nearly 11 metres. But the beam rests on no less than three metal columns flush with the facade. These, however, do not disturb the eye because they stand against the inner side of the frame uprights. Le Corbusier originally intended to match this bold architectural statement with a single structural element, by using the roof parapet to carry an over-sized lintel, but this did not find favour with the timid habits of a village builder of the 1920s.[3]

The Perret-Le Corbusier controversy
The introduction of large openings in new buildings did not pass unnoticed. Commenting on Le Corbusier and Pierre Jeanneret's buildings at the 1923 Salon d'Automne, Auguste Perret in the *Paris-Journal*[4] strongly criticised the bizarre and decorative use of windows. To his mind, the windows were far too long or too tall. Moreover, the windows were often concentrated into one part of the building, leaving other areas blank and dark. It was this comment that most infuriated Le Corbusier. Replying resentfully on the pages of the same journal,[5] he wrote:

Enfin, dernier et sanglant reproche de Perret: mes fenêtres n'éclairent pas. Ici je bondis car l'injustice est trop criante. Comment? Je m'efforce de créer des intérieurs clairs et bien . . . c'est là mon but principal, c'est là même pourquoi le dessin de mes façades peut sembler un peu bizarre aux gens routiniers (bizarrerie voulue, dit Perret; mais oui, voulue: non pas pour le plaisir même de la bizarrerie, mais pour faire entrer le plus possible, à flots l'air et la lumière dans mes maisons, la bizarrerie, ou soi-disant elle n'étant donc ici qu'une résultante de mon désir de tout plier aux nécessités vitales). [Finally, the last and bloody reproach of Perret: the windows do not shed

ル・コルビュジエは、自著『プレシジョン』のなかで、建築は「窓の物語」としても語りうることを示唆している。窓という建築の一要素が有する機能的特性の幅広さを考えれば、これはあながち驚くにはあたらない。窓の最も基本的な機能は、光と外気を室内に取り込むことである。また窓は、内部と外部の間に物理的、心理的、象徴的な境界を築き、建物の構造パターンおよび平面計画のモデュールを規定する。そのデザインには、機能上の要求にたいする分析的な評価と、技術的な解決にたいする総合的な理解が必要とされる。建物の開口部は、空間の物理的、文化的体験を定義する上で中心的な役割を果たす。ピューリスムの盛期において、ル・コルビュジエは数々の作品を通じて窓にたいする独自の解釈を発展させていった。それらの作品はその後、規範ともいえる建物として、近代運動のランドマークとなった。

革新のイメージと建物のリアリティ

コルソの「小さな家」の完成から30年の後、ル・コルビュジエは、水平連続窓の空間的、造形的役割について改めて検討を加えた。湖に面した建物の南側のファサードに取り付けられた長さ10.75mの窓は、ル・コルビュジエによれば、「ファサードの唯一の役者」であり、「この家の主役」[1]であった。この窓は、当時としてはきわめて重要な構造上の革新であったと、ル・コルビュジエは述べている。また彼は、水平連続窓は二つの基本タイプを源流としていると指摘する。第一のタイプは、（「ラ・ロッシュ-ジャンヌレ邸」にみられるように）支柱と支柱の間に伸びる、構造体と面一になったものである。[2] 第二のタイプ（「ヴィラ・シュタイン」にみられるように）、ファサードの表面から引っ込み、支柱と一直線のものである。視覚的なイリュージョンをつくりだす「小さな家」の水平連続窓は、事実上、この二つのタイプが混合したものとなっている。ファサードのイメージは、大胆な構造的な身振り、すなわち11m近いスパンに架かる巨大な梁の存在を示唆している。しかし梁は、ファサードと面一の3本の金属柱に支えられている。これらの柱は、しかしながら、垂直のフレームの内側にくっつくようにして立っているため、視覚的に水平連続窓を邪魔するものとはなっていない。ル・コルビュジエはもともとこの大胆な構造的な声明を、巨大なまぐさ材を隠す屋根のパラペットを用いて単一の構造的要素として表現することを意図していた。しかしその願いは、新しい試みにたいして消極的な1920年代の片田舎の職人たちの姿勢を前に、実現することはかなわなかったのである。[3]

ペレ-コルビュジエ論争

新しい建物に採用された大きな開口が見過ごされることはなかった。オーギュスト・ペレは『Paris-Journal』紙[4]のなかで、1923年のサロン・ドートンヌに出展されたル・コルビュジエとピエール・ジャンヌレの建物について言及し、その窓の奇怪で装飾的な扱いを手厳しく批判した。彼からすれば、その窓はあまりにも長すぎ、あるいは高すぎたのである。しかも、窓は建物の一部分に集中し、他の場所を開口部のない暗がりのままに残すことになっていた。ル・コルビュジエを激怒させたのはこのコメントであった。同じ紙上で、ル・コルビュジエは怒りを込めてつぎのように反論している。[5]
「あげくに、ペレの最後のばかげた非難はこうである。これらの窓は光をもたらさない、と。ここまでくると、その不誠実さがあまりにも度を超していて、うんざりしてしまう。なぜか？　私は、明るく、生き生きとした内部空間をつくりだそうと努力している……それが私の主な意図なのだ。そして、まさにその同じ理由から、私のファサードのデザインは、決まりきったやり方に頼りきっている人々には奇怪なものに見えるのだろう（奇をてらっているとペレはいうが、その通りなのだ。ただしそれは、奇そのものを求めているのではなく、私が設計した住宅に空気と光を最大限に取り込むためであって、この場合、奇抜さは、すべてのものを絶対に欠くことのできないものに組み込むという私の願いの結果なのだ）」。

この論争は、「小さな家」を施工した工務店との手紙[6]のやりとりがあった数週間前の、1923年12月に起った。「小さな家」の水平連続窓は、こうして公然の挑戦となった。建築家の職能団体を代表してペレは、[7]水平連続窓の使用を厳しく非難し、ル・コルビュジエは、断罪されたその要素がマニフェストとなるような作品をもってこれに応じた。それは単に時間的な偶然なのかもしれないが、ル・コルビュジエは、ペレの「パレス・オヴ・ウッド」が建てられてから半年後に起ったペレとのこの論争を、「小さな家」の水平連続窓に関連づけようと躍起になっていた。この論争は、『Almanach d'architecture moderne』誌上に、「小さな家」の紹介につづけて収められている。ル・コルビュジエは、「小さな家」の水平連続窓からみた湖のパノラマと、彼が描いた「パレス・オヴ・ウッド」の一室に光をもたらす「堂々たる水平連続窓」の前の肘掛け椅子に身を沈めるペレのスケッチとを、見開きのページに対比的に配した。[8] このスケッチは、ペレ、ジャンヌレおよびル・コルビュジエの会合の状況を説明している。ル・コルビュジエは、建物のなかで唯一この形式にあてはまる窓の前でペレがゆったりと腰を下ろす姿を目撃したことにすっかり勢いを得て、「あなたの水平窓はたいへん魅力的です！」とその水平連続窓についてペレに賛辞を贈ったのである。彼は、経験豊かな巨匠が水平連続窓を使っていることを知ってなんとも心強いとつづける。この当てこすりにたいしてペレは、縦長の窓は部屋のより奥深くまで照らすという、よく知られた彼の主張を繰り返した。しかし、なによりも興味を引かれるのはつぎの言葉である。「水平連続窓は、（分類学的な意味において）窓ではありません。窓は人間なのです……私はパノラマを嫌悪しています」。[9]ペレは、その象徴的、擬人的性格ゆえに、窓は「人間」であるという主張を保ちつづけた。「縦長の窓は、そのなかに人間を枠どり、それは彼のシルエットに合うものとなります……垂直の線は、立っている姿を暗示し、それは生命の線を体現しているのです」。[10]こうした見方は、今も進化しつづけている、古代に始まる文学と絵画の伝統全般にみられる文化的な価値体系への信頼を反映している。[11] リルケの「Les fenetres（窓）」の出だしのくだりほど、それを魅惑的にとらえているものはない。[12]

おまえは私たちの幾何学ではないのか
窓よ、その単純な形態
それは私たちの巨大な生を
やすやすと区切るのか

おまえはすべてのものになにかを与える
窓よ、私たちのしきたりの意味
ある者は、ただおまえの額縁のなかにたたずみ
待ち、とりなすだろう。

ペレが水平連続窓を否定したとすれば、それは彼が、その存在の内に「人が住む空間」のなかで「生活する」という文化と経験に深く根ざした価値観を揺るがすような、違犯的な兆候をみてとったためであった。これと同じ理由から、彼はル・コルビュジエが「素晴らしいフランスの伝統を破壊してきた」ことに憂いを示していた（『Architecture Vivante』誌の副編集長がそれを記録している）。観る者に「どこまでもつづくパノラマ」を強いる、パノラミックな視界にたいするペレの嫌悪は、この慣習的な世界観のアンチテーゼである。伝統的な窓は、内部空間を外部空間へと開いてゆく。しかし、それは同時に、場所と境界を規定する。それは空間的、感情的排除の関係をつくりだし、一枚の絵が内包する意味を与える。この価値体系にあっては、「水平に見る眼」は盲目である。ル・コルビュジエは、おそらく意図的に、彼の従弟を純真な科学者という難しい役回りを果たすように仕向けた。彼は、水平連続窓が建築と居住空間の伝統的な価値体系を破壊するという、より野心的な計画のための単なる道具 ―それは決定的なものであったが― にすぎないことを十分認識していたのである。

light. Here, I cringe as the injustice is too glaring. How? I strive to create bright and vibrant interiors . . . that is my main intent, and it is for the same reason that the design of my facades may seem bizarre to people addicted to routine (deliberate peculiarity, says Perret; yes, deliberate—not for the pleasure of peculiarity itself, but to maximize the amount of air and the light entering my houses, the peculiarity, or so being in this case only a result of my desire to incorporate everything into vital necessities).]

This exchange between Perret and Le Corbusier took place in December 1923, a few weeks before an exchange of letters with the builder of the *petite maison*.[6] The strip window of the *petite maison* thus became an outright challenge. Perret, speaking as official spokesman for the professional institute of architects,[7] had berated its use. Le Corbusier responded with a new work in which the incriminating piece became a manifesto.

It was probably only a chronological coincidence, but Le Corbusier was at pains to establish a link between the strip window of the *petite maison* and the dispute with Perret, which had a sequel half a year later around the Palace of Wood built by Perret. The dispute was reported in the *Almanach d'architecture moderne*, following the introduction to the *petite maison*. On two facing pages, Le Corbusier contrasted a view of the lake panorama from the strip window with a sketch in which he portrayed Perret seated in an armchair in front of the "masterly strip window" giving light to a room in the Palace of Wood.[8] The sketch illustrates the circumstances of the meeting between Perret, Jeanneret and Le Corbusier. Happy to have caught Perret in the act, comfortably installed in front of the only window of its sort to be found in the whole building, Le Corbusier compliments him on this strip window, "très jolies vos fenêtres en long!" [your horizontal windows are very pretty!] He goes on to say how reassuring it is to find that the strip window is used by his elderly maestro. In reply to these insinuations, Perret reiterated his well-known argument that the vertical window illuminates rooms in greater depth. But most of all, our attention is caught by these words: "La fenêtre en longueur n'est pas une fenêtre (catégorique): une fenêtre c'est un homme!" and, retorting to Jeanneret's remark that the eye sees horizontally, he said "J'ai horreur des panoramas."[9] [The horizontal window is not a window (in a categorical sense): a window is a man . . . I hate panoramas.] Perret maintained that the window "is man" because of its symbolic and anthropomorphic content: "La fenêtre verticale encadre l'homme, elle est d'accord avec sa silhouette . . . la ligne verticale est celle de la station debout, c'est la ligne de vie."[10] [The vertical window frames man, it agrees with his silhouette . . . the vertical line connotes the standing position, it embodies the line of life.] These views reflect a belief in a system of cultural values that cuts across an ancient yet still evolving literary and painterly tradition.[11] The first lines in Rilke's *Les fenêtres*, could not capture it more enchantingly:[12]

N'est-tu pas notre géometrie,
fenêtre, très simple forme
qui sans effort circonscris
notre vie énorme?

Comme tu ajoutes à tout,
fenêtre, le sens de nos rites:
Quelqu'un qui ne serait que debout,
dans ton cadre attend ou médite.

[Are you not our geometry,
window, very simple form
which effortlessly circumscribes
our enormous life?

As you add to everything,
window, the meaning of our rituals:
someone would be only standing,
in your frame, waiting and meditating.]

If Perret rejected the strip window, he did so because he recognised in it the signs of a transgression affecting values deeply rooted in the culture and experience of "living" in "inhabited space." For this same reason he showed concern that Le Corbusier "was destroying the fine French tradition" (as reported by a sub-editor on *Architecture Vivante*). Perret's aversion to the panoramic vista that condemns the viewer to a "perpetual panorama" is the antithesis of this conventional view of the world. The traditional window opens the interior towards the exterior. But at the same time it defines a place and a threshold; it establishes a relation of spatial and sentimental exclusion and gives to that which is perceived the connotations of a picture. In this framework of values, "the eye that looks horizontally" is blind. Perhaps not by chance Le Corbusier left his cousin to play the uncomfortable role of the ingenuous scientist. He was well aware that the strip window was simply a tool, though a decisive one, in a more ambitious plan to subvert the traditional system of values of architecture and inhabited space.

The strip window: an anti-perspectival device
Unlike the traditional opening, the strip window performs best as a link between the inside and the outside when the threshold effect is attenuated. The photograph of the interior of the *petite maison* published in *Almanach*[13] makes this point most graphically. All that belongs to the building is reduced to a dark background, against which the euphoric image of one of the world's most beautiful panoramas stands out, stretching from edge to edge of the image. The caption for the photograph confirms the effect of sitting in the living room: "le site 'est là' comme si l'on était au jardin."[14] [The site "is there" as if we were in the garden.] The traditional window cuts out a picture from the landscape and thereby manipulates it, giving it the aura of a view. But the strip window satisfies the demands of objectivity so dear to the Purists and the Modern Movement. It renders nature just as it is: "La fenêtre de 11 mètres introduit l'immensité du dehors, l'infalsifiable unité d'un paysage lacustre avec tempêtes ou calme radieux."[15] [the 11 meters window makes the imensity of the outside enter the house, the majesty of a lake landscape with its tempests and radiaus calm.]

But then, is it really true that the strip window does not manipulate what is perceived? Perret asserted that the vertical window (not by chance called "French" window in other cultures) offers the view of a complete space because it embraces street, garden and sky. Marie Dormoy, his faithful interpreter, in an article on Le Corbusier, points out: "la fenêtre rectangulaire en hauteur rend une pièce bien plus gaie qu'une fenêtre horizontale, puisque, grâce à cette disposition, on découvre les premiers plans, c'est-à-dire la partie vivante et animée."[16] [The vertical rectangular window makes a room much more joyful than a horizontal window because of its disposition whereby one encounters the foreground—the part that is animated and alive.] In other words, the vertical window

水平連続窓：反パースペクティヴ的装置

伝統的な開口とは違い、水平連続窓は、その境界としての効果が弱められたときに、内部と外部を結ぶものとして最大限の効果をもたらす。『Almanach』誌[13]に掲載された「小さな家」の室内写真は、この点をきわめて視覚的に証明している。建物に属するすべてのものは暗い背景となり、写真の端から端まで伸びた世界で最も美しいパノラマの幸福なイメージが浮かび上がる。この写真の説明文が、このリヴィング・ルームに腰を下ろした時の効果を確認している。「敷地が、まるで庭園のなかにいるかのように『そこにある』」。[14] 伝統的な窓はランドスケープから一枚の絵を切り取り、その結果、風景がもつ独特の雰囲気をもたらすことでそれを巧みに操る。しかし水平連続窓は、ピューリスムやモダン・ムーヴメントにとってきわめて重要であった客観性にたいする要求を満たしている。それはまさに、自然をあるがままの姿で伝えるのだ。「長さ11mの窓は外部の雄大さを住宅の内部に取り込み、湖の嵐や晴れ渡った静寂の風景が有する威厳と住宅を融合する」。[15]

しかし、水平連続窓がそれを通して知覚されるものを操作しないというのは本当だろうか。縦長の窓（この窓が他の文化圏で「フランス式」窓と呼ばれていることは偶然ではない）は、通り、庭、そして空を包含するため、空間全体の眺めをもたらすとペレは主張した。彼の忠実なる解釈者であったマリー・ドーモイは、ル・コルビュジエに関する記事のなかで次のように指摘している。「我々が、いかにして活動的で生き生きとした部分である前景と出会うかという点に関するその特性のゆえに、縦長の四角い窓は、水平の窓よりもはるかに部屋を喜びに満ちたものにする」。[16] 言い換えれば、縦長の窓は、実に多様な次元、色彩、光の度合いをもち、遠景の眺望という点で、最大限の奥行きを有する一枚の絵をランドスケープから切り取るということだ。逆に水平連続窓は、前景の視界を遮ることで、ランドスケープの実際の奥行きにたいする認識を弱めている。さらに、水平方向の視野が広く、我々の視界を制限しないために、伝統的な窓枠がもたらす視覚的な抑制の効果も失われている。

水平連続窓が、伝統的な窓によって生み出された一点透視のパースペクティヴにたいするアンチテーゼであるならば、建築におけるその機能は、本質的に反パースペクティヴ的なものである。水平連続窓から見る景色は、ほとんど窓枠に糊づけされているかのように感じられる。それは、近くにあるものと遠くにあるものとの間の移行を景色から取り去り、距離感の認識と安心して内から外の世界を静観することを妨げるのだ。

室内に侵入する水平連続窓

「たとえば完全に大きく開かれ、そのため外に向かって開き、内に入ることを許しながらなお閉ざしている近代の窓にみられるような窓のパラドックス」は、世紀の変わり目の建築家たちを困惑させた。「窓の話」は、『Panorama oder Ansichten vom19. Jahrhundert』と題する文献のなかに収められた、ドルフ・シュテルンベルガーが書いた居住空間に捧げられた章の主題であった。[17] コルネリウス・グアリットは、「大きな窓は、空間をあまりにも外の世界によって左右されるものとすることで、そのなかの静けさを奪っている」[18] と不満を訴え、ベイリー・スコットは、英国の郊外のヴィラに蔓延する大きな窓の流行を嘆き、小さなガラス面をもつ窓は視界の特性を認識させると主張した。[19]

ル・コルビュジエは、著述活動と作品とを通して、この家庭的な世界観を内密に、しかし着実に破壊してゆくことに貢献した。生活における体験と文化の根本的な転換は、突如として、明快な建築的かつ象徴的アイデンティティを与えられた。水平連続窓は室内へと外部の世界が乱入することを許し、個人を保護していたヴェール[20]をはぎとった。「小さな家」の小さな居間では、自然は時間と季節のサイクルを通じて、遺憾なくその存在を主張している。もはや壁やカーテンに遮られることなく、光は開口部を通り抜けて空間と室内の物体に降り注ぐ。感傷に浸っていた室内の物体は、ふたたび確固とした機能をもつ道具となる。[21] 光と白い漆喰の仕上げを用いて、ル・コルビュジエは、室内空間の

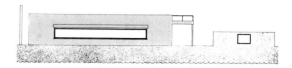

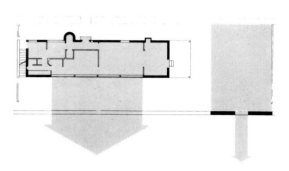

Above: Analytical drawing of Une Petite Maison.

上：小さな家の分析図。

cuts out of the landscape a picture of maximum perspectival depth with a great variety of dimensions, colours and grades of light. Conversely, the strip window, by blocking the view of the foreground, diminishes the viewer's appreciation of the real depth of the landscape. Furthermore, the effect of visual containment the traditional window frame gives is also lost because the vertical limits do not form part of our cone of vision.

If the strip window is the antithesis of the single-point perspective generated by the traditional window, its function in architecture is essentially anti-perspectival. In the strip window the view feels almost as if it were glued to the window frame. It removes from view the transition between things close and things remote, and prevents the distant and reassuring contemplation of the outside world from within.

The strip window breaks into the interior

"Die Paradoxie des Fensters, des modernen, ganz und gar durchsichtigen nämlich, das also zugleich nach draussen öffnet und Einlass gibt und doch auch wiederum absperrt" [The paradox of the window, i.e. of the modern one completely opened wide, which thereby opens towards the outside and allows entry and yet closes it] put architects in a quandary at the turn of the century. "Das störende Fenster" was the subject of a chapter by Dolf Sternberger in *Panorama oder Ansichten vom 19. Jahrhundert*, dedicated to inhabited space.[17] Cornelius Gurlitt complained that "big windows deprive spaces of their inner quietness, making them too dependent on the outer world,"[18] and Baillie Scott mocking the fashion for large windows that had spread among English suburban villas argued for windows with small panes which give that which is perceived the characteristics of a view.[19]

Through his writings and buildings Le Corbusier contributed to the underhand but steady destruction of this homely view of the world. The radical shift in the experience and culture of living was, all of a sudden, given a clear architectural and symbolic identity. The strip window ripped off the veil that safeguards the individual,[20] allowing the outside world to burst into the interior. In the tiny sitting room of the *petite maison*, nature in all its fullness, imposes its presence through the cycle of time and seasons. No longer held back by walls and curtains, light floods through the opening onto spaces and objects. Objects laden with sentiment once again become solid, functional instruments.[21] With light and whitewash, Le Corbusier totally transforms the appearance and significance of interior space. Its interiority refuses self-deception or escape into the blurred spaces of memory. Instead, the gaze is turned upon facts and things. "Quand l'ombre et les coins noirs vous entourent, vous n'êtes chez vous que jusqu'à la limite trouble de ces zones obscures que votre regard ne perce pas; vous n'êtes pas *maître de vous*. Vous serez à la suite du ripolinage de vos murs *maître de vous*."[22] [When shadows and dark corners surround you, you are at home only up to the fuzzy limits of these dark zones, which your gaze cannot penetrate; you are not the master of yourself. You will be the master of yourself only after you make proper use of the walls.]

The precariousness of modern interior space

"Mon père vécut une année dans cette maison. Ce paysage le comblait."[23] [My father lived one year in this house. This landscape fulfilled him.] That large window, flung open onto the landscape of Lake Léman, was dedicated in particular to his father, as borne out by the affectionate letter written by Le Corbusier during his father's first year in the villa: "Te voici

heureusement dans ta petite maison en face du paysage que tu aimes. S'il fait bien froid dehors, j'espère que votre chaudière fait son devoir. Ce site en hiver est extrèmement digne, vaste, plus vaste qu'en été et d'une douceur polaire impressionante. On ne voit plus les montagnes du fond, et le lac semble une mer."[24] [Here you are, fortunately, in your small house, facing the landscape you love. If it is cold outside, I hope your heater is doing its duty. This site in winter is extremely dignified and vast, more vast than in the summer with an impressive polar softness. One no longer sees the mountains in the background, and the lake seems like a sea.] The *petite maison* is a container of friendly nature, at once redeeming and consolatory (unlike Bachelard's *hütte*),[25] with its thick walls squarely protecting inner space. The strip window flung wide across the landscape projects the inhabitant into a state of unaccustomed visual and psychological ubiquity. As the intimacy between spaces and objects dissolves, and the boundaries between the polar opposites (the inhabited space and the place of desire) are blurred, the inhabitant enjoys the psychological and symbolic uncertainty of modern living space, an experience that can only be triggered by great architecture.

"Un trou carré pour proportionner"

The *petite maison* occupies a tight site, barely 12 metres wide and about 30 metres long. In the final design, the house—as seen from the lake—is situated on the left leaving space for the garden on the right, between the road and the shore. This garden was used to grow vegetables and would eventually be dominated by a majestic Paulownia tree. On the lakeside, the garden was protected by a long straight wall, erected when the embankments were rebuilt at the end of the last century. On the right, the wall was raised to form a screen, with an opening at the centre to protect or at any rate define the space furnished by a garden table and chairs.[26]

The opening in the screen limits the view: "Prise par laquelle parmi nous s'égalise le grand trop de dehors." [Intake by which the 'too much' of the outside is among us.]—again from Rilke's *Les Fenêtres*—the opening selects and detaches a view from the landscape bringing out its qualities as an image. That this opening was treated like a painting is cofirmed by the way it was photographed. In the pictures published in the *Ouevre Compléte* and in those reproduced in *Une petite maison*,[27] the photographer waited for the moment when a sailing boat happened to float into view. Le Corbusier's comment that the square hole had been designed to give a sense of proportion to the "objet à dimensions humaines" ["object with human dimensions"] seems to echo the anthropomorphic metaphor used by Perret 'une fenêtre c'est un homme.'[28] [a window is a man.]

The window as a hole in the wall

In describing the revolutionary impact that new developments in construction technology would have on architecture, Le Corbusier employed the window as a metaphor for the history of architecture.[29] Yet the large opening in the screen in the *petite maison* has more ancient origins. Nowithstanding the fact that the lintel is in (modern) reinforced concrete, the opening in a rough stone wall denotes with great eloquence an image of the traditional "hole in the wall." Its *raison d'être* resides in the language of masonry architecture. In describing the difference between modern windows and the typical windows of Hausmann's Paris, Le Corbusier notes "C'est là, l'architecture de pierre, expression d'un système constructif pur."[30] ["Here it is, the architecture of stone, expression of a pure constructive system."]

ありようとその意味を全面的に変容させている。その室内の性質は、自己欺瞞や記憶のぼんやりとした空間への逃避を拒んでいる。むしろその眼差しは、真実と事物とに転じられる。「影と部屋の隅の暗さがあなたを取り巻く時、あなたの家は、あなたの視線が貫くことのできないこの暗い領域のぼんやりとした境界まででしかない。あなたはあなた自身の主人ではない。壁を適切に用いることができてはじめて、あなたはあなた自身の主人となるのだ」。[22]

近代の室内空間の不確定性

「私の父がこの家で暮らしたのは一年にすぎなかった。だがその間、父はここの景色を存分に満喫していた」。[23] レマン湖の風景に向かって開け放たれたその大きな窓が、とりわけ彼の父に捧げられたものであったことは、このヴィラに移り住んだその年に、父に宛ててル・コルビュジエが書いた愛情あふれる手紙からもうかがえる。「幸運にも、あなたの愛する風景に面した小さな家に、あなたは身をおいています。外が寒い時に、暖房がちゃんとその役目を果たしてくれればよいのですが。冬になるとこの敷地は、限りなく高貴で、広漠たるもの、印象的な極地の安らぎをともなって、夏以上に広漠たるものとなります。彼方の山々は姿を消し、湖はまるで海のようにみえるのです」。[24] 厚い壁が内部の空間をしっかりと包み込む「小さな家」は、（バシュラールの「小屋」とは異なり）補完的であると同時に慰問的な、[25] 親しみやすい容器である。風景を横断するように広々と開く水平連続窓は、馴染みのない、視覚的、心理的に偏在する状態へと居住者を投げ出す。空間と物体の間の親しい関係は消え去り、対極にあるもの（居住空間と欲望の場）の間の境界が曖昧になるにしたがって、居住者は、偉大な建築によってのみ引き起こされうる、近代の居住空間の心理的、象徴的不確定性を楽しむようになるのだ。

「プロポーションのためにデザインされた四角い開口」

「小さな家」は、わずか幅12m、長さ30mほどの小さな敷地に建てられている。最終的なデザインでは、住宅は湖からみて敷地の左側によせて建てられており、右側には道路と湖岸に挟まれた庭のためのスペースが残されている。この庭は、野菜を栽培するために用いられていたが、最終的には堂々たる桐の木がここを支配した。庭の湖側は、19世紀末に湖岸に堤が再建された時に築かれた長い直線状の壁で守られている。右側には、壁を建てることでスクリーンが形成された。小さなテーブルとガーデン・チェアが設置された空間を守るように、あるいは少なくともその空間を定義するように、この壁には中央に開口部が設けられた。[26]

スクリーンの開口が視界を限定する。「それによって『あまりにもたくさん』の外部がもたらされてしまう」——ふたたびリルケの『窓』より——開口部は、一つのイメージとしての特質を引き出しながら、ランドスケープから風景を選び出し、切り取る。この開口が絵画のように扱われたことは、写真の撮り方から確認できる。『Ouevre Compléte（ル・コルビュジエ全作品集）』に掲載され、『小さな家』[27] に再録された写真を撮る際、写真家は視界に偶然ヨットが横切る瞬間を待った。この四角い穴は、「人のスケールをもったもの」にバランス感覚を与えるためにデザインされたというル・コルビュジエのコメントは、ペレが用いた「窓は人間である」という擬人的なメタファに響き合うものがあるように思える。[28]

壁に開けられた穴としての窓

建設技術における新たな発展が建築にもたらしうる革命的な影響力を説明するなかで、ル・コルビュジエは、建築の歴史における隠喩（メタファ）として窓を探求した。[29] そして、「小さな家」のスクリーンに開けられた大きな開口は、さらに古い起源をもっている。まぐさが鉄筋コンクリート造であるという事実にもかかわらず、自然石でつくられた壁に開けられた開口は、伝統的な「壁に開けられた穴」のイメージを雄弁に語っている。その「存在の意味」は、組積

The garden as a summer room

A hedge, an enclosing wall and the screen spatially define the garden. By erecting a limit that isolates it from the landscape, they turn it into an interior: "le jardin à gauche, clos de murs . . . sert de chambre d'été."[31] [The garden on the left-hand side, enclosed with walls . . . serves as a summer room.] Years later, after the property had been enclosed by a high wall on the road side, Le Corbusier was even more explicit about the purpose of that enclosure:

La raison d'être du mur de clôture que l'on voit ici est de fermer la vue au nord, à l'est, en partie au sud, à l'ouest; le paysage omniprésent sur toutes les faces, omnipotent, devient lassant. Avez vous observé qu'en de telles conditions, "on" ne le "regarde" plus? Pour que le paysage compte, il faut le limiter, le dimensioner par une décision radicale: boucher les horizons en élevant des murs et ne les réléver, par interruption de murs, qu'en des points stratégiques. La règle servit ici: murs nord, est et sud on "cloîtré" le tout petit jardin carré de dix mètres de côté et ils en ont fait une salle de verdure — un intérieur.[31] [The object of the wall seen here is to block off the view to the north and east, partly to the south, and to the west; for the omnipresent and overpowering scenery on all sides has a tiring effect in the long run. Have you noticed that under such conditions one no longer 'sees'? To lend significance to the scenery one has to restrict it and give it proportion; the view must be blocked by walls which are only pierced at certain strategic points and there permit an unhindered view. The following solution was chosen: the walls to the north, east, and south enclose the small garden ten meters square and convert it into a verdant room.]

Contributing to that complete image is the opening at the centre of the screen, incorporating a concrete table. Significantly, in the published photographs of this still life of inhabited space, the little table is laid and a number of domestic ornaments are set on the window sill.[32]

Interior and exterior: antithesis and paradox

In the *petite maison*, Le Corbusier confronts two different systems: the traditional window, and the new window of modern architecture. Both types of aperture perform specific, paradigmatic roles according to a precise set of parameters: functional requirements, symbolic content, technology, construction and formal composition. It is a statement of architectural opposites, an antithesis of positions.[33] The villa-garden design is based upon a set of parallel antitheses and paradoxes that confront and sustain each other in turn. This becomes clear as soon as one looks at the lakeside elevation, reproduced in a perfectly frontal view in *Almanach*:[34] a view of the building that faithfully reflects Le Corbusier's intentions. The essential compositional elements of the building — the white rectangular shapes of the elevation and the screen — stand out from the solid embankment wall. Between the screen and facade there are similarities and differences that merit detailed attention.

In formal terms the screen and facade are low, elongated rectangular solids with a single aperture. Although the proportions of the screen and of the visible portion of the facade are not quite the same, optically the difference is irrelevant. This similarity is emphasized by the choice of colour: both elements are painted white. But the materials are very different: the strip window sits within a smooth plastered wall while the hole is made in a rough stone wall.

A number of design alterations gradually clarified its paradigmatic, antithetical nature. A concrete version of the screen was abandoned in favour of stone, reflecting more directly the traditional associations of an opening in a wall. Early sketches show that Le Corbusier had intended to highlight the relationship between the two elements by using red as the unifying colour palette: pale pink for the facade and dark red for the screen.[35] But the whiteness of the screen and facade render the relationship even more striking. The rustic stone masonry screen is whitewashed, which both attenuates its naturalness and brings out its tectonic texture. The idea is reminiscent of Cubist painting techniques where an *objet trouvé* (often banel or scurrilous) is given greater visual status by amalgamating it within the painting by covering it with paint. As it turns out, the 11-metre strip window was not the pioneering structural innovation Le Corbusier claimed. Yet the composition creates the lasting impression of a mighty structure that spans a substantial distance. In contrast, the opening in the screen has all the iconographic attributes of traditional apertures that obey the rules of traditional load-bearing masonry construction. The game of antithetical oppositions is further underscored by the contradictory nature of the spaces: the inner space of habitation versus exterior garden space. The strip window, "the principal actor in the home," makes the interior become part of the exterior, "le site 'est là' comme si l'on était au jardin." [the site 'it there' as if we were in the garden.] And the opening in the screen with its view of the lake gives the enclosed space of the garden a sense of being interior, "le jardin . . . sert de chambre d'été."[36] [the garden . . . is used as a summer room.]

This double rhetorical device emphasizes the fundamentally different spatial and symbolic implications of the two openings, thus demarcating the frontier between traditional and modern architecture. It is the windows, themselves antithetical and defining antithetical spaces, that act as conduit, the *ductus subtibilis* of this architectural paradox.[37] The symmetry of the facade and screen; their elemental compositional quality and juxtaposition; the protected space of the garden (an incomplete interior or the ruins of an ancient room); all these elements combine to evoke the image of "an ancient temple on the water's edge" as Le Corbusier described the house in a letter to his fianceé Yvonne Gallis written from the building site as it was approaching completion.[38]

Corner windows: the "Dom-Ino" framework

The corner window has been perceived as a symbol, albeit often abused, of modern architecture. In his later years, Le Corbusier identified the corner window as one of the first breaks with tradition that he perpetrated: "A 17 ans et demi, je construisis ma première maison. Déjà j'avais risqué contre l'avis des sages. Une témérité: deux fenêtres d'angle."[39] [When I was 17 and a half, I built my first house. Already I took risks against the wise men's opinion. Recklessness: two angle windows.] In the Fallet house (La Chaux-de-Fonds, 1906–1907)[40] which was built when he was only 19, he designed a window with a reinforced concrete cantilever and no corner support — not quite the authentic modern corner window.

The first modern corner window — or more precisely, the first to achieve celebrity — was Walter Gropius's Faguswerke, where the German architect, if only to give substance to a ghost that was haunting the imagination of his time, resorted to a veritable structural prosthesis.[41] Several years later Le Corbusier, in the Villa Stein, used the corner window for the first time in a systematic way. Two strip windows cut across the entrance facade. As they turn the corner the windows merge into a glazed vertical slot that spans the width between the structural grid and front facade, interrupted only by the exposed floor

造の建築言語に属すものである。近代の窓と典型的なオースマン時代のパリの窓の違いを説明するなかで、ル・コルビュジエは、「これぞ石の建築、つまり純粋な構築システムの表現である」[30] と記している。

夏の部屋としての庭

障壁、囲み壁、そしてスクリーンが、庭を空間的に規定している。「壁に囲まれた右手の庭は……夏の部屋として使われる」[31] とあるように、ランドスケープから庭を切り離す境界を建ち上げることによって、庭は一つの室内へと転じている。数年後、道路側に建てられた高い壁で敷地が閉ざされた後、ル・コルビュジエは、囲い込みの目的をさらに明快なものとしている。

「ここにみられる囲い壁の存在理由は、北から東にかけて、さらに部分的に南から西にかけて視界を閉ざすためである。四方八方に広がる景色というものは圧倒的で、焦点を欠き、長い間にはかえって退屈なものになってしまう。このような状況では、もはや『私たち』は風景を『眺める』ことができないのではなかろうか。思いきった判断によって選別しなければならないのだ。すなわち、まず壁を建てることによって視界を遮ぎり、つぎに連なる壁面を要所要所取り払い、そこに水平線の広がりを求めるのである。北壁と、そして東側と南側の壁とが『囲われた庭』を形成すること、これがここでの方針である。壁に囲まれた一辺10mほどの、ごく小さな庭は室内空間に匹敵し、もう一つの緑あふれる居間となる」[31]

この完璧なイメージに貢献しているのは、コンクリートのテーブルと一体化したスクリーン中央の開口である。出版された居住空間におけるこの静物をとらえた写真のなかで、この小さなテーブルが整えられ、窓辺にいくつもの家庭的な装飾物が置かれているのはきわめて暗示的である。[32]

内部と外部：アンチテーゼとパラドックス

「小さな家」において、ル・コルビュジエは、伝統的な窓と近代建築の新しい窓という二つの異なったシステムを対比させている。この二つのタイプの開口は、どちらも規定に従ったパラメータの組み合わせに従って、独特で模範的な役割を演じている。そのパラメータとは、機能的要求、象徴的意味、テクノロジー、施工、および形態の構成である。それは、建築的に相対立するものの声明であり、たがいの立場間のアンチテーゼである。[33] ヴィラ・ガーデンのデザインは、相互に対立しつつ支え合う一組の平行したアンチテーゼとパラドックスの組み合わせにもとづいている。このことは、『Almanach』誌[34] に掲載された、真正面から見た湖側の立面を見れば、たちどころに明らかになる。その建物の眺めは、ル・コルビュジエの意図を忠実に映し出している。この建物の欠くことのできない構成上の要素—白い四角形のファサードとスクリーン—は、重厚な堤壁からひときわ屹立している。スクリーンとファサードの間には、より詳細に分析するに値する類似性と差異とが認められる。

形態についていえば、スクリーンとファサードは、一つだけ開口をもった低く長く伸びた四角い立体である。スクリーンとファサードの目に見える部分のプロポーションはまったく同じというわけではないが、視覚上この差異は重要ではない。その類似性は、どちらの要素も白色に塗るという、色彩の選択によって強調されている。しかし、用いられている材料はまったく異なる。水平連続窓がなめらかな漆喰仕上げの壁に開けられているのにたいし、穴は自然石の壁に設けられている。

何度もデザインを変更するうちに、徐々にその模範的で、アンチテーゼ的な本質が明確になった。壁に設けられた開口にたいする伝統的な連想をより直接的に反映するという理由で、スクリーンをコンクリートでつくるという案は取りやめられ、最終的には石が用いられた。初期のスケッチは、ル・コルビュジエが、淡いピンクをファサードに、また深みのある赤をスクリーンに使い、[35] 赤を統括的な色彩として用いることによって二つの要素の関係性を強調しようとしていたことを示している。しかし、スクリーンとファサードの白さは、この

関係性をより際立たせている。粗い石でつくられた組積造のスクリーンは漆喰で仕上げられているが、その仕上げは、スクリーンの自然な風合いを弱めると同時に、テクトニックな質感を引き出している。その発想は、オブジェ・トゥルヴェ、すなわち流木など人手を加えない美術品（それはしばしば陳腐な、あるいはとるに足りないものである）を絵の具で覆うことで絵画に融合させ、そのオブジェ・トゥルヴェにより高い視覚的地位を与えようとしたキュービストの絵画技法に似ている。

やがて、その11mの水平連続窓は、ル・コルビュジエが主張していたような先駆的な構造的発明ではなかったことが明らかになる。しかしその構成は、かなり長い距離に及ぶ偉大な構造物という不変の印象をつくりだしている。対照的に、スクリーンに設けられた開口は、荷重を支える伝統的な組積造の法則に従った伝統的な開口の図像的属性をすべて有している。アンチテーゼ的な相対立するもの同士のゲームは、居住の内部空間にたいする外部の庭空間という、空間の相反する性質によってさらに強調されている。「住宅の主役」である水平連続窓は、室内を外部の一部とし、「敷地が、まるで庭園のなかにいるかのように『そこにある』」ものとしている。そして、スクリーンに設けられた湖の風景を臨む開口は、庭の閉じられた空間にあたかも室内にいるような感覚をもたらし、「庭は……夏の部屋として使われる」のだ。[36]

この二重のレトリック上の装置は、二つの開口の本質的に異なった空間的、象徴的意味合いを強調し、かくして、伝統的な建築と近代建築との境界を規定している。その仲介役を担っているのは、それ自体アンチテーゼ的であり、また空間を規定している窓であり、それがこの建築的なパラドックスを生み出している。[37] ファサードとスクリーンの左右対称の構成、それらの本質的な構成上の特性と並置、庭の保護された空間（不完全な室内あるいは古代の部屋の廃墟）、これらすべての要素が、完成間近の現場からフィアンセのイヴォンヌ・ガリに宛てた手紙[38] のなかでル・コルビュジエがこの住宅について描写していたように、「水辺の古代神殿」のイメージを惹起するように組み合わされたのである。

コーナー・ウインドウ：「ドミノ」構造

しばしば非難されてはきたが、コーナー・ウインドウは、近代建築の一つのシンボルと考えられてきた。ル・コルビュジエは晩年、彼が伝統を打ち破った最初のものの一つとして、このコーナー・ウインドウを挙げている。「私は17歳と6ヵ月のときに最初の住宅を建てた。その時、私はすでに、賢者の知恵に逆らうという危険を冒した。向こうみずな二つの勾配窓がそれである」。[39] 彼が弱冠19歳にして設計した「ファレット邸」（ラ・ショー・ド・フォン、1906〜07年）において彼は、鉄筋コンクリートの片持ち梁をもち、角に支持材のない窓—正真正銘の近代的コーナー・ウインドウとはいいがたいものではあったが—をデザインしていた。[40]

最初の—あるいはより正確には、最初に広く知られるようになった—近代的コーナー・ウインドウは、ウォルター・グロピウスの「ファグス靴工場」であった。このドイツ人建築家は、この建物で、当時たびたび出没していたイマジネーションの亡霊に実体を与えたにすぎなかったとはいえ、垂直の構造上の人工補綴物をあえて用いている。[41] 数年後、ル・コルビュジエは「シュタイン邸」において、はじめて系統だった方法でコーナー・ウインドウを用いた。ここでは、二つの水平連続窓が入り口側のファサードを横断している。それが建物の角を回り込むと、窓はガラス張りの垂直の切り込みに合流する。この垂直の切り込みは、構造上のグリッドと正面ファサードの間の幅にまたがり、剥き出しの床スラブによってのみ中断される。この建物を横からみると、ファサードは構造上のグリッドの上に貼りつけられた蓋のような印象を与える。ル・コルビュジエが記しているように、「スラブは窓の腰壁を支持するファサード上の柱を越えて張り出し、1.25mの幅のバルコニーを形成している。窓のアーキトレーヴは、上階の床スラブから『吊られている』」。[42] フレームは建物の外被と面一となり、コーナーの直立面は、腰壁と同じ最小の厚みをもつため、ソリッド

slabs. A lateral view of the building gives the impression that the facade is an infill, pasted onto the structural grid. As Le Corbusier noted: "The slabs project beyond the pillars on the facade, forming balconies 1.25-metres wide, which support the window parapets. The window architraves are "suspended" from the floor slabs above."[42] Since the frames are flush with the outer skin and the corner uprights have the same minimal thickness as the parapet, the solid and void (glazed) elements are reduced to simple rectangular shapes that play an equal role in the composition of the facade; an accurate example of the breaking down of the wall surface into planes, defined by La Roche-Jeanneret as similar to de Stijl in its formal approach.[43] Le Corbusier said: "la façade . . . n'est plus qu'un voile de verre ou de maçonnerie clôturant la maison!"[44] [the facade . . . becomes only a curtain of glass or of masonry enclosing the house!] Two balconies of different width, but similar depth, stand out from the main facade. The structural grid of the building is organised in alternating structural bays that follow an ABABA rhythm, where A is 5 metres and B is 2.5 metres. The central balcony occupies the wider bay, the smaller balcony the narrower bay. Both balconies have a solid frontal parapet and railings on either side, reproducing the composition of the corner windows at a different scale. The defining elements of the Dom-Ino frame are thus revealed: cantilevered slabs, non-load-bearing facade and sub-divided structural grids.

A reticent architecture

It is useful to compare the Villa Stein with another, equally famous yet very different, example of the corner window that reveals the potential of the reinforced concrete frame. The immense three-storey glazed surface that forms the northeast corner of Gropius's Bauhaus, completely exposes the structural system. There is a total separation between cladding and structure. A steel and glass curtain wall forms the outer skin, while a reinforced concrete frame with projecting floor slabs forms the structural support for the building.

While the structure of the Villa Stein and the Bauhaus are not substantially different, the architectural manifestation of that structure is.[45] In the Bauhaus the solution is literally and figuratively transparent: the structure is fully exposed just as it is. The corner window has clear semantic content. Its function is to express a more general principle.[46] In the Villa Stein the structure can only be inferred from clues discernible to the expert eye. Le Corbusier's design perfectly illustrates his earlier critique of the poverty of an architecture reduced to mere structural manifestation. He concluded that the structural frame should be inferred or hinted at, not fully exhibited; "Qu'un os parût aux poignets ou aux cheville, et l'esprit s'en délecterait."[47] [That a bone appears at the wrists or at the ankles, the mind would be delighted.]

Pierre Fontanier's definition of the effects of the "figures d'expression par réflexion" [figures of expression through reflection] is particularly relevant to Le Corbusier's use of the Dom-Ino frame in the Villa Stein, "Pour charmer encore l'esprit des autres en l'exerçant, nous ne présenterons la pensée qu'avec un certain détour, qu'avec un air de mystère; nous la dirons moins que nous la ferons concevoir ou deviner, par le rapport des idées énoncées avec celles qui ne le sont pas, et sur lesquelles les premières vont en quelque sorte se réfléchir, sur lesquelles du moins elles appellent la réflexion, en même temps qu'elles les réveillent dans la mémoire."[48] [In order to charm still the mind of others by exercising it, we shall present the thinking only with through a certain detour, only with an air

of mystery; we shall speak about it less than we shall make it cerebral or implied, through the relationship between the expressed ideas and the unexpressed ones, and which the first will in some way be reflected upon, which at least call them into reflection and are awoken within memory.] By rendering the reading of the building more difficult, Le Corbusier felt that the "lecture de l'oeuvre"[49] [the reading of the work] would gain in richness and awareness. "Etre caressé par des formes, puis savoir comment elles répondent à une intention qui devient évidente, comment elles se classent dans la collection qu'on s'est constituée, d'image électives. Mesurer, comparer en son esprit, voir . . ."[50] [To be caressed by forms, then to know how they respond to an intention which becomes obvious, how they are classified in the collection we have put together, of elective images. To measure, to compare in its own spirit, to see . . .] The ability of Le Corbusier's buildings to suggest more than they show could be seen as an architectural manifestation of Fontanier's "figures d'expression par réflexion" which demonstrate that rare quality of "reticence."[51]

The modular window

In the booklet introducing Le Corbusier's experimental houses at the Stuttgart Weissenhof, Alfred Roth explains how the module of the frame was inferred from the dimensions of the sliding window: a single bay in length and a double bay in width, from column to column.[52] The development of the window element demonstrates Le Corbusier's interest in raising the discipline of architecture to the ranks of modern technology and science, a precursor of pars pro toto the total industrialisation of building construction.

The dimensions of the windows are a synthesis of all structural, tectonic, spatial, functional and economic considerations. As Roth explains, two 2.5-metre bays give the optimum 5-metre span for a reinforced concrete frame. 2.5 metres is the minimum width for a decent living space, made up of two 1.25-metre elements, each the length of a human arm thus facilitating the operation and cleaning of the window. The dimensions of the metal frame, 1.1 metres by 2.5 metres, optimise costs and construction. The wings of the sliding window are highly functional in so far as they do not invade the interior space, do not rattle in the wind, and allow natural ventilation. Given its wide range of applications and need to satisfy such diverse requirements, the window is an ideal candidate for industrialisation and mass production. In his "Appel aux industriels," [Call to the industrialists,] Le Corbusier urged the manufacturers to use industrialised building techniques, pointing to the window as "l'élément mécanique-type de la maison . . . nous contenterons fort bien d'un module fixe. Avec ce module nous composerons."[53] [the mechanical-type element of the house . . . we would be well satisfied with a fixed module. With this module, we will compose.] He used graphs to illustrate how openings of different shapes and sizes could be obtained by simply juxtaposing single units horizontally or vertically. The granting of patent number 619.254 to the design of his Weissenhof windows confirmed the considerable econonomic potential for mechanisation.[54]

The composition of the facade and the disposition of its windows tells the story of the internal organisation of a building in section. In the distinctive Citrohan house, the pan de verre on the south elevation indicates the location of the main double-height living room, while the strip windows indicate the three levels of the other living spaces. The "élément mécanique-type de la maison" [mechanical-type element of the house] affects the internal distribution of spaces

な要素とヴォイド的な（ガラス張りの）要素は、ファサードの構成において同等の役割を演じる単純な四角形へと還元されている。それは、ラ・ロッシュ-ジャンヌレが形式的アプローチという点でデ・スティルに類似していると定義した、壁面を平面へと解体してゆく手法の的確な例である。[43] ル・コルビュジエは「ファサードは……単に住宅を包み込むガラスあるいは組積造のカーテンになる！」[44] と述べている。また、同じくらいの奥行きと異なる幅をもつ二つのバルコニーが、正面のファサードから張り出している。建物の構造上のグリッドは、Aを5m、Bを2.5m幅とするABABAという交互のリズムの柱間によって構成され、中央のバルコニーが幅の広いほうの柱間を占め、小さいバルコニーは狭いほうの柱間を占めている。これらのバルコニーはともに、正面にはしっかりとした手摺壁が、両側面には手摺が取り付けられ、異なるスケールでコーナー・ウインドウの構成を再生している。かくして、片持ち梁のスラブ、非載荷のファサード、そして細分化された構造上のグリッドという、ドミノ構造を規定する要素がここにすべて登場するのである。

寡黙な建築

「シュタイン邸」を、鉄筋コンクリート構造の可能性を明らかにする、同様に有名であるがまったく異なったもう一つのコーナー・ウインドウの例と比較してみることは参考になる。グロピウスが設計したバウハウス校舎の北東角を形成する巨大な3階建てのガラス張りの外装は、その構造システムを完全に剥き出しにしている。鉄とガラスのカーテン・ウォールが外被を形成し、その一方で、張り出した床スラブをもつ鉄筋コンクリートの骨組が建物を構造的に支えている。

「シュタイン邸」とバウハウス校舎の構造は実質的には違わないが、その構造が表明する建築的なマニフェストは大きく異なっている。[45] バウハウス校舎においては、その解決法は文字どおり、また造形的にも透明である。その構造は、ありのままの姿を完全に剥き出しにしている。そのコーナー・ウインドウは、明快な意味論上の趣旨をもっている。すなわちその役目は、より一般的な原理を表現することにある。[46]「シュタイン邸」の構造は、専門家の目だけが認識しうる手がかりによってのみ推測することが可能である。ル・コルビュジエのデザインは、単なる構造的な表現へと矮小化された建築の貧困に向けられた、彼の初期の批評を完璧に例証している。彼は、構造的な骨組は完全に露出すべきではなく、推測されるか、あるいはほのめかされるべきものだと結論づけている。「骨が手首や足首に現れ、心は喜びに満たされよう」。[47]

「沈思を通した表現の造形」の効果に関するピエール・フォンタニエの定義は、とりわけ「シュタイン邸」におけるル・コルビュジエのドミノ構造の使用にあてはまる。「それを実践することによって、ほかの人々の心を喜びあふれるものとするために、我々は、ある種の回り道を経てのみ、また神秘の空気をもってのみ、考えを提示すべきである。表現された考えと、表現されていないものとの間の関係を通じて、我々はそれについて語るよりも、知的なもの、あるいは意味のあるものとすべきである。そして、まず何らかの仕方で投影され、少なくとも沈思のなかに呼び込み、記憶の内で呼び覚まされる」。[48] ル・コルビュジエは、建物の読解をより困難なものとすることによって「作品の読み取り」[49]が豊かさと理解を獲得すると感じていた。「形態と戯れ、それからそれらの形態がどのような意図に対応するのかを知ること。いかにそれらの形態が、我々が一つにまとめた選び抜かれたイメージのコレクションのなかで分類されるか。それ自身の精神で計り、比較し、そして見るために……」。[50] 目に見える以上のものを示唆するル・コルビュジエの建築がもつ力は、「寡黙さ」という、あの類い稀なる特質を実践した、フォンタニエの「沈思を通した表現の造形」の建築的な顕現とみることができる。[51]

モデュラー・ウインドウ

シュトゥットガルトのヴァイゼンホーフにおけるル・コルビュジエの実験住宅

Above: Villa Stein de Monzie, Garches, Le Corbusier, 1926. Below: Bauhaus, Dessau, Walter Gropius, 1926.

上：モーンジーのヴィラ・シュタイン、ガルシュ、ル・コルビュジエ、1926年。下：デッサウのバウハウス校舎、ウォルター・グロピウス、1926年。

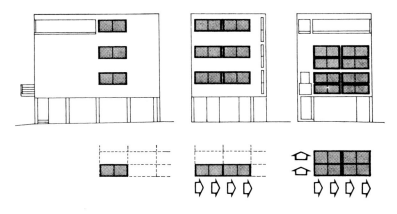

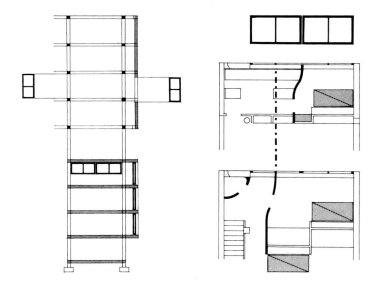

Above: Elevations of the one-family house demonstrate the compositional pattern of the basic window.
Middle: Weissenhofsiedlung. Citrohan single-family house on the left, two-family houses on the right, Le Corbusier, 1927. Below left: The window module determines the constructional interaxes. Below right: The free plan also undergoes the law of industrially manufactured units.

上：1家族住宅の基本的な窓割りパターンによる立面構成。中：ヴァイゼンホーフジードルング。左手にシトロアン1家族住宅、右手は2家族住宅、ル・コルビュジエ、1927年。下左：窓のモジュールによって構造軸が決定される。下右：フリー・プランは工業生産されたユニットの規準の影響を受ける。

in plan. The length of a bed or the width of a cupboard may be determined by the disposition of internal partitions, but if these elements face an external, wall, they establish a direct relationship with the geometry of the window and its compositional elements. Le Corbusier's *plan libre* responds to individual functional requirements, but is in turn subjected to the laws of the mass-produced window.

Nothing could be less industrial than the timber frames of the Weissenhof houses. But in this experimental project, the laying down of facts mattered less than setting the scene for the future industrialisation of the building process. As the exhibition's organisers had clearly specified, perhaps counting too much on the public's intelligence: ". . . die Siedlung [kann] nicht selbst die Methode des rationellen Serienbaus sondern lediglich ein Modell-Vorarbeit dazu vorführen."[55] [. . . the *Siedlung* [can] not be itself a method for rational serial building, but should show a purely preliminary model.]

An aperture as a painting

The ramp in the Villa Savoye extends to the solarium, pointing straight to an opening that frames the surrounding landscape and the river Seine. "La vue principale est au nord" [The main view is to the north] in the highest point of the house.[56] To the south, the solarium space opens directly onto the landscape, spatially circumscribed and without surprises. Stanislaus von Moos has convincingly compared this aperture to a naturalist painting.[57]

Prior to the Villa Savoye, Le Corbusier had shown interest in the kinetic potential of architecture. Never, however, had this been expressed so explicitly. The Villa Savoye must be appreciated by walking through it.[58] A compulsory route is imposed by the ramp: De l'intérieur du vestibule, une rampe douce conduit, sans qu'on s'en aperçoive presque, au premier étage, où se déploie la vie de l'habitant: réception, chambres, etc . . . Du jardin suspendu, la rampe, devenue extérieure, conduit sur le toit, au solarium . . . La circulation fournit des impressions architecturales d'une diversité qui déconcerte tout visiteur étranger aux libertés architecturales apportées par les techniques modernes.[59] ["From inside the entrance, a ramp leads easily, hardly noticed, up to the first floor, where the life of the inhabitants goes on: reception, bedrooms, etc. . . . From the hanging garden, the ramp, now on the outside, leads to the solarium on the roof. . . . Circulation furnishes architectural impressions of such diversity that they disconcert visitors ignorant of the architectural liberties brought by modern techniques."]

The slow, continuous ascent to the roof requires a device to reduce speed and to conclude the walk. In the early designs for the house the ramp reached an enclosed space with a spiral staircase leading to an upper terrace that acted as roof to Madame Savoye's private rooms. In character with the figurative ethos of the time, the spiral stairs "wound the movement of the walk around itself," introducing the visitor to the circular panoramic vista from the terrace.

As built, the ability of the inert architectural forms to suggest motion and guide perception is even more convincing. Physical movement is translated into virtual, perceptive movement. The human gaze looks towards increasingly distant horizons. The window replaces the spatial and perspective illusion of a naturalist painting. It is the inventive interrelationship between reality and image, facts and signs, architectural text and pictorial figuration, that renders the *promenade architecturale* of the Villa Savoye one of the most superbly poetic openings of modern architecture.

を紹介した小冊子のなかで、アルフレッド・ロートは、長さが柱間一つ分、幅が柱間二つ分の引き違い窓の寸法から、構造のモデュールがどのように推測できるかについて説明している。[52] 窓の要素の発展は、建築学を近代テクノロジーと科学の地位にまで引き上げようとしたル・コルビュジエの意図を立証している。そしてそれは、建設の総合的な工業化の先駆的な例となった。

窓の寸法は、構造的、架構技術的、空間的、機能的、そして経済的な考察すべての総合体である。ロートが説明するように、二つの2.5mの柱間が、鉄筋コンクリート構造に最適な5mのスパンとなっている。二つの1.25mの要素からなる2.5mという寸法は、適切な居住空間をつくりだす上での最小限の幅である。1.25mというのは人間の腕の長さであり、それゆえに窓の操作と清掃を容易にする。また、1.1m×2.5mという金属フレームの寸法は、経費と施工を最も効率のよいものとする。引き違い窓は、室内空間を侵さず、風のなかでもガタガタ鳴ることなく、また自然の換気を促す限りにおいて、きわめて機能的なものである。その用途の幅広さと、このような様々な要求を満たす必要性とを考えた時、窓は工業化と大量生産の理想的な対象となる。「産業資本家への呼びかけ」のなかでル・コルビュジエは、「住宅における機械的な種類の要素」として窓を指し、「我々は、規格化されたモデュールに十分満足するだろう。このモデュールを用いて我々は組み立ててゆくのだ」[53] と述べ、工業化された施工技術を用いるよう製造業者を説得した。彼は、一つのユニットを水平方向あるいは垂直方向に並置するだけで異なった形態と寸法の開口部がいかにしてつくりだされるか、グラフを用いて説明した。彼がヴァイゼンホーフで用いた窓のデザインにたいして特許第619,254号が認められたことは、機械化がもつ大きな経済的可能性を確認するものとなった。[54]

ファサードの構成と窓の配置が、断面に現れた内部の組み立てを物語る。有名な「シトロアン住宅」では、南側の立面のパン・ド・ヴェーレが2層分の高さをもつメインの居間の位置を示し、一方で水平連続窓が3層からなる他の居住空間を示している。「住宅における機械的な種類の要素」が、平面計画における内部の空間配分にも影響を及ぼしている。ベッドの長さやカップボードの幅は内部の間仕切りの配置によって定められることもあるが、これらの要素が外壁に面した場合には、窓の幾何学とその構成上の要素と直接的な関係をもつ。ル・コルビュジエの自由な平面は、個々の機能的要求に対応しているが、それはまた、大量生産された窓の法則に従属することとなる。

ヴァイゼンホーフの住宅の木造軸組みほど工業的でないものも少ない。しかしこの実験的なプロジェクトにとっては、事実を並びたてることよりも、建設プロセスの工業化の未来像を定めることのほうが重要だったのである。この展覧会の主催者がはっきりと明記しているように、おそらく大衆の知性にあまりに多くを期待しすぎていたのであろう。「……ジードルングは、合理的な連続的建物の手法となりうるだけでなく、純粋に準備としてのモデルを提示すべきである」。[55]

絵画としての開口

「サヴォア邸」の斜路は、周囲のランドスケープとセーヌ川を枠どる開口にまっすぐ向かって、サンルームへと伸びている。この住宅の最も高い部分の「主な景色は北向き」である。[56] 南に向かって、サンルーム・スペースは、空間的に囲まれなんの驚きもないランドスケープに直接的に開けている。スタニスラウス・フォン・モースは、この開口と自然主義的な絵画との説得力のある比較を行った。[57]

「サヴォア邸」に先立って、ル・コルビュジエは建築がもつ動的な可能性に興味を示していた。しかしながら、この住宅ほど、それを明確に表現したものはなかった。「サヴォア邸」を理解するには、その空間を経験しなければならない。[58] 通るべき経路は斜路が規定している。「エントランスの内に入ると、斜路がごく自然に、ほとんど意識されることもないままに、レセプション、寝室といった居住者の生活が営まれる2階へと導く。空中庭園からは、この時点で

は屋外にある斜路が、屋上のサンルームへと導く。近代技術によってもたらされた建築的な自由を知らぬ訪問者たちを戸惑わせるこのように多様な建築的印象を、その動線はもたらしている」。[59]

屋上へと向かうゆるやかで連続的な上昇は、その速度をゆるめ、歩みに終止符をうつ装置を必要としている。この住宅の初期のデザインでは、斜路は、サヴォア夫人の私室の屋根となる上層のテラスへと通じる螺旋階段をもった閉じた空間へと伸びていた。当時の造形的精神を感じさせる特質をもったその螺旋階段は、来訪者にテラスから円形のパノラミックな景色をみせながら、「それ自身のまわりを歩く動きを巧みに織りなした」。

不動の建築的形態が有する動きを誘導し、知覚を導くという能力は、それが実際に建てられた場合、より説得力のあるものとなる。肉体的な動きは、仮想の知覚的な動きへと翻訳される。人の眼差しは、ますます遠くへと広がる水平線に向けられる。窓が、自然主義的な絵画の空間的、遠近法的なイリュージョンに置き換わる。「サヴォア邸」のプロムナード建築を近代建築のなかでも最もすぐれて詩的な開口の一つとしているのは、現実とイメージ、事実と象徴、建築的テキストと図像的造形の間の発明的な相互関係なのである。

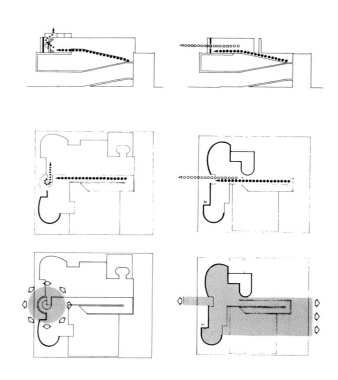

Above: Diagrammatic sketches illustrating the "promenade architecturale" of two versions of the Villa Savoye, 1928 and 1929.

上：サヴォア邸。1928年、1929年の「プロムナード建築」2案の図解。

Notes

1. Le Corbusier, "Une petite maison, 1923," *Les Carnets de la recherche*, Series 1 (Zurich, 1954), pp. 30–31 and p. 36.

2. In a lecture given by Le Corbusier at the Sorbonne on 12 June 1924, he explained: Désormais la nouvelle maison à étages va se présenter en façade sous la forme d'une nouvelle grille. See "L'Esprit Nouveau en Architecture," *Almanach d'architecture moderne* (Paris, 1926).

3. Letter from Le Corbusier to building contractor, Albert Colombo, 2 June 1924, " . . . nous avons supprimé les trois petites colonnes de fonte prévues dans l'avant projet enfin de simplifier la construction en vous permettant de faire une seule grande poutre, la hauteur du linteau de la grande fenêtre étant largement suffisant"

4. Le Corbusier and Pierre Jeanneret exhibited a model and drawings of the La Roche-Jeanneret house at the Salon d'Automne of 1923. See "M. Auguste Perret nous parle de l'Architecture au Salon d'Automne," *Paris-Journal*, 1 December 1923. The interview, which occupied nearly two columns of the paper, was a direct attack by Perret on Adolf Loos and Le Corbusier.

5. "Une visite à Le Corbusier-Saugnier," *Paris-Journal*, 14 December 1923.

6. Letter to Colombo, 10 January 1924, Fondation Le Corbusier, dossier Le Lac, 570.

7. The *Paris-Journal* article notes that Perret is "an authority on architecture;" Le Corbusier, in his reply, pays homage to the "savant technicien." But in a personal letter to Perret, the respect gives way to sarcasm: "un Dieu de l'Olympe va parler . . ." (letter, 13 December 1923).

8. Le Corbusier, "Petite contribution à l'étude d'une fenêtre moderne," in *Almanach*, pp. 95–97.

9. Le Corbusier, op. cit. p. 96.

10. Marcel Zahar, *Auguste Perret* (Paris, 1959), p. 15.

11. J. A. Schmoll gen. Eisenwerth, "Fensterbilder, Motivketten in der europäischen Malerei," in *Beiträge zur Motivkunde des 19. Jahrhunderts* (Munich, 1970).

12. Rainer Maria Rilke, *Les Fenêtres* (Paris, 1927).

13. Le Corbusier, *Almanach*, p. 94.

14. Le Corbusier, *Une petite maison, 1923*, p. 9, and *Almanach*, p. 94.

15. Le Corbusier, "Précisions sur un état de l'architecture et de l'urbanisme," *L'Esprit nouveau* (Paris, 1930) p. 130.

16. Marie Dormoy, "Le Corbusier" in *L'Amour de l'Art*, Paris, May 1930, no 5, p. 213

17. Dolf Sternberger, *Panorama oder Ansichten vom 19. Jahrhundert* (Frankfurt, 1974), p. 156.

18. Cornelius Gurlitt, *Im Bürgerhause* (Dresden, 1888), p. 166, quoted by Dolf Sternberger, op. cit. p. 156.

19. M. H. Baillie Scott, *Häuser und Gärten* (Berlin, 1912), p. 35, original edition, *Houses and Gardens* (London, 1906).

20. Walter Benjamin, *Parigi: Capitale del XIX secolo* (Turin, 1962), p. 148.

21. Le Corbusier, *L'art décoratif d'aujourd'hui* (Paris, 1925), p. 69.

22. Le Corbusier, ibid p. 191.

23. Le Corbusier, *Une petite maison, 1923*, p. 15.

24. Le Corbusier to his father, 29 November 1925, letter in the Bibliothèque de la Ville, La Chaux-de-Fonds.

25. Gaston Bachelard, "La maison, de la cave au grenier: le sens de la hütte," in *La poétique de l'espace* (Paris, 1957).

26. The first sketches for the screen wall can be seen on an early site plan on page 67 of the Cahier de dessins, no. 9, Fondation Le Corbusier (FLC) 5085. It is not featured in the project drawings produced during the winter of 1923–1924, although it is fully defined by May 1924.

27. Le Corbusier, *Oeuvre Complète 1910–1929*, eds W. Boesiger and O. Stonorow, (Zurich, 1974), p. 74, and Le Corbusier, *Une petite maison,1923*, p. 50.

28. While this quotation is from *Précisions* (p. 53 and fig. 55), the concept had already been developed in the lecture given at the Sorbonne in 1924: "Je viens de dire que portes et fenêtres sont des déterminantes de l'architecture; ce n'est pas un paradoxe et l'on peut s'en assurer en étudiant l'histoire de la fenêtre." *Almanach*, p. 30.

29. Le Corbusier, *Précisions*, p. 54; cf also Le Corbusier, "Une maison, un palais," *L'Esprit Nouveau* (Paris, 1930), p. 100.

30. Le Corbusier, *Précisions*, p. 130.

31. Le Conbusier, *Une petite maison, 1923* p. 22. ff.

32. Le Corbusier, *Oeuvre Complète 1910–1929*, p. 74

33. Pierre Fontanier, *Les figures du discours* (Paris, 1968) p. 379; first published between 1821 and 1830. Fontanier classifies the antithesis between the "figure de style par rapprochement" and defines:

"l'Antithèse oppose deux objets l'un à l'autre, en les considérant sous un rapport commun, ou un objet à lui-même, en le considérant sous deux rapports contraires." Angelo Marchese, in *Dizionario di retorica e di stilistica* (Milan, 1978) states: "Antithesis: a logical figure consisting in the juxtaposition of two words or phrases of opposite meanings."

34. Le Corbusier, *Almanach*, p. 92.

35. Original coloured drawings FLC 9419 and sheets FLC 5102 and 5103 of the *Cahiers de dessins no 9*.

36. Le Corbusier, *Précisions*, p. 130.

37. Paradox: the word is derived from the Greek "para" (contrary, opposite) and "doxa" (opinion). In literary rhetoric a paradox designates the effects of estrangement, of simulation that calls reality into question, making us believe that things are not what they are; cf. Heinrich Lausberg, *Elementi di retorica* (Bologna, 1969) p. 28–7, p. 50 and p. 66. J. Dubois, F. Edeline, J. M. Klinkenberg, P. Minguet, F. Pire, H. Trinon, in *Rhétorique générale* (Paris, 1970), pp. 142–143 define paradox as a logical device and note that its strong relationship with oxymoron and antiphrase (*op. cit.* p. 121). Angelo Marchese defines paradox as "a logical figure consisting of an apparently absurd affirmation contrary to common sense."

38. Le Corbusier, letter to Yvonne Gallis, 11 September 1924, FLC, Courrier de Famille, box 35(2): "La petite maison sera comme un temple antique au bord de l'eau."

39. Le Corbusier, "Mise au point," *Forces Vîves* (Paris, 1966), p. 13.

40. The Villa Fallet at La Chaux-de-Fonds, 1906–1907, is Le Corbusier's first built work designed at the age of 19. In fact, the design was the fruit of a collaboration between Le Corbusier, a local builder (René Chapallaz) and L'Eplattenier's atelier.

41. Cf. Helmut Weber, "Die Form," *Walter Gropius und das Faguswerk*, p. 71. ff. and the photograph of the second floor corner interior, p. 70.

42. Le Corbusier and Pierre Jeanneret, *Précisions*, p. 33. "Les planchers sont projetés au delà des poteaux, en façade, en forme de balcon de 1m 23: ces balcons reçoivent les allèges des fenêtres. Les linteaux des fenêtres 'sont suspendus' au plancher qui les domine."

43. Cf. Bruno Reichlin, "Le Corbusier vs de Stijl," *De Stijl et l'architecture en France* (Liège, 1985).

44. Le Corbusier, *Oeuvre Complète 1910–1929*, p. 140.

45. The comparison between Gropius's Bauhaus building and the Villa Stein has already been suggested in C. Rowe, R. Slutzky, B. Hoesli, *Transparenz, Le Corbusier Studien 1* (Basel and Stuttgart, 1968), p. 21 ff.

46. Umberto Eco, *Trattato di semiotica generale* (Milan, 1975), para 3.6.3: Ostensione, pp. 294–295.

47. Le Corbusier, "Ce Salon d'Automne," *L'Esprit Nouveau*, no 28, January 19.

48. P. Fontanier, *Les figures du discours*, p. 123.

49. Le Corbusier, *Une maison, un palais*, p. 5: "Et c'est au delà de la sensation brutale physique que provoque en nous la chose considérée qu'intervient cette 'lecture de l'oeuvre' qui est en vérité ce que vent dire le mot architecture. Eblouissante, riche sans limites, l'intention devient claire. Et dans l'esprit de celui qui contemple, se reconstitue, étape par étape, l'événement créateur. L'admiration trouve ses bases."

50. Le Corbusier, *Urbanisme* (Paris, 1925), p. 59.

51. "La Reticence consiste à s'interrompre et à s'arrêter tout-à-coup dans le cours d'une phrase, pour faire entendre par le peu qu'on a dit, et avec le concours des circonstances, ce qu'on affecte de supprimer, et même souvent beaucoup au delà," Pierre Fontanier, *Figures*, p. 135.

52. Cf. Alfred Roth, *Zwei Wohnhäuser von Le Corbusier und Pierre Jeanneret* (Stuttgart, 1927) pp. 10–13.

53. Le Corbusier, *Almanach*, pp. 102–103.

54. Alfred Roth, op. cit. drawing p. 14.

55. *Werkbund-Ausstellung DIE WOHNUNG, Stuttgart*, a confidential document handed to participants.

56. Le Corbusier, *Précisions*, pp. 136.

57. Stanislaus von Moos, *Le Corbusier — Elemente einer Synthese* (Frauenfeld and Stuttgart, 1968), p. 364

58. "L'architecture arabe nous donne un enseignement précieux. Elle s'apprécie 'à la marche,' avec le pied: c'est en marchant, en se déplaçant que l'on voit se développer les ordonnances de l'architecture. C'est un principe contraire à l'architecture baroque qui est conçue sur le papier, autour d'un point fixe."

59. Le Corbusier, *Précisions*, pp. 136–138.

[Additional translation of quotes on pp. 80-90 by Marc E. Bretler, a+u editorial associate.]

原註

1-ル・コルビュジエ、「Une petite maison（小さな家）、1923」、『Les Carnets de la recherche』、シリーズ1、（チューリッヒ、1954年）30〜31頁および36頁。

2-1924年6月12日、ソルボンヌにおける講演。「L'Esprit Nouveau en Architecture」、『Almanach d'architecture moderne』（パリ、1926年）参照。

3-ル・コルビュジエが施工請負業者のアルベール・コロンボに宛てた、1924年6月2日付の手紙による。

4-ル・コルビュジエとピエール・ジャンヌレは、1923年のサロン・ドートンヌに、「ラ・ロッシュ-ジャンヌレ邸」の模型とドローイングを出展した。「M. Auguste Perret nous parle de l'Architecture au Salon d'Automne」、『Paris-Journal』（1923年12月1日号）参照。紙面のほぼ二段を占めたインタヴューは、ペレによるアドルフ・ロースとル・コルビュジエにたいする直接的な攻撃であった。

5-「Une visite à Le Corbusier-Saugnier」、『Paris-Journal』（1923年12月14日号）。

6-コロンボに宛てた、1924年1月10日付の手紙、ル・コルビュジエ財団、dossier Le Lac、570。

7-『Paris-Journal』紙に掲載された記事は、ペレを「建築の権威」と記している。また、ル・コルビュジエは彼の反論のなかで「学識のある技術者」に敬意を表しているのだが、ペレに宛てた私信（1923年12月13日付の手紙）では、「un Dieu de l'Olympe va parler ...」と記し、敬意のかわりに皮肉をこめている。

8-ル・コルビュジエ、「Petite contribution à l'etude d'une fenêtre moderne」、『Almanach』、95〜97頁。

9-ル・コルビュジエ、『Almanach』、96頁。

10-Marcel Zahar、『Auguste Perret（オーギュスト・ペレ）』（パリ、1959年）、15頁。

11-J. A. Schmoll gen. Eisenwerth、「Fensterbilder, Motivketten in der europäischen Malerei」、『Beiträge zur Motivkunde des 19. Jahrhunderts』（ミュンヘン、1970年）。

12-ライナー・マリア・リルケ、『Les Fenêtres（窓）』（パリ、1927年）。

13-ル・コルビュジエ、『Almanach』、94頁。

14-ル・コルビュジエ、「Une petite maison, 1923」、9頁、および、『Almanach』、94頁。

15-ル・コルビュジエ、「Précisions sur un état de l'architecture et de l'urbanisme」、『L'Esprit nouveau』（パリ、1930年）、130頁。

16-マリー・ドーモイ、「Le Corbusier（ル・コルビュジエ）」、『L'Amour de l'Art』（パリ、1930年5月）、第5巻、213頁。

17-ドルフ・シュテルンベルガー、『Panorama oder Ansichten vom 19. Jahrhundert』（フランクフルト、1974年）、156頁。

18-コルネリウス・グアリット、『Im Bürgerhause』（ドレスデン、1888年）、166頁。ドルフ・シュテルンベルガー、前掲書、156頁での引用による。

19-M・H・ベイリー・スコット、『Häuser und Gärten』（ベルリン、1912年）35頁。オリジナル版は『Houses and Gardens』（ロンドン、1906年）。

20-ヴァルター・ベンヤミン、『Parigi: Capitale del XIX secolo』（トリノ、1962年）、148頁。

21-ル・コルビュジエ、『L'art décoratif d'aujourd' hui』、パリ、1925年、69頁。

22-ル・コルビュジエ、同書、191頁。

23-ル・コルビュジエ、『Une petite maison, 1923』、15頁。

24-ル・コルビュジエが父に宛てた、1925年11月29日付の手紙。Bibliothèque de la Ville, La Chaux-de-Fonds収蔵。

25-ガストン・バシュラール、「La maison, de la cave au grenier: le sens de la hütte」、『La poétique de l'espace』（パリ、1957年）。

26-スクリーン壁の最初のスケッチは、『Cahier de dessins』、no 9、Fondation Le Corbusier(FLC)5085、67頁の初期の配置図に見ることができる。それは、1924年5月には完全に決定されているが、1923〜24年にかけての冬の時点のプロジェクト図面には描かれていない。

27-ル・コルビュジエ、『Ouevre Complète（ル・コルビュジエ全作品集）1910-1929』、W. BoesigerおよびO. Stonorow編（チューリッヒ、1974年）、74頁、および、ル・コルビュジエ、『Une petite maison, 1923』、50頁。

28-この引用は『Précisions』、53頁および図55からのものであるが、そのコンセプトは、1924年にソルボンヌで行われた講演においてすでに展開されていた。『Almanach』、30頁。

29-ル・コルビュジエ、『Précisions』、54頁。また、ル・コルビュジエ、「Une maison, un palais」、『L'Esprit Nouveau』（パリ、1930年）、100頁を参照せよ。

30-ル・コルビュジエ、『Précisions』、130頁。

31-ル・コルビュジエ、「Une petite maison, 1923」、22頁。

32-ル・コルビュジエ、『Ouevre Complète 1910-1929』、74頁。

33-ピエール・フォンタニエ、『Les figures du discours』、パリ、1968年、379頁。初版は1821年から1830年の間に刊行された。フォンタニエ同様、アンジェロ・マルケスは『Dizionario di retorica e di stilistica』（ミラノ、1978年）のなかで、「アンチテーゼ：相対立する意味をもつ二つの言葉あるいはフレーズの並置からなる論理的な思考」であると述べている。

34-ル・コルビュジエ、『Almanach』、92頁。

35-オリジナルの彩色されたドローイングは、『Cahiers de dessins』、no 9、FLC 9419、および、シートFLC 5102ならびに5103。

36-ル・コルビュジエ、『Précisions』、130頁。

37-パラドックス：この言葉は、ギリシャ語の「para」（逆の、反対の、の意）と「doxa」（意見の意）から派生した言葉である。文学のレトリックにおいては、パラドックスは、相反の効果、あるいはリアリティに疑問を投げかけ、物事はそれらがあるがままのものではないと信じ込ませるように見せかける効果を示すものである。Heinrich Lausberg、『Elementi di retorica』、（ボローニャ、1969年）、28〜27頁、50頁および66頁を参照せよ。J. Dubois、F. Edeline、J. M. Klinkenberg、P. Minguet、F. Pire、H. Trinon、『Rhétorique generale』（パリ、1970年）、142〜143頁において、パラドックスを論理上の装置として定義しており、パラドックスがもつ矛盾語法や語意反用との強い関係性について言及している（同書、121頁）。Angelo Marcheseは、パラドックスを「学識とは反する明らかに不合理な肯定からなる論理的思考である」と定義している。

38-ル・コルビュジエ、1924年9月11日付のイヴォンヌ・ガリへの手紙、FLC、Courrier de Famille、box 35(2)。

39-ル・コルビュジエ、「Mise au point」、『Forces Vives』（パリ、1966年）、13頁。

40-ラ・ショー・ド・フォンの「ヴィラ・ファレット」（1906〜07年）は、ル・コルビュジエが19歳の時にデザインした、彼の最初の実作である。実際には、そのデザインはル・コルビュジエと地元の大工（René Chapallaz）、そしてL'Eplattenierアトリエとの共同によるものである。

41-Helmut Weber、「Die Form」、『Walter Gropius und das Faguswerk』、71頁および、70頁の3階の室内の隅の写真を参照。

42-ル・コルビュジエとピエール・ジャンヌレ、『Précisions』、33頁。

43-ブルーノ・ライヒリン、「Le Corbusier vs de Stijl」、『De Stijl et l'architecture en France』、リエージュ、1985年を参照。

44-ル・コルビュジエ、『Ouevre Complète 1910-1929』、140頁。

45-グロビウスのバウハウス校舎と「ヴィラ・シュタイン」の比較は、C・Rowe、R・Slutzky、B・Hoesli、『Transparenz, Le Corbusier Studien 1』（バーゼルおよびシュトゥットガルト、1968年）、21頁においてすでに示唆されている。

46-ウンベルト・エコ、『Trattato di semiotica generale』（ミラノ、1975年）、3.6.3節。「Ostensione」、294〜295頁。

47-ル・コルビュジエ、「Ce Salon d'Automne」、『L'Esprit Nouveau』、第28号。

48-ピエール・フォンタニエ、『Les figures du discours』、123頁。

49-ル・コルビュジエ、「Une maison, un palais」、5頁。

50-ル・コルビュジエ、『Urbanisme』、パリ、1925年、59頁。

51-ピエール・フォンタニエは『Figures』、135頁で、「センテンスの途中で突然さえぎり、止まった時の寡黙というのは、多くを語らず、しばしばその背後に多くのことを隠している」と記している。

52-アルフレッド・ロート、『Zwei Wohnhàuser von Le Corbusier und Pierre Jeanneret』（シュトゥットガルト、1927年）、10〜13頁を参照せよ。

53-ル・コルビュジエ、『Almanach』、102〜103頁。

54-アルフレッド・ロート、前掲書、ドローイング、14頁。

55-『Werkbund-Ausstellung DIE WOHNUNG, Stuttgart』。これは参加者に支給された内々の文書である。

56-ル・コルビュジエ、『Précisions』、136頁。

57-スタニスラウス・フォン・モース、『Le Corbusier - Elemente einer Synthese』、フラウエンフェルトおよびシュトゥットガルト、1968年、364頁。

58-「アラビアの建築は、貴重な教えを与えてくれる。それは、歩くことによって味わうことができるのだ。歩き、動くことで、建築的な秩序が発展するのがわかる。これは、紙の上の固定された視点から考えられたバロック建築と相反する原理である」。

59-ル・コルビュジエ、『Précisions』、136〜138頁。

Rietveld Schröder House
Utrecht, The Netherlands 1924
Gerrit Thomas Rietveld

リートフェルト・シュレーダー邸
オランダ、ユトレヒト　1924
ヘリット・トマス・リートフェルト

The Rietveld Schröder house was built in 1924 by Gerrit Thomas Rietveld for the widow Truus Schröder-Schrader. After her husband died, she wanted to live in a smaller house with her three children. She had known Rietveld's work for some years and in 1921, she commissioned him to redesign her personal study in her family's existing 19th century house. The new house was Rietveld's first commission for more than a facade or an interior alteration. He was originally trained as a cabinet maker in his father's business and started his own workshop in 1917. There he made the unpainted prototypes of what would become the Red Blue chair. The design was published in *de Stijl* in 1919, where Rietveld emphasized its spatial aspects in the accompanying text. The separate elements are joined without any deformations, so that no one part is dominant or is subordinate to another. As a result, the design clearly and freely occupies space as a single entity, the form being more important than the material itself. Four years later, under the influence of *de Stijl*, Rietveld started painting his furniture in the primary colors red, yellow and blue, combined with white, black and grey. He also experimented with asymmetrical compositions for his furniture—and architectural designs.

The design for the Schröder house is in every way a realization of the ideas of *de Stijl* and at the same time an elaboration of Rietveld's views on architecture. The flowing transition between the inner and the outer space, the open plan of the second level and the visually dominant use of color are the three main characteristics of the house. Rietveld achieved the first element by expressing the walls as three-dimensional compositions of lines and planes. The juxtaposition of these elements can be compared with the composition of the Red Blue chair and leads to the same spatial clarity. At some places the plane of the facade is completely broken up, as in the corner window on the second level with the missing mullion. The windows at this point form a corner of 90 degrees when closed, but when open this delineation disappears. On the second level, Rietveld also realized the ideal of a fully open living room. At Schröder's request, he implemented a system of sliding partitions to separate corners for sleeping and dining. On the ground level, he linked the rooms with clerestory windows. Rietveld used the colors to strengthen the spatial effect of the design. Conversely, he consistently denied the tactile materiality of the resultant composition. Red, yellow, blue, white, grey and black lines and planes visually dominate. Outer and inner walls and furniture have the same finish and therefore form one unified composition.

After completing the house, Rietveld's style changed. His work became more restrained, using mainly white, black and grey. Nevertheless, the open plan and asymmetrical composition continued to be important elements of his architectural idiom. The principal client, Truus Schröder, lived in the house until her death in 1985. She and Rietveld kept working together. Rietveld's office was in fact situated in one of the rooms on the ground floor for about nine years. They were friends and lovers and they lived together in the house from 1958 to 1964. The house is now owned by a foundation and maintained under the auspices of the Centraal Museum in Utrecht.

(Ida van Zijl, *Adjunct Director/Curator Applied Arts, Centraal Museum*)

Above:View from an open polder on the east, c. 1926. Today the polder is covered by an expressway viaduct. Opposite top: View of southeast facade with main entry. Opposite bottom: View of southwest facade.

上：かつて干拓地のあった頃の光景。東からみる。今日、この干拓地の上には高速自動車道が建設されている。右頁、上：メイン・エントランスのある南東側ファサード。右頁、下：南西側のファサード。

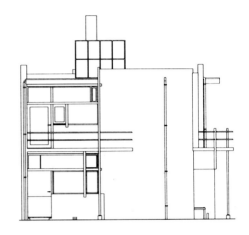

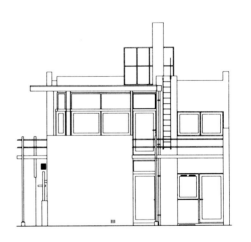

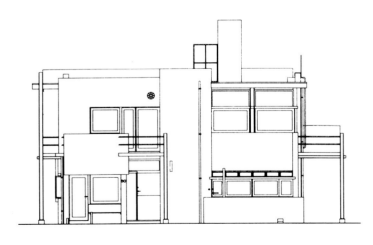

Top to bottom: Southwest elevation, northeast elevation, southeast elevation with main entry just left of central axis. Opposite: Detail of the southwest facade.

上から：南西側立面図。北東側立面図。南東側立面図、左右中心軸の左側にメイン・エントランスがある。右頁：南西側のファサードの詳細。

リートフェルト・シュレーダー邸は、1924年、ヘリット・トマス・リートフェルトによって、未亡人であったトゥルース・シュレーダー・シュラーダーのために建てられた。夫の死後、彼女は三人の子どもたちとそれまでよりも規模の小さい住宅に住むことを望んだ。シュレーダー夫人は、1921年に、当時家族とともに暮らしていた19世紀の住宅にある彼女の書斎を改装する仕事を依頼して以来、リートフェルトを知っていた。それはリートフェルトにとって、単にファサードや内装を変更する以上の、初の本格的なインテリア・デザインの仕事であった。彼はもともと父親の仕事を継いで家具職人として修業を積み、1917年に自らの工房を始めた。ここで彼は、後のレッド・ブルー・チェアのプロトタイプ（色を塗っていない状態）をつくった。そのデザインは1919年の『デ・スティル』誌に掲載され、リートフェルトは解説文のなかで、その空間的な側面を強調している。各要素は変形することなく結合しているため、支配的、あるいは従属的な要素はない。結果としてそのデザインは、明確に、そして自由に、一つの自立したものとして空間を占め、形態が材料そのものよりも重要になる。4年後、デ・スティルの影響の下、リートフェルトは白、黒、グレイと、組み合わされた基本的な色である赤、黄色、青で椅子を着色した。彼はまた、家具デザインにおいて非対称の構成を試み、それは建築デザインにも応用された。シュレーダー邸のデザインは、あらゆる点で、デ・スティルの思想を実現したものであり、同時にリートフェルトの建築にたいする考えを忠実に形にしたものであった。内部空間と外部空間の間の移行、2階のオープン・プラン、そして視覚的に顕著な色の使用の3点は、この住宅の最大の特徴である。リートフェルトは、第一の特徴を、線と面の3次元構成として壁を表現することによって実現した。これらの要素の並置は、レッド・ブルー・チェアの構成と比較することが可能であり、それは同じ空間的明快さをもたらしている。ある部分では、ファサードの平面が完全に壊れている。たとえば、2階のコーナーの窓には方立がない。この部分の窓は、閉じている時は90°のコーナーを形成しているが、開放するとこの図形は消えてしまう。2階において、リートフェルトは完全にオープンな居間を実現した。シュレーダー夫人の要望に応えて、住宅のコーナーを寝室およびダイニングとして引き違いの間仕切りで仕切るシステムを採用した。また1階では、高窓によって部屋をつなぎあわせた。

リートフェルトは、デザインの空間的効果を強化するために色を使った。言い換えれば、彼は合成された構成における素材の質感を徹底的に否定したのである。赤、黄色、青、白、グレイ、黒の線と面は視覚的に支配的である。外部と内部の窓と家具は同じ仕上げであり、したがって一つの統一された構成を形づくる。この住宅が完成した後、リートフェルトのスタイルは変化した。彼の作品はより抑制され、主に白、黒、グレイが使われた。それでもオープン・プランと非対称の構成は、彼の建築言語の重要な要素でありつづけた。

施主であるトゥルース・シュレーダーは、1985年に亡くなるまでこの家で暮らした。彼女とリートフェルトは、一緒に仕事をした。実際リートフェルトの事務所は、約9年間、この住宅の1階の一室に置かれた。彼らは友人として、また愛人として、1958年から1964年までこの家でともに暮らした。この住宅は現在、財団が所有し、セントラル・ミュージアム・ユトレヒトの援助を受けて管理されている。

（イダ・ヴァン・ジール、セントラル・ミュージアム、応用芸術キュレーター）

*Above: Windows of the
sitting/dining area at the east
corner. Opposite top: Detail of the
east corner. Opposite bottom: Detail
of the southeast facade with signs
that read: "Goods delivered here"
and "Ring first; if no answer, use
speaking tube." (visible on the left
wall.)*

上：東隅の居間／食堂の窓が開いている。
右頁、上：東隅の詳細。右頁、下：南東
側ファサードの詳細。サインには、「ここ
で、配達物を受け取ります」「ベルを鳴ら
して返事のないときには、送話管（左手
の壁に穴が開いている）を使ってくださ
い」と書かれている。

Left column, top to bottom: 2nd
floor plan with all sliding
partitions opened; 2nd floor plan
with all sliding partitions closed;
ground floor plan. Right column,
top to bottom: Northwest section,
southeast section, northeast
section. Opposite: Axonometric
drawing of the 2nd level by
Rietveld, undated.

左、上から：引き込み式の間仕切りを開
いた状態の2階平面図。引き込み式の間仕
切りを閉じた状態の2階平面図。1階平面
図。右、上から：北西側断面図。南東側
断面図。北東側断面図。右頁：リートフ
ェルトによる2階アクソノメトリック図。
制作年不明。

Opposite: Entrance hall with
wardrobe and stairs to the upper
level to the right. Above: Kitchen
on the ground floor with Military
chair, 1923, on the left.

左頁：エントランス・ホール。正面に洋
服掛け、右手に2階への階段がみえる。
上：1階の台所。ミリタリー・チェア
（1923年）が右手にみえる。

pp. 104–105: View from the
daughters' room with sliding
partitions opened. Staircase and
landing in the foreground,
sitting/dining area in the middle,
son's room on the right, and
Mrs. Schröder's room on the left.
Above: Daughters' room.

104〜105頁：娘たちの寝室からみる。引
き込み式の間仕切りが開いた状態。手前
に階段室と踊り場、その奥に食堂・居間、
右手に息子の寝室。左手にシュレーダー
夫人の寝室がみえる。上：娘たちの寝室。

Above: Sitting/dining area. View to the east originally looked onto an open polder.

上：食堂・居間。以前は東側に干拓地が眺められた。

Opposite: View of the sitting/dining area from the son's room. Sliding partitions partially closed.
Above: View from the sitting/dining area of the son's room with Red Blue chair and daughters' room behind the half-closed sliding partitions.

左頁：息子の寝室から食堂・居間をみる。引き込み式の間仕切りは部分的に閉まっている。上：食堂・居間から半開きの引戸越しに、レッド・ブルー・チェアのある息子の寝室、娘たちの寝室をみる。

How House
Silver Lake, California, USA 1925
Rudolph Schindler

ハウ邸
米国、カリフォルニア州、シルヴァー・レイク　1925
ルドルフ・シンドラー

In this house, built for the socially progressive client James Eads How and his wife, Rudolph Schindler explored geometric compositional ideals similar to those of the Dutch *de Stijl* group, but within the regional context of Southern California. Earlier in his career, Schindler had been active in Adolf Loos's studio-salon in Vienna, and had joined Frank Lloyd Wright's Chicago office in 1918. He moved to Los Angles in 1919 to manage Wright's California office and supervise the construction of the Barnsdall "Hollyhock house." Schindler established his own practice in 1921.

The plan of the How house is organized by diagonal bilateral symmetries along an east-west axis, with views of the Los Angeles River and San Gabriel Mountains illuminated at sunrise, and Silver Lake and the Hollywood Hills at sunset. The horizontality of the concrete base and redwood siding contrasts dramatically with the verticality of the surrounding Eucalyptus trees. At street level the house appears to be single-storied, but actually consists of four levels descending a steeply sloping site. The entry is sharply compressed by a deeply cantilevered roof at door-head height, but inside the space opens onto a double-height living space with an L-shaped gallery above, used for additional sleeping and musical performances. Schindler himself explained the plan: "the rooms form a series of right angle shapes placed above each other and facing alternatingly (east and west). This scheme provides sufficient terraces necessary for outdoor life. The angles are further placed in such a way as to frame an open shaft between them. This shaft illuminates the hall downstairs. It affords a direct view from the lowest floor to the highest ceiling of the living room, thus emphasizing the spatial unity of the structure."

Schindler, who had been hired by Wright to work on the foundations of the Imperial Hotel, designed the How house structure to withstand Los Angeles earthquakes. The lower portion was constructed of monolithic concrete, executed with his "slab-cast" system. Concrete was poured in 16″ (0.4 m) daily increments into reusable 2″ (5 cm) thick redwood plank formwork that was finally incorporated into the wood-frame structure above. Schindler placed windows in the wooden structure by substituting horizontal pieces of plate glass for redwood planks, between vertical drip strips. While two integral chimney stacks stabilize the structure against shear forces during earthquakes, the living room is spanned by a single beam from which secondary beams hang in a herringbone pattern.

Following Wright's example, Schindler created a total living environment, designing redwood furniture and light fixtures for the house. He also designed elements such as a cantilevered terrace roof with drainage slots, which create a raindrop curtain around the corner light, where water falls to the terrace before streaming under built-in planters and cascading to the garden below. This vision has been revived and lives on today. Current owners Lionel March and Maureen Mary have reconstructed many pieces of Schindler's furniture and removed unauthorized 1926 additions, such that the How house is now one of Schindler's best preserved houses from the twenties, and a lasting expression of his vision for modern living.   (KTO)

進歩的な社会思想をもっていたジェイムズ・イーズ・ハウとその妻のために建てられたこの住宅において、ルドルフ・シンドラーは、オランダのデ・スティル派と類似した幾何学的構成の理想を南カリフォルニアという地域的文脈において探求した。シンドラーは、建築家としてまずはウィーンのアドルフ・ロースのサロン的スタジオで意欲的に活動し、1918年にシカゴにあるフランク・ロイド・ライトの事務所に加わった。1919年には、ライトの事務所を運営し、かつバーンズドール「ホリーホック」邸の現場を監督するためにロサンゼルスに移った。そして、シンドラーは1921年に独立し、自らの事務所を設立した。

ハウ邸の平面計画は、東一西方向の軸に沿った対角線を挟んで左右対称に構成され、日の出にはロサンゼルス・リヴァーとサン・ガブリエル山脈の景色を、また日没にはシルヴァー・レイクとハリウッド・ヒルの景色を望めるよう考慮された。コンクリート基礎とアメリカスギの羽目板の水平性が、周囲のユーカリの木々の垂直性と劇的な対比を生み出している。道路のレヴェルからは平屋に見えるが、実際には、急勾配の傾斜地に建つ4階建ての建物である。奥行きのある片持ち屋根によって圧縮された狭い入口を入ると、予備の寝室や演奏室として使われたL字型のギャラリーをもつ吹抜けのリヴィング・スペースへと空間が開ける。シンドラー自身は平面計画について次のように説明している。「部屋は、一連の直角にくの字の形態を形成し、それぞれが重なり合い、交互に（東と西）向かい合っている。この案は、屋外での活動に必要なテラスを十分確保することを可能にする。このくの字型は、その間に吹抜けのシャフトを形づくるようにさらに積み上げられる。このシャフトは、下の階のホールを明るく照らしている。また、このシャフトを通して最下階から居間の最も高い天井まで見通せるため、建物の空間的なまとまりを強化している」。

帝国ホテルの基礎計画のためにライトに雇われていたシンドラーは、ハウ邸の構造をロサンゼルスの地震に耐えうるようにデザインした。下部は、モノリシックなコンクリート構造でつくられ、彼が考案した「スラブ・キャスト」システムによって施工された。コンクリートは1日16インチ（0.4m）が流し込まれ、厚さ2インチ（5cm）のアメリカスギの型枠は何度も再利用され、コンクリート工事が終了した後は上部の軸組構造に組み込まれた。またシンドラーは、上部の木造の部分で、垂直の水切りの間にあるアメリカスギの板を単に横長の板ガラスに取り替えることによって窓をつくった。二本の構造上不可欠な煙突が地震の際のせん断力にたいして構造を安定させる役目を果たしているのにたいし、居間はヘリングボーン状の補助的な梁が吊られている一本の梁が架けられているだけである。

ライトの住宅建築の例に倣い、アメリカスギを使った家具や照明器具などをデザインすることによって、シンドラーはトータルな生活環境を創造した。彼はまた、排水溝付きの片持ちルーフ・テラスといった要素もデザインした。これは、角に取り付けられた照明の周りに雨水のカーテンをつくり、その水がテラスに落ち、造り付けの鉢の下を流れ、最終的に滝のように下の庭に落ちるという仕掛けになっていた。

シンドラーのこのヴィジョンは甦り、今日まで生きつづけている。現在のオーナーであるライオネル・マーチとモウリーン・メアリーは、シンドラーの家具の大部分を再建し、1926年に施主の独断で増築された部分を取り除いた。その結果、ハウ邸は1920年代に建てられたシンドラーの住宅のなかでも現在最もよい状態で維持されており、彼のモダン・リヴィングにたいするヴィジョンを今も力強く表現している。   (KTO)

pp. 110–111: View of the entrance
side from the west. Above: View
from the terrace on the east side.

110〜111頁：西からみたエントランス側
全景。上：東側のテラスからみる。

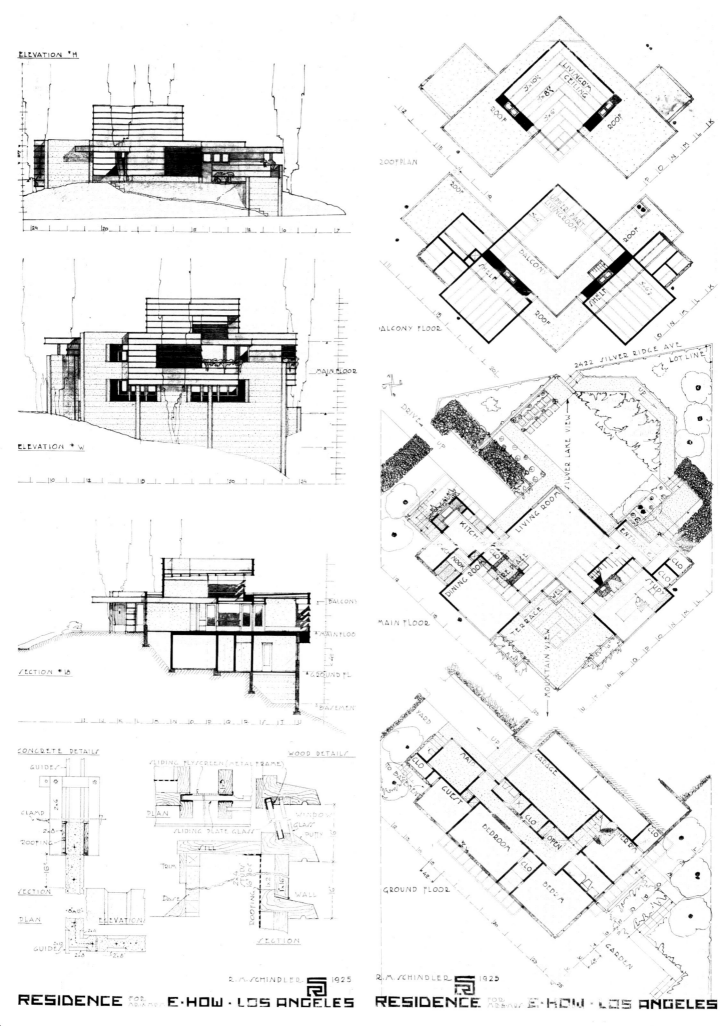

ELEVATION #H

ELEVATION #W

MAIN FLOOR

SECTION #18

BALCONY
MAIN FLOOR
GROUND FL
BASEMENT

CONCRETE DETAILS

WOOD DETAILS

GUIDES

SLIDING FLYSCREEN (METAL FRAME)

PLAN

CLAMP

SLIDING PLATE GLASS

WINDOW

GLASS
PUTTY

ROOFING

STEEL

TRIM

SECTION

PLAN

ELEVATION

WALL

ROOFING

GUIDES

SECTION

R.M. SCHINDLER 1925

RESIDENCE FOR E·HOW·LOS ANGELES

ROOF PLAN

ROOF

LIVINGROOM CEILING

ROOF

BALCONY FLOOR

ROOF

SHELF

UPPER PART LIVINGROOM

BALCONY

SHELF

ROOF

2422 SILVER RIDGE AVE.
LOT LINE

DRIVE
UP

UP

LAWN

KITCH

LIVING ROOM

ENT

CLO

NOOK

CLO

DINING ROOM

TERRACE

WELL

UP

MAIN FLOOR

MOUNTAIN VIEW

YARD

UP

CLO

MAID

GARAGE

TO BASEMENT

GUEST

CLO
OPEN

CLO

BEDROOM

CLO

BED·M

GROUND FLOOR

GARDEN

R.M. SCHINDLER 1925

RESIDENCE FOR E·HOW·LOS ANGELES

114

Opposite left column, top to bottom: Northwest elevation, southeast elevation, section looking northeast through living and dining, and concrete and wood details. Opposite right column, top to bottom: Roof plan, balcony floor plan, main floor plan, ground floor plan (Note: direction arrow on opposite page original drawing is wrong. It should be turned to the left 90 degrees). Above: Approach to entrance with exterior of the living room on the right.

左頁、左、上から：北西側立面図。南東側立面図。居間・食堂を通る北東側断面図。コンクリート部分・木部詳細図。左頁、右、上から：屋根伏図、バルコニー階平面図、主階平面図、1階平面図（左頁のオリジナル図面の方位は誤って記入されている。正しくは、時計回りに90度回転されねばならない）。上：エントランスへのアプローチ。右手に居間の外部がみえる。

*Above: Exterior fenestration of the
living room. Terrace on the east is
visible across the living room.
Opposite: View of the living room
with light-well toward the terrace.*

上：居間外部の窓割り。ガラス窓を通し
て居間の向こうに東側のテラスがみえる。
右頁：光井戸のある居間。テラス方向を
みる。

pp. 118–119: View of the living
room toward the dining room.
Above: View of the northwest
interior elevation of the living
room. Opposite top: Dining room
with door to the terrace on the left.
pp. 120–121, bottom: Furniture and
light fixture in the living and
dining rooms by Schindler.

118〜119頁：居間。食堂方向をみる。
上：居間。北西側の隅をみる。右頁、
上：食堂。左手の扉はテラスへの出入口。
120〜121頁、下：居間・食堂の、シンド
ラーのデザインによる家具、天井照明。

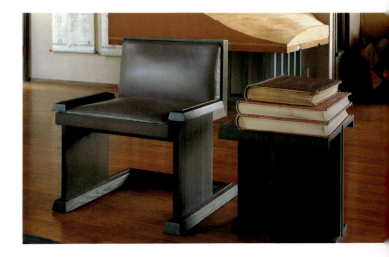

Melnikov House
Moscow, Russia 1929
Konstantin Stepanovich Melnikov

メルニコフ邸
ロシア、モスクワ　1929
コンスタンティン・ステパーノヴィッチ・メルニコフ

Few people passing by know the story of this bewildering double-cylinder house sheltered behind a wooden fence on an ancient Moscow side street — not to mention the story of its architect, whose name is boldly inscribed on the cornice of the front facade. With the rise of many taller buildings, the house's neighborhood has witnessed radical change in the 70 years since its completion, leaving few traces of the ancient thriving European city. Today, it is difficult to imagine that any architect could build his own house in the center of Moscow, moreover in such an unusual form. Although the city government initially hesitated to give the site to Melnikov, then a world-renowned architect of the USSR Pavilion at the Paris Exposition des Arts Décoratifs (1925), his determination saved this unique project that would become the greatest modern house in Russia.

Limited financial resources forced Melnikov to rely on his profound knowledge of building construction methods to realize his long-held dream of creating a communal home and studio for he and his family. He reduced building costs by two-thirds through the use of an efficient circular form and an original method of laying the structural brick wall, which used construction refuse and broken bricks as additional infill. He also eliminated the need for interior columns by using a wooden egg-crate lattice floor structure. Although the project was approved before construction, Melnikov experimented continuously while building the house and amazed all through his innovative use of space. For example, once during construction he was bewitched by the sunlight filtering through the holes of the walls and decided to make it into a special octagonal window to allow the evening sunlight to animate the space and preserve the view the church of Nicolas the Carpenter.

Private Space
The family of four lived their daily lives on the well-organized ground floor, adapted to the family members' individual and communal needs. After approaching the house on the north-south axis and entering the door, the axis shifts 45 degrees and one is effortlessly led to the right side of the cylinder. From here one encounters the stair leading to the living room and two hexagonal windows. A double swinging door allows direct access to the family's private spaces or it can be closed to directly lead the guest to the living room and studio above. The main room on the ground floor is a dining-room (17 m²) with two hexagonal and one rectangular window looking out to the street. This was the family room with the "kiot" altar, which still contains the betrothal candles of Konstantin Stepanovich and his wife Anna Gavrilovna. This room is connected by an open corridor through floor-to-ceiling doorways to the kitchen, dressing room, lavatory, and study rooms as an uninterrupted continuity of spaces. The dressing room has two wardrobes: one for mother and daughter to the right of the entrance and one for father and son to the left. The family changed clothes here before going sleep in the bedroom on the floor above, which originally lacked any additional furniture besides dressing-gown hooks. Melnikov, who considered sleep an important time to dream, created a unique communal family bedroom (43 m²) consisting of three built-in beds and two partitions to ensure visual privacy. In the evening, summer sunlight would be modulated by twelve hexagonal windows.

Public Space
One does not enter the living room space directly, but rather first passes through a lower transitional space at the intersection of the two cylinders. One then enters the expansive living space dominated by the masterpiece of an oversized window-screen, which appears very light despite its heavy frame. The arrangement of the room is very simple — a sofa, working table, pictures by his artist-son (left of the entrance) and works of Konstantin Melnikov himself (on the right). This space now serves as a space in dialogue between father and son, two friends, two masters, where he devoted his life to the pursuit of art. The window stands strong and gives scale to this acoustically-fine entertainment space, where famous musicians performed. The studio is also a double-height space of similar proportions (50 m² with 4.7 m ceilings), but completely different in character. Here 38 hexagonal windows create a symphony of light and shadow. For Melnikov, proportions of spaces were not absolute but rather in relationship to each other. The studio was Melnikov's personal workspace. The loft above was his own favorite place from where he could look at his own works spread out on the floor below and also sketch. From here, one could access the outdoor roof terrace where one could relax and drink tea during the summer months.

This small house, whose composition is created by simple geometrical form, is an architectural masterpiece. The astonishingly diverse and dynamic spatial expressions are difficult to imagine from the outside. There were many hindrances along the way to constructing Melnikov's dream, except his own unyielding talent. Its realization is proof that there were no boundaries for his ingenuity and bold way of thinking. Today the story of Melnikov's house has become one of the most fortuitous ones that will not be forgotten by those who know its secret.

(Rishat Mullagildin)

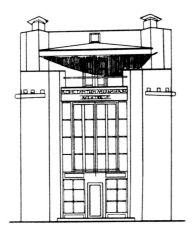

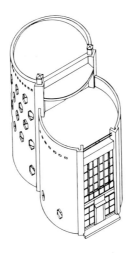

*Opposite: South elevation and ·
axonometric drawing. Above: View
of the front facade from
Krivoarbatesky Lane.*

左頁：南側立面図およびアクソノメトリ
ック図。上：クリヴォアルバトスキ通り
からみた正面ファサード。

Above and opposite: Front facade and elevations of the two penetrating cylinders with 65 hexagonal openings.

上：二つの円筒が重なりあった外観。円筒の外壁には65の六角形の開口が穿たれた。

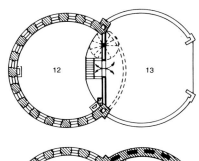

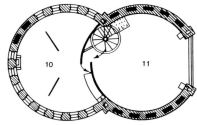

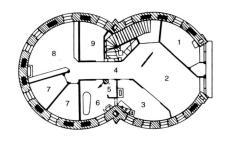

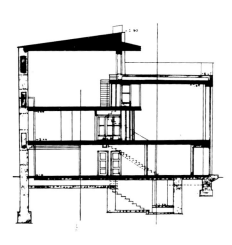

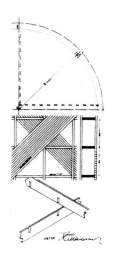

モスクワの小さな旧道に面した、この円筒が重なり合った不思議な住宅について知る通行人はほとんどいないであろし、ましてや正面ファサードにその名が刻まれた建築家を知る人はいないだろう。現在では、背の高い建物が建ちならび、この70年の間に古き良き時代のヨーロッパの面影はほとんど失われてしまった。今日のモスクワでは、街の中心に建築家が自邸を建てるというのはきわめて例外的であり、ましてこのような見慣れない形態で建てることなど考えられない。当初、市当局は、メルニコフにこの敷地を与えることに難色を示したが、彼の強い決意が、最も偉大なロシアのモダン・ハウスとなるこのプロジェクトを救った。

家族と自分のための住宅とスタジオをつくるという長年の夢を実現する上で、経済的な制限から、メルニコフは建設技術に関する自らの知識を駆使する必要があった。効率的な円という形態と、廃材や壊れた煉瓦を補助の充填材として使うという独自の煉瓦積みの手法によって、建設費の2/3が削減された。また内部で柱を使わなくてよいように、格子状の木の床構造を用いた。建設が始まる前にすでに認可はおりていたが、メルニコフは建設期間を通して様々な実験を行い、その革新的な空間は彼にとって驚きの連続だった。たとえばある時、建設中に壁の穴から漏れる太陽の光に魅了された彼は、夕日を取り入れ、ニコラス聖堂の眺めを確保するために、この穴を特別な八角形の窓とした。

四人の家族は、家族の個人的および共通の必要を満たしてくれる1階で日々の生活を送った。南北の軸に沿ってこの住宅に入ると、軸は45度転換し、円筒の右側へと自然に誘導される。ここに居間へとつながる階段がある。二つの前後に開くドアは、家族の私的な空間へのアクセスでもあり、またそこを閉めると、来客を上階の居間とスタジオへ誘導することができる。1階の中心は、道に面して二つの六角形の窓と一つの菱形の窓をもつ食堂（17㎡）である。ここは祭壇のある家族室で、この祭壇には今もコンスタンチン・ステパーノヴィッチと彼の妻のアナ・ガブリオヴナの婚約を記念する蝋燭が飾られている。この部屋は、床から天井までの高さのドアがある廊下によって、台所、更衣室、洗面所、そして書斎と空間的に連続している。更衣室には、母と娘の衣装箪笥が右手に、父と息子の衣装箪笥が左手にある。上階の寝室にはナイト・ガウン掛け以外に家具がなかったため、家族は寝る前にここで衣服を着替えた。就寝は夢を見るための大切な時間と考えたメルニコフは、三つの造り付けベッドと視覚的なプライヴァシーを守るための二つの間仕切りが設けられたユニークな家族共有の寝室（43㎡）を設計した。そして、12個の六角形の窓が夏の夜の光を調整した。居間へは直接ではなく、二つの円柱が交差する天井の低い移行空間を通って入る。ついで、巨大な窓が設けられた開放的な居室へと至る。部屋のアレンジはきわめて簡素で、ソファ、作業机、画家である息子が描いた絵（入口の左）、メルニコフ自身の作品（入口の右）が置かれているだけである。メルニコフが自らの人生を芸術に捧げたこの空間は、現在、父と息子の対話の空間となっている。窓は強烈な印象を与えると同時に、著名な音楽家がしばしば演奏した音響の優れたこの空間にスケール感を与えている。スタジオは、居間とほぼ同じプロポーション（床面積50㎡、高さ4.7m）だが、空間的性格はまったく異なっている。ここでは、38個の六角形の窓が光と影の交響曲を奏でている。メルニコフにとって、空間のプロポーションは絶対的なものではなく、その関係性をより重視した。スタジオは彼の個人的な作業空間であった。ロフトは、床に並べられた彼の作品を眺め、スケッチすることができる彼のお気に入りの場所であった。このロフトはルーフ・テラスへとつながっている。

空間構成が単純な幾何学形態によってつくられたこの小さな住宅は、建築的傑作である。驚くほど多彩で力強い空間表現は、外からは想像することが難しい。メルニコフの夢を実現する道のりには数多くの困難があったが、この住宅の実現は、彼の発明の才と大胆な着想に際限がなかったことを証明している。今日、メルニコフの家の物語は、その秘密を知る者にとって忘れがたいものとなっている。

（リシャット・ムラギルディン）

Opposite, top to bottom: 3rd floor plan, 2nd floor plan, ground floor plan, section, detail of floor structure (left) and the house under construction with Melnikov and his wife at right. Above left: A hexagonal window. Above right: View through a hexaganal window. Legend of the floor plans:
1) Entrance hall, 2) Dining room, 3) Kitchen, 4) Corridor, 5) Toilet, 6) Bathroom, 7) Children's study rooms, 8) Dressing room, 9) Work room, 10) Bedroom, 11) Living room, 12) Studio, 13) Roof terrace

左頁、上から：3階平面図。2階平面図。1階平面図。断面図。床の構造図（左）と工事中のメリニコフ邸、右手はメルニコフ夫妻。左上：六角形の窓。右上：六角形の窓からみた外部の光景。
平面図凡例：1）エントランス・ホール、2）食堂、3）台所、4）廊下、5）洗面所、6）浴室、7）子ども室、8）更衣室、9）作業室、10）寝室、11）居間、12）スタジオ、13）屋上テラス

*Above left: Ground floor entrance
on left, dining room on right.
Above right: Spiral staircase to the
living room on the 2nd level.*

左上：左手に1階エントランス、右手に食
堂。右上：螺旋の階段室、2階の居間へと
導かれる。

Above left: Spiral staircase at 2nd level. Above right: Enrty to the living room from the staircase.

左上：2階の螺旋の階段室。右上：階段室から居間への入口。

pp. 130–131: Melnikov's 3rd level studio. pp. 132–133: View of the 2nd level communal bedroom clockwise along the curved wall of the cylinder.

130～131頁：3階にあるメルニコフのスタジオ。132～133頁：2階にある家族共同の寝室。円筒の曲壁に沿って、時計回りにみる。

Above: Living room on the 2nd
level with special octagonal
window at left. Central alcove
leads to the bedroom.

上：2階居間。左手に他とは異なる八角形
の窓がみえる。中央のアルコーヴに寝室
への入口がある。

Above: 2nd level living room.　　　　　　上：2階居間。

Opposite: Living room. Upper
curved wall defines the 3rd level
studio. Above: Glass wall of the
living room facing the street.

左頁：居間。3階スタジオとの境界壁が半
円筒となって、居間上部に現われる。
上：通り側に面した居間のガラス壁。

Dialogue with Kenneth Frampton
The Modern House /A Response to Nine Questions
Interviewer: Ken Tadashi Oshima

A residence must only serve for living. The site, the exposure to the sun, the program of rooms, and the building materials are the essential factors for the design of a residence. The building is to be formed in response to these conditions. Old familiar pictures may disappear, but in their place residences will arise that are functional in all respects. The world did not become poorer when the stagecoach was replaced by the automobile.

Mies van der Rohe, *"Building Art and the Will of the Epoch," 1924*

Above: King's Road house, Los Angeles, Rudolph Schindler, 1922. Bottom: Health House, Los Angeles, Richard Neutra, 1929.

上：キングス・ロードの住宅、ロサンゼルス、ルドルフ・シンドラー、1922年。
下：健康住宅、ロサンゼルス、リチャード・ノイトラ、1929年。

Question 1

Oshima: In the 20th century, the "modern house" has become defined in many ways — from a functional definition highlighting hygiene, to forms derived from new materials and modes of production, to an aesthetic style of abstraction. Based on your own experience as both an architect and a historian, what do you feel is the most meaningful definition of such a "modern house"?

Frampton: The modern house is ultimately inseparable from the modern project in the Jürgen Habermas sense of the term and in fact, as you know, Habermas lives in a modern house. I am alluding to the idea that the house should be liberative, that is it should be "a machine for living-in" as Le Corbusier put it in his 1923 Manual of the Dwelling. Permit me to cite three precepts from this document that still seem to be valid: "Demand one really large living room instead of a number of small ones. (Demand) built-in fittings to take the place of much of the furniture. Demand concealed or diffused lighting, etc." Aside from such dicta, (one thinks of all the domestic specifications set forth by Rudolf Schindler) the modern house as such is difficult to define. Of course, we may say that it is a house built in this century, let us say, for us, in the span of time between 1918 and the present. Recently when I was choosing 35 modern houses for an anthology entitled *American Masterworks* (Rizzoli 1995), I was motivated mainly by the following criteria; first of all, the house had to have strong character; that is to say it had to be a particularly rich condensation of a particular era or approach; second, the house had to be lived-in or maintained according to the way of life implicit in the design of the house; third, the house had to manifest and/or suggest a new way of life or a new mode of production or preferably both. This explains why I featured Schindler's King's Road house of 1922 with its new form of family life, emphasizing the sovereignty of each individual, combined with the concrete lift-slab technique used for the construction of the perimeter walls. In fact many of the houses included in this anthology met these "masterwork" criteria; among them, Schindler's Lovell house (1926), Neutra's Health House (1929), Wright's Fallingwater (1937), Gropius' House in Lincoln, Massachusetts (1937), Wright's Sturgis house (1939), Mies's Farnsworth (1951) and Johnson's Glass House (1949). These last two are the most abstract of the set, of course, but they still meet the Corbusian demand for built-in storage and a single large room.

Question 2

Oshima: Lewis Mumford wrote in 1941: "Life without order is chaotic; but order without life is the end of everything, and eventually the end of order, too, since the purpose of order in building is to sustain human life." In other words, architecture ideally should strive for a balance between the logic of building and the logic of life. In what way do modern houses in

ケネス・フランプトンとの対話
─ モダン・ハウス / 九つの質問にたいする回答

インタヴュア：ケン・タダシ・オオシマ
木下壽子訳

住宅は、生活のためだけにある。敷地、採光、部屋の計画、そして建築材料は、住宅設計の基本となる要素である。建物はこれらの条件に応じて形づくられる。馴染みのある光景は姿を消すかもしれないが、かわりにあらゆる面で機能的な住宅が生まれるだろう。馬車がその役割を自動車にとってかわられた時、世のなかが貧しくなることはなかった。

ミース・ファン・デル・ローエ、「建築芸術と時代の意志」(1924)

Above: Fallingwater, Bear Run, Pennsylvania, Frank Lloyd Wright, 1937. Below: Glass House, New Canaan, Connecticut, Philip Johnson, 1949.

上：落水荘、ペンシルヴェニア州、フランク・ロイド・ライト、1937年。下：ガラスの家、コネティカット州、フィリップ・ジョンソン、1949年。

訳註1-ユルゲン・ハーバーマス(1929-)。フランクフルト学派第二世代に属し、現在最も影響力のあるドイツ人哲学者、社会学者の一人として知られている。啓蒙批評のプロジェクト、あるいは彼がいうところの「モダニティの哲学的ディスコース」を擁護し、その回復を主張した。主な著書に『Knowledge and Human Interests』(1972)、『コミュニケーション的行為の理論／上・中・下』(未来社、1985、1986、1987)、『近代：未完のプロジェクト』(岩波現代文庫、2000)がある。

質問　1

オオシマ： 20世紀において、衛生面に注目した機能的定義から、新しい材料と生産方法によってもたらされた形態、あるいは抽象性を追求した美的なスタイルといったものまで、「モダン・ハウス」は様々な定義がなされてきました。建築家、そして建築史家としてのあなた自身の経験から、「モダン・ハウス」の最も適切な定義とはどのようなものだとお考えですか。

フランプトン： モダン・ハウスは結局、ユルゲン・ハーバーマス[訳註1]が言うところの近代のプロジェクトと切り離すことのできない存在であり、実際、ハーバーマス自身がモダン・ハウスに住んでいたことはご承知の通りです。私が言おうとしているのは、住宅というのは人間を解放するものであるべきだということです。つまり1923年に出版された『住まいの手引き』のなかでル・コルビュジエが言い表したように、住宅は「住むための機械」であるべきだということです。ここで、いまだ有効と思われるこの文献のなかから三つの教訓を引用したいと思います。「いくつもの小さな部屋のかわりに、一つの十分に広い居間を要求しなさい。たくさんの置き家具にかわって造り付け家具（を要求しなさい）。間接照明か拡散照明を要求しなさい、等々」。このような格言（ルドルフ・シンドラーが説いた家事に関するあらゆる詳細な事項が思い浮かびますが）を除けば、モダン・ハウスそれ自体を定義するのは困難です。もちろん、今世紀に建てられた住宅だということもできるのですが、より正確に、ここでは1918年から現在までに建てられた住宅ということにしておきましょう。最近出版された『American Masterworks（米国の名住宅）』(Rizzoli 1995)という本のために、私は35軒のモダン・ハウスを選んだのですが、その際、主に次のような基準を念頭におきました。まず第一に、その住宅が強い個性をもっている、つまりある特定の時代やアプローチをとりわけ濃密に凝縮したものであること。第二に、その住宅デザインが意図する生活スタイルにそって住まわれているか、維持されていること。第三に、その住宅が新しい生活スタイルか新しい生産方法のどちらか、あるいはできればその両方を具体的に表現しているか提案しているということです。個人の主権を強調した新しい家庭生活のあり方と外壁の施工に用いられたコンクリートのリフト・スラブ技術が結びついた、シンドラーのキングス・ロードの家(1922)をとりあげたのはこのような理由からです。実際、この本でとりあげている住宅の多くが、以上のような「名住宅」の基準を満たすもので、そのなかには、シンドラーのロヴェル邸(1926)、ノイトラの健康住宅(1929)、ライトの落水荘(1937)、マサチューセッツ州リンカーンにあるグロピウスの自邸(1937)、ライトのスタージス邸(1939)、ミースのファンズワース邸(1951)、そしてジョンソンのガラスの家(1949)などが含まれています。もちろん最後の二つの住宅はこのなかで最も抽象的ですが、それでも造り付けの収納と一つの広い部屋をもつというコルビュジエの要求に応えています。

質問　2

オオシマ： ルイス・マンフォードは1941年に次のように書いています。「秩序のない生活は混沌としている。

the 20th century embody this notion? Do you believe a house is a vehicle for life to unfold or rather does a house imply a particular conception of life? Assuming the validity of the first premise, how may an architect particularly facilitate a way of life through the design of the house?

Frampton: It is obvious that neither the Farnsworth house nor Johnson's Glass House come close to satisfying Mumford's principles. Alvar Aalto's Villa Mairea on the other hand potentially does since clearly this house is capable of accommodating the vicissitudes of everyday life without losing its cultural depth and aesthetic coherence. One never feels that Aalto is either precious or unduly polemical. Something similar may be claimed for his Hansaviertel apartments that on balance are more accessible to everyday middle-class occupation than the duplex units of Le Corbusier's Unité block at Marseilles. In fact, not many of the houses included in the book *American Masterworks* would respond to Mumford's demand. Strangely enough, Pierre Chareau's Maison de Verre (1932) does meet his challenge in an unconventional way, as does Eileen Gray's house, E1027. Look for example how easily different styles of furniture seem to fit within the Maison de Verre. The later houses of Neutra were also open and flexible from this point of view. I am thinking of his Nesbitt and Tremaine houses of 1942 and 1946 respectively.

Question 3

Oshima: Can a house be seen to facilitate a way of life on both a macro and microspatial scale? To what extent do elements such as furniture, doors and windows have on such a life?

Frampton: It is obvious that the micro-spatial details of a house are absolutely crucial to the fulfillment of function and the provision of sensuous pleasure. This can already be felt in the traditional Japanese house, but it is also intensely present in the mature work of Eileen Grey and in the Purist furniture that Le Corbusier designed with Charlotte Perriand — see for instance the sublimely sensuous environment that they created for the Salon d'Automne of 1929. The same combination of small-scale richness, coherence and flexibility is also evident in the Maison de Verre and in Wright's Usonian houses. These last may also be seen as the last real effort to render the American suburb as a place of culture. In the field of collective housing this kind of micro-spatial sensitivity is also present in Alfred Roth's Siedlung Neubuhl of 1932. This is particularly marked in the way the windows are detailed. They are designed to serve as sensitive filters between the interior and the exterior. In this respect it would seem that we have lost as much in the culture as we have gained. For instance, why do we not use roller sun-blinds anymore or wooden lattice adjustable sunblinds? The sliding window wall surely was another 20th century triumph, which we seem to have forgotten how to use.

Above: Villa Mairea, Noormarkku, Alvar Aalto, 1937–39. Below: House at Riva San Vitale, Ticino, Mario Botta, 1971–73.

上：ヴィラ・マイレア、ノールマルック、アルヴァ・アアルト、1937〜39年。リヴァ・サン・ヴィターレの住宅、ティチーノ、マリオ・ボッタ、1971〜73年。

Question 4

Oshima: More specifically, how does/should the modern house intersect with the exigencies of everyday life and vernacular culture?

Frampton: In the first instances we may follow Mario Botta's early slogan "building the site" in the effect that every house should transform the site while at the same time being inscribed within it so that the terrain and the house amount to a mutually reinforcing synthesis. This should go without saying, even if the integration of the site does not always correspond with the exigencies of everyday life. Tadao Ando's critical strategy of the introspective courtyard house (a strategy that he shared at one moment with Ito and Hara) was surely a response to the stress of daily commutation and the psycho-social chaos of the modern megalopolis. In this case the house was meant to serve as a restorative micro-

しかし、建物における秩序の目的が人間生活を維持することにある以上、生活のない秩序はすべての終わりであり、つまりは秩序の終わりである」。言い換えると、理想的には、建築は建物の論理と生活の論理の間の調和を保つべく努力すべきだということだと思います。20世紀のモダン・ハウスは、どのような方法でこの概念を実現しているのでしょうか。住宅とは生活を発展させるための道具であるとお考えですか。それともむしろ、住宅はある特定の生活にたいする概念を暗示しているのでしょうか。さきほどの前提が有効だとすると、どのようにすれば、建築家は住宅のデザインを通して人々の生活を向上させることが可能なのでしょうか。

フランプトン：　ファンズワース邸もジョンソンのガラスの家も、マンフォードの原則を満たすにはほど遠いことは明白です。一方、アルヴァ・アアルトのマイレア邸は潜在的にこれを成し遂げています。というのも、明らかにこの住宅は、その文化的な奥深さと美的一貫性を失うことなく、日常生活の変化を許容できるからです。アアルトがもったいぶった人物だとか、議論好きだと思う人はいないでしょう。同様に、アアルトが設計したハンザ・フィエルテルの集合住宅のほうが、コルビュジエがマルセイユのユニテで試みたメゾネット型のユニットよりも、結局、一般の中産階級には受け入れられやすいといえるかもしれません。実際、『American Masterworks』に収められた住宅のなかで、マンフォードのこの原則を満たすものは多くないはずです。興味深いことに、ピエール・シャロウのガラスの家（1932）は、アイリーン・グレイ の住宅E1027同様、独自のかたちでマンフォードの要求に応じています。たとえば、異なるスタイルの家具がいかに容易にガラスの家に収まるかを見てみるといいでしょう。ノイトラの後期の住宅、私の頭にあるのはネズビット邸（1942)とトレメイン邸(1946)ですが、これらもこうした観点からいえばオープンかつフレキシブルです。

質問　3

オオシマ：　マクロとミクロ両方のスケールにおいて、住宅は生活のあり方を向上させると考えることは可能ですか。家具、扉、そして窓といった要素は、どの程度そのような生活に影響を与えるのでしょうか。

フランプトン：　住宅のミクロ空間のディテールが、機能を満たし、気持ち良さを与える上で決定的に重要であることは明らかです。これは伝統的な日本の住宅にすでに見出すことができますが、同様に、最盛期のアイリーン・グレイの作品、そしてル・コルビュジエがシャルロット・ペリアンとともにデザインした純粋主義の家具にも歴然と存在しています。たとえば、1929年のサロン・ドートンヌ[訳註2]のために彼らがつくりだした究極的に感覚に訴えかける環境をご覧なさい。同じような小さなスケールの豊かさ、一貫性、そして柔軟性の組み合わせは、ガラスの家とライトのユーソニアン住宅にもはっきりと見出せます。このユーソニアン住宅は、文化的な場所として米国の郊外を描こうとした最後の試みだったとみることもできます。集合住宅の分野でいうと、こうしたミクロ空間への感受性は、1932年のアルフレッド・ロートによるノイブール・ジードルングにも見出せます。特に窓のディテールのデザインにそれが顕著に表われています。窓が内部空間と外部空間を仕切る繊細なフィルターとしてデザインされています。この点からいうと、我々は文化的に得たものと同じだけ失ったものもあるように思えます。たとえば、なぜ私たちはローラー式のブラインドや調整可能な木製格子のブラインドを使わなくなってしまったのでしょう。引き違いのガラス戸はまちがいなく20世紀が生んだもう一つの素晴らしい功績だったにもかかわらず、今ではその使い方すら忘れられてしまったかのようです。

質問　4

オオシマ：　もう少しテーマを絞って、モダン・ハウスは、日常生活の要求と土着の文化とどのように相互作用する、あるいはすべきものなのでしょうか。

フランプトン：　たとえば、マリオ・ボッタが初期に唱えていた「サイトを建設する」というスローガンに従うと、いかなる住宅も、地形と住宅が相互に強化し合う複合体となるように敷地のなかに住宅が刻み込まれると同時に、敷地を変容させねばならないということになります。たとえこのような敷地との融合が日常生活の

*Above: Unité d'Habitation,
Marseilles, Le Corbusier, 1947-52.
Below: Katsura, Kyoto, 1620-25.*

上：ユニテ・ダビタシオン、マルセイユ、
ル・コルビュジエ、1947〜52年。
下：桂離宮古書院、京都、1620〜25年。

訳註2-サロン・ドートンヌ。フランスの美術展の一つで、1903年にフランツ・ジュールダンをリーダーとし、マティス、マルケ、ルオー、ヴュイヤールらによって創立されたサロン。サロン・ナショナルの保守性に反発してつくられたもので、毎年秋にパリで開かれる。設立から数年後には、このサロンからフォービスムやキュービスムが生まれた。絵画の他、彫刻、装飾芸術など多くの部門を有している。

cosmos. In some respects this seems to echo what Adolf Loos used to say — "the house should be rich on the interior and austere without." As to vernacular culture? Well surely this may only be referenced today through the notion of *répétition differente*. In general the introspective courtyard house is not popular today because with this type the house fails to arrive at an adequate representative image of the bourgeois high-style dwelling. By definition the generic courtyard house does not display its status and as such it is not an "identifiable commodity" so that the real estate industry doesn't know how to market it. It is not a spectacular object that may be readily mortgaged and sold. In this specific sense it harkens back to the vernacular in that it is potentially a continuous part of a residential fabric in as much as we still find such fabric in pre-industrial, agricultural or fishing villages, etc.

Above: Row House at Sumiyoshi, Osaka, Ando Tadao, 1976.

上：住吉の長屋、大阪、安藤忠雄、1976 年。

Question 5

Oshima: To what extent can one say that the regional inflection of the site and surrounding landscape determine the house — or conversely, to what extent does the house determine the landscape?

Frampton: Siedlung Halen, dating from 1960 and occupied by an upwardly mobile, well-educated Swiss middle-class, was in fact composed of narrow courtyard houses set side by side on a terraced slope. It was heavily planted from the beginning and is currently so covered with greenery that you can hardly see it, let alone photograph it. It has practically disappeared. It is both building and landscape at one and the same time. Visiting it in high-summer a few years ago I began to wonder whether these houses had been built by the Egyptians or by some other antique civilization. However there is simply no answer to this chicken and egg question. As Alvaro Siza points out and as the Canadian architects John and Patricia Patkau demonstrate through their practice, on some occasions one opposes the site in order to bring it into focus, at other times one makes the house flow into the morphology of the surrounding landfall, so as to create a harmonious continuity, as in traditional agrarian building where homes and farms were acutely responsive to topography and to the path of the sun and the direction of the wind, etc.

Question 6

Oshima: Do you believe it is possible to search for universal forms and still not lose sight of the local and the particular? What architects might embody this concept and how might their expressions vary across the world?

Frampton: Well one should try to achieve both, but this is not always possible. One could hardly call Aalto's Maison Carré a vernacular piece and yet it responds to the sense of local character implicit in the shape of the site. On the other hand, one could not identify it as particularly French. At the same time, we may perhaps say that the Villa Shodhan is more Indian than the Maison Carré is French, although perhaps this is not saying very much! One may point to the sun canopies, to the evocation of Fatepur Sikri but does this make it Indian in a profound sense? If one sets a perfect cube into an undulating site without the use of *pilotis* some kind of terraced earthwork has to be constructed to receive it.

Question 7

Oshima: To what extent is a house's tectonic expression, as a play between material, craftwork and gravity, its primary form?

要求と常に一致しなくとも、いうまでもなくこれは当然起こるべきことです。外にたいして閉じた中庭をもつ住宅を設計した安藤忠雄の批判的戦略（かつて伊東や原とも分かち合った戦略）は、まちがいなく日々のコミュニケーションや近代的大都市の社会心理的なカオスから発生するストレスへの一つの回答でした。この場合、この住宅は元気を回復させるためのミクロコスモスとして機能するよう意図されています。いくつかの点で、これはアドルフ・ロースがかつて言っていた「住宅とはその内部空間が豊かで、外観は質素であるべきだ」という考えと共鳴するように思えます。次に土着の文化にたいしてですか。それについては、差異のある繰り返し、つまりフランス語でいうところの「repetition differente」の概念を通して今日語ることができると思います。外にたいして閉じた中庭の家は、現在ではあまり関心をもたれていません。このようなタイプの住宅は、中産階級の最先端の住居を代表する適切なイメージとはなりえないからです。定義上、一般的な中庭をもつ住宅はそのステイタスを示せず、またそれ自体「身分を確認できる商品」ではないため、不動産業界はそれをどう市場で売買すればよいのかわからないのです。このような住宅は、たやすく抵当に入れ、売ることができる見世物的な物件ではないのです。そういう意味でいうと、このような中庭をもつ住宅は土着的なものに立ち戻っています。なぜなら、こうした住宅はおそらく集落のような家々の集合体の延長上にあるのであり、我々はこのような集合体を今も工業化以前の村、農村、あるいは漁村などに見出すことができるからです。

質問 5

オオシマ： 敷地と周囲のランドスケープの地域的な特色は、住宅のあり方をどの程度決定するといえるのか、また逆に、住宅はどの程度ランドスケープを決定するといえるのでしょうか。

フランプトン： 1960年に始まり、居住者の多くが経済的に豊かになりつつある教育水準の高いスイスの中産階級であったハーレン・ジードルングは、テラス状の斜面に細長いコートヤード・ハウスが並んだ構成となっています。最初からかなりの量の植栽が施され、現在では草木ですっかり覆い隠されているため、まったく見えず、ましてや写真が撮れないのはいうまでもありません。事実上、姿を消してしまっています。それは建物であると同時にランドスケープでもあるのです。数年前、夏の盛りにここを訪れた時、私はこれが古代エジプト人、あるいは他の古代文明によって建設されたものではないかと感じたほどでした。しかしながら、この「卵が先か、鶏が先か」という問いにたいする答えはありません。アルヴァロ・シザが指摘し、カナダ人建築家のジョン・パトコーとパトリシア・パトコーが彼らの仕事を通して実践しているように、時には敷地を中心テーマとするためにそれと対立する場合もありますし、またある時は、住居と農場が、地形、太陽の動き、風の向きなどに敏感に対応した伝統的な農家の建物のように調和的な連続性を生み出すために、住宅を周辺の地形に溶け込ませるケースもあります。

Above: Halen Siedlung, near Bern, Atelier 5, 1955–61. Below: Villa Shodhan, Ahmedabad, Le Corbusier, 1956.

上：ハーレン・ジードルング、ベルン近郊、アトリエ5、1955〜61年。下：ショーダン邸、アーメダバッド、ル・コルビュジエ、1956年。

訳註3-ファテプル・シークリー。アーグラーの南西約40kmに位置するシークリーに16世紀後半に建設されたムガル朝アクバル帝の都。イスラム建築とインドの土着的な建築技術が融合し、石を木のように扱った架構が特徴的である。チャンディガールの設計を行っていたル・コルビュジエは、ファテプル・シークリーを訪れ、その建築に感銘を受けた。

質問 6

オオシマ： 地域性とその土地の特徴を失うことなくユニヴァーサルな形態を探求することは可能だと思いますか。また、どのような建築家がこのような考えを実現し、またその表現は国によってどのように異なるのでしょう。

フランプトン： その両方を成し遂げる努力をすべきだと思いますが、それがいつも可能だとは限りません。たとえば、アアルトのメゾン・カレを土着的な建物だということはできませんが、この住宅は敷地の形態に潜む地域的特質が意味するものに対応しています。その一方で、それが特にフランス的だと判断することもできません。同時に、メゾン・カレがフランス的である以上にヴィラ・ショーダンがインド的であるということはできるかもしれませんが、これはたいして説明になっていないかもしれません。インドのファテプル・シークリー訳註3を思い起こさせるものとしてその庇に注目する人がいるかもしれませんが、しかしそれが真の意味でこの住宅をインド的にしているでしょうか。もし完璧な立方体を、ピロティを使わずに起伏のある敷地に置こうとするならば、それを受け止めるためにある種のテラス状の敷地造成を施さねばなりません。

Frampton: I don't think that the tectonic aspect can ever be the total point of departure for the primary form; not even the vaults in Le Corbusier's Maison Week-End fully account for its form. However, the poetry of any given work surely does depend in most instances on the tectonic articulation of its apriori form. In a work of quality it is invariably difficult to say where the one begins and the other ends.

Question 8

Oshima: Walter Benjamin once wrote, "The world is beautiful — therein is unmasked the posture of a photography that can endow any soup can with cosmic significance but cannot grasp a single one of the human connections in which it exists."* In terms of architectural photography, to what extent do you believe photographs of houses tend to promote an understanding more related to abstract formalism than humanism? What role do you believe architectural photography plays in one's understanding of modern houses?

Frampton: Well this question doesn't just apply to houses, it is a paradox that affects the representation of architecture in general. At the end of the first edition of *Modern Architecture: a Critical History*, I wrote: "The veil that photo-lithography draws over the architecture is not neutral. High-speed photographic and reproductive processes are surely not only the political economy of the sign but also an insidious filter through which our tactile environment tends to lose its concrete responsiveness. When much of modern building is experienced in actuality, its photogenic sculptural quality is denied by the poverty and brutality of its detailing. Time and again an expensive and ostentatious display of either structure or form results in the impoverishment of intimacy, in that which Heidegger has recognized as the loss of 'nearness.' How rarely do we encounter a modern work where the inflection of a chosen tectonic penetrates into the innermost recesses of the structure, not as a totalizing force but as the declension of an articulate sensibility. That modern society still possesses a capacity for such inflection finds confirmation in the finest work of Aalto . . . ." This is not exactly the Benjamin position but it is the closest I have come to it. Thus one needs to represent buildings as much through readable plans and through details as through photos. As of now, *a +u* does a brilliant job in this regard, but in general most architectural magazines can be faulted for their imprecise documentation of work though their undue emphasis on the photographic image.

Question 9

Oshima: What legacies do modern houses in the 20th century offer for architects of the 21st century? And what do you believe is the greatest challenge for architects designing houses today?

Frampton: Let me answer this aphoristically with the immortal words of certain figures for instance Mies who said, "I don't want to be interesting, I want to be good. I get lots of interesting ideas, I have to get rid of them," or Loos' "the house is conservative and the work of art is revolutionary . . . and so the man loves his house and hates art," or Baudelaire's "*La tout n'est pas qu'ordre et beauté, luxe, calme et volupté*" (There all is order, beauty, luxury, calm and sensuousness); his belief that civilization does not depend on technology but in the elimination of all traces of original sin, a precept that may surely be applied to the design of bathrooms, etc. that are invariably reduced, even the most expensive houses to hygienic cubicles. Finally there is Luis Barragan, whose sensibility sticks in my mind for his aphorism: "an architecture which does not achieve tranquillity fails in its spiritual mission." Hence the task remains, as I have suggested elsewhere, how to combine vitality with calm? It is a challenge that applies as much to houses as to any other modern building and as much today and in the future as in times past.

Note:
* Walter Benjamin, "A Short History of Photography," in *Screen* No. 13 (Spring 1972), p. 24.

質問 7

オオシマ： 実用と美の両面から考えられた構造上の表現、つまり住宅のテクトニックの表現は、材料、工芸、重力の相互関係として、どの程度その住宅の根源的な形態なのでしょうか。

フランプトン： テクトニックという側面が、根源的な形態への出発点になるとは思いません。ル・コルビュジエの週末住宅のヴォールト天井ですら、完全にはその形態の出発点とはなっていません。しかしながら、作品の詩的な部分は、確かにほとんどの場合、その先天的な形態のテクトニックな相互関係によっています。質の高い作品はどれも、どこから始まりどこで終わるかを見きわめるのは困難なものです。

質問 8

オオシマ： ベンヤミンはかつてこう書いています。「世界は美しい──そこに露見するのは、どのようなスープ缶にも無限の重要性を与えることはできても、無限の重要性が存在する人間関係を一つも捉えられない写真の有り様である」。*　建築写真は、人間性よりも抽象的な形式主義につながる理解をどの程度深める可能性があるのか、また、モダン・ハウスを理解する上で、建築写真はどのような役割を果たすとお考えですか。

フランプトン： その質問は、建築表現全般に関わるパラドックスです。『近代建築：その批評的歴史』^{訳註4}の最後に私は次のように書いています。「写真が建築にかぶせているヴェールは中立的ではない。高速度の写真撮影と複製プロセスは、記号の政治経済であるだけでなく、我々の実体的な環境から具体的な反応を失わせかねない油断のならないフィルターでもある。近代建築の多くは、実際に体験すると、その写真うつりのよい彫刻的な魅力が細部の貧しさといい加減さによって否定される。構造や形態にお金をかけてこれ見よがしに誇示することによって、しばしば親密さが失われる。ハイデッカーはこれを『親密さ』の喪失と認識したのだ。ゆるぎなく一体化した選ばれたテクトニックが、支配的な力としてではなく、調和的な感性として構造の最も深い部分にまで浸透した近代建築に出会うことがいかに希であることか。しかし、近代社会が今なおこのような一体性を受け入れる能力を有していることは、アアルトの最も優れた作品が立証している」。正確にはベンヤミンの見解と異なりますが、これが彼の見解に最も近づいた私の考えです。このように、写真だけでなく、分かりやすい平面図と詳細図を通して建物を説明する必要があります。一般的に、建築雑誌の多くは、写真のイメージを過度に強調することで不正確な記録を残すという失敗をおかす可能性があります。

質問 9

オオシマ： 20世紀のモダン・ハウスは、21世紀の建築家にどのような遺産を残せると思いますか。また、今日住宅設計に携わる建築家にとって最大の挑戦は何だと考えますか。

フランプトン： その質問にたいしては、何人かの建築家たちが残した格言をいくつか引用しながら答えたいと思います。たとえば、「私は興味深いと思われたいのではなく、よい仕事をしたいのだ。興味深いアイディアは次々と思い浮ぶが、私はそれらを払いのけねばならない」といったミース。あるいは「住宅は保守的なものであり、芸術作品は革命的である……だから人は住宅を愛し芸術を嫌うのだ」といったロース。「あるのは、秩序、美、贅、静寂、そして感性である」といったボードレール。彼は、文明は技術によってではなくあらゆる原罪の痕跡の排除に左右されると信じ、この教訓は、最も高級な住宅においてでさえ一様に衛生的な立方体に還元された浴室のデザインなどにまちがいなく適用されました。最後に、ルイス・バラガンです。「静穏を生み出せない建築は、それが果たすべき精神的使命を果たしていない」といった彼の言葉に表れた感受性が心に残ります。どこかで述べたと思うのですが、いかにして活力と安らぎを融合させるか、という仕事が今も残されています。これはあらゆる近代建築と同様に住宅にもいえることであり、過去と同じく、今日、そして未来にも当てはまる挑戦だと思います。

Above: Chapel for the Capuchinas Sacramentarias del Purismo Corazan de Maria, Tlalpan, Luis Barragan, 1952–55.

上：カプチン派の礼拝堂、トラルパン、ルイス・バラガン、1952〜55年。

原註
＊ 『screen』誌 No.13（1972年春）、ヴァルター・ベンヤミン、「A Short History of Photography」、24頁。

訳註4-原題『Modern Architecture: A Critical History』。「現代建築への道程」というタイトルで、『a+u』1985年1月号から1988年7月号まで中村敏男訳により26回に渡って掲載された。

Tugendhat House
Brno, Czech Republic 1930
Ludwig Mies van der Rohe

トゥーゲントハット邸
チェコ共和国、ブルノ　1930
ルードヴィッヒ・ミース・ファン・デル・ローエ

The Tugendhat house, designed at the same time as Mies van der Rohe's landmark Barcelona Pavilion (1929), adapted that building's dynamic spatial conception to a domestic program. Four hundred and twenty-five extant drawings (primarily details, furnishings, and working drawings) attest to the refinement of the resulting building. Working on a steeply sloping hillside site in the suburbs of the castle town of Brno, Mies van der Rohe suggested a two-story scheme with entry and bedrooms above and main living space below. He created a spatial composition whereby walls organize space but do not bear weight, by using a steel skeleton structure with reinforced concrete floors. All of Fritz and Grete Tugendhat's living and bedroom spaces face south, with individual access to ample travertine terraces. The living and dining areas face a wall entirely of glass. Two of the large panes can be mechanically retracted to the floor below, thereby converting the interior living space into a belvedere open to the natural elements. To prevent this glass wall from excessive nighttime reflection, Mies specified natural raw silk curtains that could be drawn along the entire wall. Further, individual areas like the dining area could be closed off with velvet curtains to prevent the transmission of sounds and smells without disrupting the unity of the space.

More than a composition of lines and planes, Mies's residential design provided a framework for appreciating nature. While the floor-to-ceiling glazed walls framed and intensified the view of the natural landscape, the conservatory served for cultivating plants all year round. Inside, the natural grain of Macassar ebony wood-veneer walls and doors provide both a sense of animation and of opulence. Moreover, the golden onyx wall, while depicting fossilized nature, also reflects the views of nature and of the adjacent plants across its shiny surface. Through this integration of organic life and form, Mies expressed the belief that "life intensity is form intensity" (as articulated by religious philosopher Romano Guardini, whom Mies read assiduously).

Following Mies's belief that design is a life process, the Tugendhat house itself has gone through a course of decay and rebirth in the years following its completion. In regard to the habitability of the house, Grete Tugendhat publicly stated, "We are very happy living in this house, so happy that we find it difficult to think of taking a trip, and we feel liberated when we come back from confining rooms into our large, restful spaces once again." However as Wolf Tegethoff notes in the following essay, the Tugendhats were forced to flee the country in 1938 during the Nazi-German occupation. The house fell into disrepair under subsequent occupants, and was only partially restored to its original condition later. Nevertheless, Mies himself recalled in 1966 that "what gives the building its quality is the proportions.... For the most part it is the proportions between things; it is not even the things themselves." While the proportions are grand, with 3-meter-high cruciform columns, they nevertheless provide a timeless frame for living.

(KTO)

ミース・ファン・デル・ローエの歴史に残る名作、バルセロナ・パヴィリオン（1929）と同じ時期にデザインされたこのトゥーゲントハット邸において、バルセロナ・パヴィリオンのダイナミックな空間概念が住生活のプログラムに応用された。現存する425におよぶドローイング（主として、ディテール、家具類、施工図）は、最終的にできあがった建物の精巧さを裏づけている。城下町ブルノ郊外にある斜面の敷地にたいして、ミースは、上階に入口と寝室、下階にメインの居室がある2階建ての住宅を提案した。鉄筋コンクリート造の床をもつ鉄骨造を用いることによって、耐力壁ではない壁によって空間を組織化する空間構成をつくりだした。フリッツおよびグレテ・トゥーゲントハットの居室と寝室はすべて南に向き、広々としたトラヴァーチンのテラスへ個々にアクセスできるようになっている。居室にある巨大なガラス張りの開口のうち二つは自動的に下階に引き込まれるようになっており、これが開け放たれた時、居室は自然にたいして開かれた見晴らし台となる。夜の過度の反射からこのガラスの壁を守るために、ミースは生糸のカーテンで壁全体を覆うことを条件とした。さらに、空間のまとまりを壊すことなく音や匂いの伝達を防ぐために、食堂をはじめとする個々のエリアが、ヴェルヴェットのカーテンによって閉じられるようにした。単なる線と平面の構成以上に、ミースの住宅デザインは、自然を楽しむためのフレーム・ワークとなった。床から天井までのガラス張りの壁が自然のランドスケープを縁どり、その景色を強調する一方で、温室では植物が一年を通して育てられた。内部では、マカッサル黒檀の化粧張りを施した壁とドアの自然な木目が活気と華やかさをもたらしている。さらに金色のオニックスは、化石化した自然を描き出すと同時に、その光沢のある表面には自然の景色と近くにある植物が映し込まれた。このような有機的な生活と形態の融合を通して、ミースは「生活の強度は形態の強度である」（ミースが熱心に読んだ宗教哲学者のロマーノ・ガルディーニが述べているように）という信念を表現した。

デザインは生きたプロセスであるというミースの信念のとおり、トゥーゲントハット邸は衰微の過程を経て、再生した。この住宅の住みやすさという点に関しては、グレテ・トゥーゲントハットが公式に次のように述べている。「我々はこの家に住んでいてたいへん幸せです。あまりに幸せで、旅に出ることなど思い浮かばず、閉ざされた部屋からふたたびこの大きくて落ち着いた空間に戻ってくると、我々は開放されたように感じます」。しかしながら、ヴォルフ・テゲトフが彼のエッセイのなかで述べているように、トゥーゲントハット一家はナチス・ドイツの占領下だった1938年に、祖国から逃れることを余儀なくされた。その後の占有者のもとでこの住宅はかなりの破損をきたした。ミースは1966年、「この住宅に優れた質を与えているのは、そのプロポーションである」と回想している。ほとんどの部分においてそれは、物と物とのプロポーションであって、物そのものが重要なのではなかった。高さ3mの十字断面の柱をもつそのプロポーションは雄大だが、それは生活のための時を超越したフレームとなっている。

(KTO)

pp. 146–147: View from the garden
on the south. Above: North street
facade. Entrance with curved glass
wall and passageway to the
southern terrace on the right.

146〜147頁：南側の庭からみた全景。
上：通り側のファサード。曲面のガラス
壁の入口と右手に南側のテラスへの通り
抜けがみえる。

Above: Entrance hall and staircase to the living space on the lower level. Opposite: Forecourt with curved glass wall of the entrance hall on the left.

上：エントランス・ホールと階下のメインの居室への階段室。右頁：エントランス・ホールの曲面を描くガラス壁のある前庭。

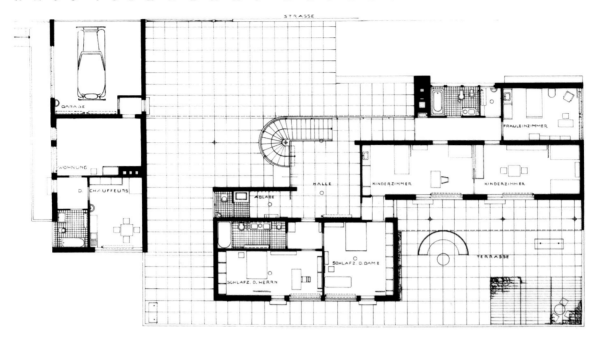

OBERGESCHOSS.

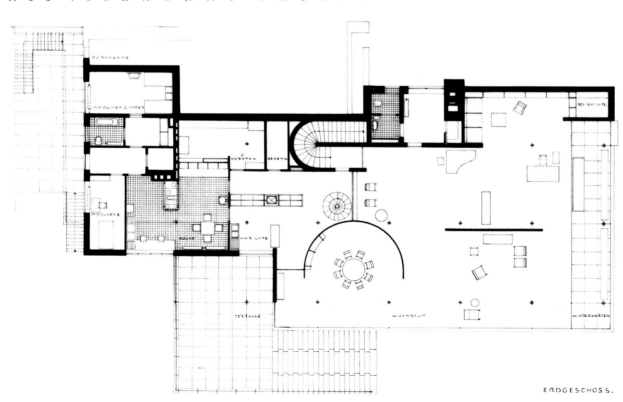

ERDGESCHOSS.

Opposite top: Street level plan.
Opposite bottom: Lower level plan.
Above: Detail of the entry staircase
handrail.

左頁、上：ストリート・レヴェル（上階）
平面図。左頁、下：下階平面図。上：下
階への階段室の手摺のディテール。

pp. 154–155: Living and dining area looking toward the west. Left above: View of living toward dining space with golden onyx wall to the right. Left below: View from living toward garden and Spilberk Castle through floor-to-ceiling retractable windows. Opposite: View from library, of onyx wall, Macassar ebony veneer dining wall, and chrome-faced cruciform columns. Light wall is far right.

154～155頁：下階の居間・食堂（メインの居室）西側に向かってみる。左上：居間から食堂をみる。右手にオニックスの壁がみえる。左下：天井高いっぱいの、格納式上げ下げ窓を通して居間から庭の光景とスピルベルク城をみる。右頁：北東の隅にあるライブラリーからみる。オニックスの壁、食堂のマカッサル黒檀の壁、クロム仕上げの十字柱、右手前方に光壁がみえる。

Above: Library at the northeast corner of the lower level. Opposite: Original Macassar ebony wood bookshelves and Tugendhat Chair in the library.

上：下階北東隅のライブラリー。右頁：
ライブラリーの当時のままのマカッサル
黒檀の書棚とトゥーゲントハット・チェ
ア。

Ludwig Mies van der Rohe's Tugendhat House:
A Model Home of Its Time?
Wolf Tegethoff

ルードヴィッヒ・ミース・ファン・デル・ローエのトゥーゲントハット邸
時代を映す住宅
ヴォルフ・テゲトフ
中田雅章訳

By the end of 1930, after more than two years of planning, construction work, and interior furnishing, Ludwig Mies van der Rohe's largest private commission had finally reached completion. Grete and Fritz Tugendhat had given him an almost free hand in the design of their new house in Brno, sited at the upper end of the park-like property of Mrs. Tugendhat's parents. The southward sloping site offered a spectacular view of the Baroque city, by then a prominent industrial center for the young Czechoslovakian Republic.

The house is entered from the north front on Schwarzfeldgasse (today cernopolni ulice) through an expansive forecourt to a covered passageway set between the receding walls of the upper floor. The opening between these walls resembles a stage set, with the Brno landmark, Spilberk Castle, as its programmatic backdrop. Otherwise, the structure appears hermetically closed. The curving frosted glass wall of the entrance hall lacks the transparency usually associated with glass, completely hiding the interior from view. Moreover, its projecting curve, which encases the turning staircase to the lower main floor, deliberately conceals the entrance door behind, making it difficult for the unaccustomed visitor to find his or her way in. The garage and servants' wing to the right, with a simple metal door as its only opening into the forecourt, enhances the rather forbidding character of the street front. Were it not for the clear-cut lines of its blank walls, and the carefully arranged prospect at the end of the passageway, the house would hardly attract much interest.

Whether this deliberate understatement responded to a particular whim of the client or reflected the architect's intention remains a point for further discussion. In any case, and contrary to what is still taken as a key dogma of Modern Architecture, Mies van der Rohe's masterpiece does not reveal itself to the general public easily. As had generally been the custom with European town houses for centuries, the upper floor of the two-story structure (set upon a full basement floor equipped with the usual facilities), was mainly reserved for the private quarters of the family. Due to the particular requirements of the steeply sloping site, however, the house was entered from above, and any cross-over between the formal entrance and the family's private sphere had to be carefully avoided. This accounts for the hermetic quality of the upper floor as it faces Schwarzfeldgasse. For the ordinary passer-by, the main floor below remains almost completely hidden from view. The house thus produces the erroneous, but possibly desired effect of a smaller structure than is actually present. The Tugendhat house has a total floor area of some 1,250 square meters, including terraces.

Following the conventional arrangement of an elevated *belle*

Above: Winter garden on the east side of the lower level.　　　上：下階東側のウインター・ガーデン。

計画から2年以上が過ぎた1930年の暮れ、ミース・ファン・デル・ローエにとって個人から依頼されたものとしては最大規模のこの作品は、家具調度を含め、完成を迎えていた。トゥーゲントハット夫妻は、夫人の両親が所有する公園のように美しい敷地の小高い丘の上に建てられるブルノの新しい住宅のデザインについて、基本的にミースにそのすべてを任せていた。南に向かって傾斜したその場所からは、当時、新生チェコスロヴァキア共和国の重要な工業の中心地となっていた「バロック」の街、ブルノの素晴らしい風景を望むことができた。住宅へは、シュヴァルツフェルト通り（今日のチェルノポルニ・ウリーチェ）に面した北側正面から入り、広々とした前庭を通って、奥まった上層階の壁面に挟まれた通路へとつながっている。この壁面に挟まれた開口は、ブルノのランドマークであるスピルベルク城を背景幕とする舞台のセットのようだ。しかしそれを除けば、この建物はきわめて閉鎖的であるようにみえる。エントランス・ホールの湾曲したガラスの壁面は、ガラス本来の透明性を欠いており、内部の視線を完全に遮っている。さらに、階下のメイン・フロアへと通じる階段の折返し部分を包む張り出した曲面は、エントランスの扉をその背後に意識的に隠しており、不慣れな来訪者にはどこから入るべきか少々わかりにくいものとなっている。通りからみて右手には、前庭への唯一の開口として一枚の簡素な鉄の扉をもつガレージと使用人棟があり、これが通り側のファサードのどちらかというと近づきがたい性格をより一層強めている。開口部のない壁面の明快なラインと、使用人棟と住居部分の間にある通路の端から見渡せる巧みに構成された眺望がなければ、この住宅はさして興味を引くものとはならなかったであろう。

この意図的な控えめな表現が、施主の特別な考えに応えたものなのか、あるいは建築家の意図なのかという点については、さらなる議論を必要とするであろう。いずれにせよ、今日なお近代建築の重要な教義とされているものとは対照的に、このミースの傑作は、一般の人々から容易に理解されうるものではない。幾世紀にもわたって典型的なヨーロッパのタウンハウスが慣習としてきたように、上下二つのフロアからなるこの建物の上層階は、一般的な設備を備えた下層階の上に置かれ、主に家族のためのプライヴェートな領域とされた。しかし、傾斜の厳しい敷地という特殊性ゆえに、住宅には上層階から入らなければならず、また表玄関と家族のプライヴェートな領域が交差することは、注意深く避けられねばならなかった。そのため、シュヴァルツフェルト通りに面した上層階は、閉鎖性の高いデザインとされたのである。逆に下のメイン・フロアは、道行く人々の視線からほぼ完全に隠されている。トゥーゲントハット邸のテラスを含めた総床面積はおよそ1250㎡もあるが、こうして実際の建物よりもはるかに小さな建物にみえるという、事実とは異なるが、おそらく適切であろう効果を生み出している。

上に持ち上げられた美しい舞台の伝統的な構成に倣って、家族のためのプライヴェートな領域を上層階に配したこの住宅の内部空間の配置計画は、19世紀以

étage topped by family quarters on the upper floor, the interior disposition of the house still reflects many typical aspects of upper-class residences of the preceding century. This certainly applies to the hierarchical sequence of forecourt, *porte cochère*, entrance hall, and staircase. This sequence demands a formality of approach that continues, surprisingly, in the single large living area on the lower main floor, always regarded as an utterly modern example of Mies's residential architecture. While breaking down the traditional *enfilade*, with its formal sequence of reception, dining, and drawing rooms, the single, continuous space has still been structured to accommodate the various social functions once required in the formal entertainment of guests. In fact, early floor plans of the Tugendhat house reveal the labels *"Empfangsraum"* (reception room) for the immediate entry from the main staircase, and *"Herrenzimmer"* (gentlemen's drawing room) for the study section and library niche. These terms were surely considered both utterly bourgeois and completely outmoded by avant-garde circles at the time. Needless to say, in the operation of a house like this many a helping hand was needed, so that ample staff quarters had to be provided for in the adjoining service wing.

Given these facts, Mies's apodictic statement of 1931 that the home for our time does not yet exist, even though living conditions have changed in such a way so as to demand its realization, may thus appear as a defensive response to the growing negative critique of the Tugendhat house. To achieve this end, so his paragraph continues, there has to be above all *"a clear idea of what our living requirements really are. Overcoming today's discrepancy in our living conditions between actual needs and false pretensions, between genuine demand and inadequate supply, is a burning economic challenge, and a precondition to the advancement of culture."* The enormous space of the living area, with its luxurious display of furnishings, did arouse concern among Mies's contemporaries, despite the fact that the rather unspectacular, conventionally-shaped sleeping rooms on the upper floor provided privacy for the individual members of the family (the only consequential change the clients had asked of Mies's original design). Justus Bier, for example, seriously questioned whether the Tugendhat house was habitable. Its dazzling atmosphere and the amazing view to be gained by the continuous glazing of the garden front notwithstanding, there were serious doubts about the house's contribution to the pressing issues of current living conditions, issues which Mies was claiming to address.

Yet the Tugendhats, while not committed to official receptions or extensive entertaining (and therefore lacking the compulsion

Above: View of the upper level terrace with Brno city center to the right.

上：上階のテラス。右手にブルノの市街がみえる。

前の上流階級の住宅にみられる典型的な特徴をいまだ反映している。これはまちがいなく、前庭、車寄せ、エントランス・ホール、そして階段室の秩序だったシークエンスに当てはまる。このシークエンスは、アプローチの形式を尊重することを要求し、驚いたことに、それはこれまでミースの住宅建築のなかでもまったく近代的だと常に考えられてきたリヴィング・スペース（メインの居室）においても継続している。レセプション、ダイニング、応接間という形式にそったシークエンスをもつ伝統的な配列を解体してはいるものの、来客を正式にもてなす必要が生じた時には、様々な社交的機能を果たせるように構成されている。実際、トゥーゲントハット邸の初期の平面図をみると、メインの階段室からリヴィング・スペースに入ってすぐのところに「レセプション・ルーム」、そして書斎とライブラリーのコーナーには「殿方の応接間」という室名が記されているのである。これらの言葉は、いずれもきわめてブルジョア的で、当時の前衛的な人々の間では完全に流行遅れとなっていたことは確かである。このような住宅を維持していくためには、多くの人手が必要で、隣接するサーヴィス棟には使用人のための十分な領域を備えていなければならなかったことはうまでもない。

こうした事実を考え合わせると、1931年にミースが述べた、我々の時代の住宅は、居住環境が変化しその実現を求めているにもかかわらず存在しないとする彼の必然的な発言は、トゥーゲントハット邸に向けられた批判の高まりにたいする、自己防衛的な対応であったとも考えられる。彼がさらにつづけて述べているように、この目的を達成するためにはまず、「我々の居住の要求が実際どのようなものなのかについてのはっきりとした考え」がなければならず、また「我々の居住環境における、実際のニーズと見せかけの根拠のない主張、真正な要求と不適切な供給との間に横たわる、今日の決定的な食い違いを克服することは緊急の経済的課題であり、文化の発展のための前提条件である」のだ。上層階に配された、そして魅力的でもなく、保守的ともいえる寝室（これは唯一、ミースのオリジナルのデザインにたいして施主が変更を求めた結果なのだが）が家族の一人一人にプライヴァシーをもたらしているのにたいし、豪華な家具を配した下層階のリヴィング・スペースの巨大な空間は、ミースの同時代の人々を困惑させた。たとえばユスタス・バイアは、トゥーゲントハット邸が本当に居住可能なのかどうか、真剣に疑った。その息を呑むような雰囲気と、庭に面した連続的なガラス面がもたらす素晴らしい眺望にもかかわらず、そこには、ミース自身が問題提起したように、この住宅が当時の居住環境をめぐる緊急の問題の解決に本当に貢献しているのか、という大きな問題が残された。
いまだ公式なレセプションや社交的な催しはまだあまり開かれていなかったが（したがって、見せかけの根拠のない主張の受け入れを強いる機会には欠けていたが）、トゥーゲントハット家の人々は、彼らの新しい住宅にたいする深い親愛の情を感じはじめていた。当時の論争にたいして彼らが発表した声明のなかではっきりと述べられているように、この住宅は彼らが建築家に求めた心地

Above: Door to the entrance hall reflecting of upper level terrace.

上：エントランス・ホールへの扉に映り込んだ上階テラス。

to adopt false pretensions), developed a deep-felt sympathy for their new home. As they emphasized in statements addressed to the contemporary debate, it offered all the comfort and privacy they had asked from their architect. Setting aside the question of space allocation and personal consumption at a time when much of the population still faced a serious housing problem, the Tugendhat house did, in fact, advance the cause of *Modern Architecture* in more than one respect. First, by breaking up traditionally separate rooms in favor of a continuous space loosely subdivided for a variety of daily functions, Mies introduced a new concept which could be easily adapted to future changes in living conditions. Second, here Mies explored a new inside-outside relationship, expanding various interior spaces either physically (as with the roof terrace on the upper floor) or purely visually (as with the completely glazed garden front of the lower living area), without ever sacrificing the sheltering, protective qualities generally expected from a private house. For both achievements, skeleton frame construction, which had rarely been used in residential architecture before, was an indispensable prerequisite. More specifically, Mies invented his unique system of slender cruciform columns with elegant chromium-plated sheathings, a key motif of his mature German period. Thanks to these innovations, as well as to the meticulous care paid to the design of even the smallest detail, the Tugendhat house has stood up exceedingly well to the test of time, and looks as "fresh" today as it did in 1930. It is thus rightly considered one of the few masterpieces of twentieth-century modern architecture.

Faced with growing racist and military aggression from Nazi-Germany, the Tugendhats, as Jews, were forced to flee their country in 1938. During the years of German occupation

よさとプライヴァシーをそなえていた。ほとんどの人々がいまだきわめて深刻な住宅問題に苦しんでいた時代におけるこの住宅の空間配分と個人的消費額の問題はともかくとして、トゥーゲントハット邸がいくつかの点で、近代建築を前進させたことは確かである。まず第一に、様々な日常的な機能を満たすために緩やかに区画された連続的な空間を求めて、伝統的な小割りされた部屋の構成を解体したことで、ミースは将来の居住環境の変化により容易に対応できる新しいコンセプトを導いた。第二に、ミースは、個人の住宅に一般に求められる保護的な性格を犠牲にすることなく、様々な内部空間を物理的（上層階のルーフ・テラスのように）に、あるいは純粋に視覚的に（下層階のリヴィング・スペースの、ガラス張りの庭園側のファサードのように）拡張することによって、新しい内と外の関係性を探求した。この二つを達成するためには、これまで住宅建築でほとんど使われることがなかった鉄骨構造を導入することが不可欠の条件であった。より具体的にいうならば、成熟したドイツ時代のミースの作品のキー・モチーフの一つともいえる、クロムめっきに覆われた、十字型断面の独特のエレガントな細身の柱のシステムをつくりだしたのである。これらの発明としての側面と、最も小さなディテールにまで払われたデザインへの細心の心配りゆえに、トゥーゲントハット邸は、時の試練に驚くほどよく耐え、今日に至ってもなお、1930年当時と同じくらい「新鮮」にみえる。こうしてこの住宅は、当然のごとく、20世紀における数少ない近代建築の傑作の一つとみなされてきた。

ますます悪化する人種差別と、ナチス・ドイツの軍事力による圧政を前に、ユダヤ人であったトゥーゲントハット一家は、1938年に祖国を逃れることを余儀なくされた。ドイツ占領下の数年間（1939～45）に、彼らがかつて住んでいた住宅には大幅な改造が加えられ、またかつてミースのコンセプトにとって不可欠な部分であったオリジナルの家具はほとんどが失われてしまった。長く続いた共産主義政権の時代には、この住宅は当初の目的とはまったく異なった用途に用いられることになったが、おおむね、ていねいに扱われた。

Left above: View of garden from the west. c. 1936. Right above: View of the living space from lower landing of staircase, looking east, 1931.

左上：庭。西からみる。1936年頃。右上：下階のメインの居室。階段室から東側をみる。1931年頃。

Above: South facade with fully retractable windows.

上：南側のファサード。ガラス窓全体が
上げ下げ可能で格納される。

(1939–1945), their former home suffered severe alteration, losing most of the original furniture that had formed an integral part of Mies van der Rohe's concept. For many years under the communist regime, the house had to serve quite different functions than originally intended, but was, by and large, well taken care of. A major restoration campaign in the early 1980s removed the most awkward disfigurements and later additions but, in many respects, failed to meet today's standards for restoration. Since 1994, when the care of the house was entrusted to the municipal museum in Brno, it has been open to visitors. With public interest growing ever since, the house awaits the international support needed for its preservation and a careful restoration of its major interior parts.

Note:

The quotation from Mies has been translated from his inauguration address for the opening of the 1931 Berlin Building Exposition reprinted in *Der Deutsche Tischlermeister* XXXVII, 30, June 23, 1931, p. 1038. For the contemporary debate on the Tugendhat house cf. *Die Form* VI, nos. 10, 11, 12, Oct.–Nov. 1931, which also gives the original statements by Grete and Fritz Tugendhat (pp. 437–438). For a translation of these as well as much broader analysis of the subject in general see the English edition of Daniela Hammer-Tugendhat, Wolf Tegethoff (eds.), *Ludwig Mies van der Rohe: Das Haus Tugendhat*, Vienna and New York (Springer), 1999.

1980年代初頭に起こった大々的な修復キャンペーンによって、目に余る改築部分と増築部分が取り除かれたが、しかしなお多くの面で、それは今日の修復の基準に見あうものではなかった。1994年以降、この住宅はブルノ市立博物館が管理するところとなり、一般に公開されている。その後のこの住宅にたいする関心の高まりとともに、内部の主要な部分の保存と注意深い修復に必要な国際的な支援が待たれる。

原註：

ミースの引用は『Der Deutsche Tischlermeister』第37巻30号、1931年6月23日、1038頁に収録された、1931年ベルリン建築博覧会の開幕式典の基調講演から訳出したものである。トゥーゲントハット邸をめぐる当時の論争については『Die Form』第6巻10、11、12号、1931年10〜11月を参照されたい。また同誌には、グレテ・トゥーゲントハットならびにフリッツ・トゥーゲントハットによるオリジナルの文章が掲載されている（437〜438頁）。これらの翻訳およびこのテーマについてのより一般的な広範な分析については、ダニエラ・ハマー-トゥーゲントハット、ヴォルフ・テゲトフ共編、『ルードヴィッヒ・ミース・ファン・デル・ローエ：トゥーゲントハット邸』（英語版）、ウィーンおよびニューヨーク（スプリンガー）、1999年を参照されたい。

Left: Mies van der Rohe in the still uncompleted Tugendhat house, winter 1930.

左：ミース・ファン・デル・ローエ、未完のトゥーゲントハット邸にて。1930年、冬。

Maison de Verre
Paris, France 1932
Pierre Chareau with Bernard Bijvöet

ガラスの家
フランス、パリ　1932
ピエール・シャロウ（ベルナルド・ベイフォートと共同）

This renovation of an eighteenth-century Parisian townhouse was designed as a medical office and residence for Doctor Jean and Madame Annie Dalsace. It provided an innovative and practical solution to the problem of lighting a narrow building set back in a courtyard. Pierre Chareau, trained as a furniture designer, together with collaborator Bernard Bijvöet, a Dutch architect, faced the task of building within the 2-story volume of the townhouse while preserving the existing third level for its elderly resident, who was unwilling to move. The two designers in collaboration with master craftsman Louis Dalvet solved the problem by demolishing the first two levels and underpinning the third with a steel structure. The resulting void was divided into three levels: the first for Dr. Dalscace's medical practice centered around a glazed-in nurse's station, the second being a vast split-level volume given over to living, and the third being the private bedrooms overlooking the living space below. Chareau also experimented with transparent and frosted glass to provide light and privacy for the interior space. Externally he opted for the recently-developed "Nevada-type" square glass lens block that refracted light evenly. While glass blocks had been used in the late nineteenth century in glass slabs to allow light to filter through floors, its residential use as a vertical screen supported by a steel framework was unprecedented and could not be guaranteed by its manufacturer.

The glass blocks, assembled in 4- by 6-unit panels, formed a modular order repeated throughout the house, but with specific and varying uses. In fact, doors, balustrades, book racks, storage units, and fenestration were all designed as modular units of a grid running throughout the house. However such a modular attitude was never allowed to become unduly dominant. The stairs, for example, were designed in five distinctly different incarnations, including a retractable ship's ladder, a stringless stair integrated structurally with its balustrade, and the main stair with treads bracketed off steel string beams. Further, different types of floor tile indicate spatial function: studded off-white tile for active public spaces, black ceramic tile for semi-public quiet spaces, wooden strip tile for the dining area and gallery, and off-white ceramic tile for the kitchen and medical examination suite.

While the Maison de Verre took some four years of arduous design and construction, for Chareau the house was a "model made by artisans with a view towards standardization."[1] The design was not entirely preconceived, as the virtual lack of existing working drawings seems to imply, but rather part of an exploratory building process adapted to meet specific needs. As Kenneth Frampton has stated, the house could be seen as a "grossly enlarged piece of furniture." Its implications transcend the limitations of an elite domestic space.

Although virtually ignored by scholarship for more than three decades after its completion, the house was rediscovered through the publication of an extensive 1965 survey by Kenneth Frampton. In a 1966 essay in *Domus*, Richard Rogers proclaimed, "The 'house of light' is possibly the least known and the greatest of 20th century houses." While the house is finite as an exquisite object, it continues, as Frampton notes, "to offer through the fluidity of its plan, the standardization of its components and the mobility of its parts and through its clear assembly of public and private spaces within a single envelope, a general model from which to evolve solutions to some of the indeterminate problems of our epoch."[2]　　(KTO)

Notes:
1. Julient Lepage, "Observations en visitant," *L'Architecture d'Aujourd'hui* No. 9, November/December 1933, p. 15.
2. Kenneth Frampton, "Maison de Verre," *Perspecta* (The Yale Architectural Journal), No. 12, 1969, p. 83.

Opposite: Night view of the glass block wall from the forecourt.

右頁：前庭からみたガラス・ブロックの壁。

この18世紀のタウンハウスの改築は、医師のジャン・ダルザスとマダム・アニー・ダルザスの診療所および住宅として計画された。そのデザインは、中庭にセットバックした細長い建物にいかに十分な採光を確保するかという課題にたいし、革新的かつ実用的な解決策を示した。家具デザイナーとして教育を受けた建築家、ピエール・シャロウは、オランダ人建築家のベルナルド・ベイフォートとともに、立ち退きを拒んだ高齢の住人のために既存の3階部分を残しつつ、タウンハウスの1、2階のヴォリュームにこの住宅と診療所を建てるという困難な仕事に取り組むことになった。彼らは、熟練の職人、ルイ・ダルヴェと共同で、1、2階を取り壊し、3階を鉄骨構造で支えることによってこの問題を解決した。その結果得られた空間を三つのレヴェルに分割し、1階をガラスに囲まれたナース・ステーションを中心とするダルザス氏の診療所、2階を中2階のある広々とした居室、3階を下階の居室を見下ろすプライヴェートな寝室とした。シャロウは、内部空間の採光とプライヴァシーを確保するために、透明ガラスとすりガラスを使って実験を行った。外壁として、彼は光を均等に屈折させる当時開発されたばかりの「ネヴァダ型」の四角いガラス・レンズ・ブロックを採用した。ガラス・ブロックは、床を通して光を取り入れるためのガラス・スラブとして19世紀末から用いられたが、この材料を鉄骨で支えられた垂直のスクリーンとして住宅建築に使用するというのは先例がなく、製造者による保証は得られなかった。

4×6単位のパネルとして整理されたガラス・ブロックは、住宅全体を通して繰り返される寸法体系の秩序を形成しているが、その使われ方は独自かつ多様であった。実際、ドア、手摺、本棚、収納ユニット、採光用の開口は、すべて住宅全体におよぶグリッドの寸法体系ユニットとしてデザインされた。しかし、このような寸法体系は、決して過度に支配的になることはなかった。たとえば階段を見ると、船の折り畳み可能なはしご、手摺と構造的に一体となった側桁

のない階段、踏板がスティール製の中桁から張り出したメインの階段など、五つのまったく異なるデザインがなされている。また、異なる種類の床タイルが空間の使われ方を示唆している。ちりばめられたオフ・ホワイトの磁器質タイルは活動的なパブリック・スペースに、黒の磁器質タイルはセミ・パブリックの静かな部屋に、木片タイルはダイニングとギャラリーに、オフ・ホワイトの磁器質タイルはキッチンと医療診察室に使われた。

ガラスの家はこの困難な設計と建設に4年の月日を要したが、シャロウにとってこの住宅は、「標準化を念頭に職人がつくったモデル」であった。実施図面がほとんど存在しないという事実からも推測できるように、このようなデザインは最初から考えられていたものではなく、特定のニーズに適用された実験途中の建設プロセスの一部なのである。ケネス・フランプトンも示唆しているように、この住宅はまるで「著しく拡大された家具」のように建設されたとみることも可能である。この住宅が意味するものは、単なるエリートの住空間を超越している。

「ガラスの家」は、完成後30年以上にわたって、事実上、研究者から無視されてきたが、1965年のケネス・フランプトンによる詳細な調査の出版を通して再発見された。1966年に『ドムス』誌に掲載されたエッセイのなかでリチャード・ロジャースは、「この『光の家』は、おそらく最も知られていない最も偉大な20世紀の住宅であろう」と述べた。この上なく美しいオブジェとしては限りあるものだが、フランプトンが述べているように、この住宅は「平面の流動性、構成要素の標準化、部分の可動性を通して、そして一つのまとまった空間におけるパブリックとプライヴェートの明快な組み立てを通して、我々の時代が直面する未解決の問題が解答を引き出しうる一般的なモデル」として存在しつづけるであろう。　　　　　　　　　　　　　　　　　　　　　（KTO）

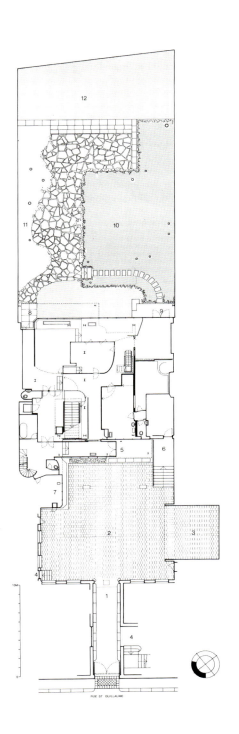

Opposite left: Original town house before the demolition for remodelling. Opposite right: View after the demolition of the 1st and 2nd levels. Left: Site plan. Above: Main forecourt facade. Legend of the site plan: 1) Tunnel entrance, 2) Forecourt, 3) 2-car garage, 4) Existing 18th century building, 5) Entrance to house, 6) Entrance to house upper level, 7) Service wing, 8) Garden access, 9) Consulting room terrace, 10) Ground ivy, 11) Grass and shrubs, 12) Gravel play court

左頁、左：解体前のタウンハウス。左頁、右：解体後の1・2階。左：配置図。上：前庭からみる。
配置図凡例：1）入口のトンネル、2）前庭、3）車庫、4）18世紀の既存建物、5）ガラスの家エントランス、6）上層階の住宅エントランス、7）サーヴィス棟、8）北側の庭への出入口、9）診察室前テラス、10）植栽／カキドゥシ、11）植栽／草木、12）砂場

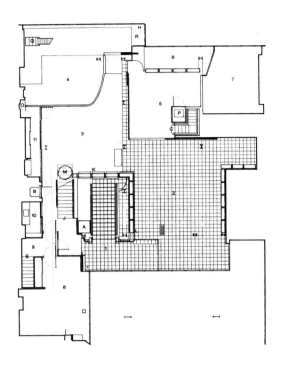

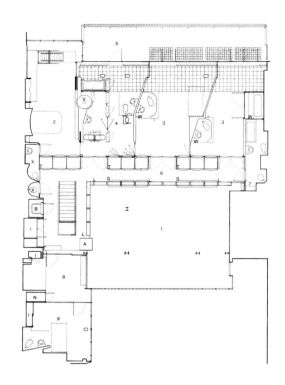

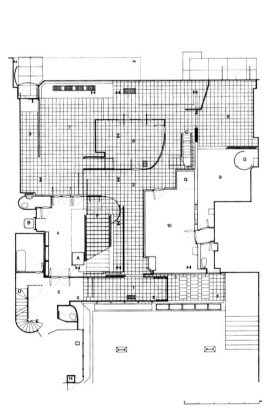

Left Above: 2nd floor plan. Right above: 3rd floor plan. Left: Ground floor plan. Opposite: Salon.
Legend of the plans:
A) Dumbwaiter, B) Passenger elevator, C) Auxiliary stair to study, D) Stair to basement, E) Stair to kitchen, F) Main stair to salon, G) Changing cubicle, H) Refuse, waste disposal, I) Cupboard, J) Storage unit, K) Storage unit, L) Book rack, M) Rotary cleaning cupboard, N) Cleaning cupboard, O) Passage, P) Telephone kiosk, Q) Retractable stair to master bedroom, R) Plant conservatory, S) Storage unit, T) Wardrobe unit, V) Shower, W) Toilet unit, X) W. C.
Legend of the 3rd floor plan:
1) Void over salon, 2) Master bedroom, 3) Bedroom, 4) Master bathroom, 5) Terrace, 6) Gallery access, 7) Guest bathroom, 8) Workroom, 9) Maid's bedroom
Legend of the 2nd floor plan:
1) Main landing, 2) Salon, 3) Dining area, 4) Day room, 5) Study, 6) Void over foyer, 7) Void over consulting room, 8) Kitchen, 9) Kitchen entrance, 10) Laundry, 11) Storage wall
Legend of the ground floor plan:
1) Entrance lobby, 2) Central corridor, 3) Garden corridor, 4) Service foyer, 5) Maid's entrance, 6) Receptionist, 7) Waiting room, 8) Consulting room, 9) Examination room, 10) Attendance room

左上：2階平面図。右上：3階平面図。左下：1階平面図。右頁：2階のサロン。
平面図凡例：A）ダムウェーター、B）エレヴェータ、C）書斎への補助階段、D）地下室への階段、E）台所への階段、F）サロンへの主階段、G）更衣室、H）ごみ処理、I）食器入れ、J）物入れユニット、K）物入れユニット、L）書棚、M）回転式食器洗い機、N）食器洗い機、O）通り抜け、P）電話室、Q）主寝室への階段（格納式）、R）温室、S）物入れユニット、T）衣装入れユニット、V）シャワー、W）洗面所ユニット、X）便所
3階平面図凡例：1）サロン上部吹抜け、2）主寝室、3）寝室、4）主浴室、5）テラス、6）ギャラリーへの出入り口、7）客用浴室、8）作業室、9）使用人寝室
2階平面図凡例：1）主階段昇降口、2）サロン、3）食堂、4）娯楽室、5）書斎、6）フォワイエ上部吹抜け、7）診察室上部吹抜け、8）台所、9）台所出入り口、10）洗濯室、11）物入れ
1階平面図凡例：1）エントランス・ロビー、2）主廊下、3）庭への通路、4）勝手口、5）使用人用入口、6）受付、7）待合室、8）診察室、9）検査室、10）付き添い人室

Above: View of the 2nd floor salon
with the study in the rear. Below:
Section through main stair.

上：2階のサロン。奥に書斎がみえる。
下：主階段を通る断面図。

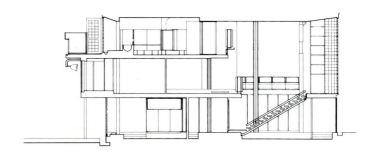

Above: Bedroom on the 3rd floor.
Below: Section through the salon.

上：3階寝室。下：サロンを通る断面図。

*Above left: Detail of standard
bookrack balustrating to main stair
well. Above right: Detail of steel
grill and perforated metal
assembly.*

左上：スティールの書棚の詳細。右上：
スティールの格子と有孔金属板の組み合
わせ。

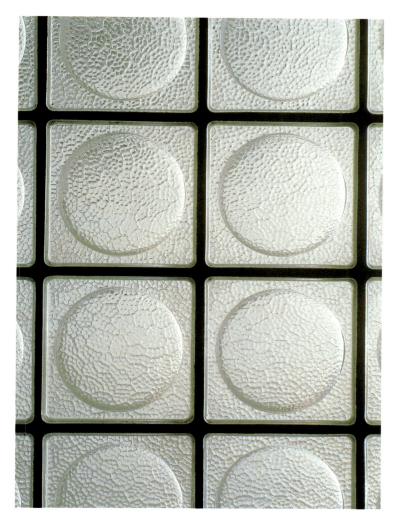

Above: Detail of the "Nevada-type" glass lens block wall.

上：ネヴァダ型のガラス・レンズ・ブロック壁の詳細。

Dammann House
Oslo, Norway 1932
Arne Korsmo with Sverre Aasland

ダマン邸
ノルウェー、オスロ　1932
アルネ・コルスモ（スヴェール・アースランドと共同）

This house was designed in 1930 and completed in 1932 for businessman Axel Dammann, a client willing to create a "new dwelling" in tune with the time. In this house, Arne Korsmo sought to translate the necessities of a domestic program into compositions of symbolic forms like the sphere, cube, and tower. This composition stands at the end of Havna allé, a development of 15 houses all designed by Korsmo, and assisted by his partner Sverre Aasland. As indicated in Korsmo's diagram, one approaches this house from the northeast. A long pergola leads from the garden to a tower-like entrance, then up an entry stair to a cross-axial living space spanning the brow of the hill. The public spaces (one-room living/dining, semi-circular study, and terrace) face southwest towards a view of the fjord in a plan closely connected both with the logic of the site and human life. Korsmo designed the continuous clerestory windows running along the southwest facade of the living/dining room to light the Dammann's art collection. As one-time owner and Korsmo protégé Sverre Fehn noted, sunlight also enlivens the spatial composition, because the house functions like a large sundial.

In this house, the architect aimed to intensify architectural experience through a logical sequence of structures. Building on the compositional ideas developed by Rietveld and in the work of Dudok, among others, Korsmo created his own synthetic free plan as a play of tensions between large and small, high and low, closed and open. The dynamic composition of the fireplace provides an inner core to the building, like that of Frank Lloyd Wright's Robie house. Similarly, Korsmo liberated the house from any traditional static equilibrium. He designed much of the furniture himself, with the same poetic and functional sensibility with which he would later design household objects such as glasses and flatware. According to Christian Norberg-Schulz, fellow member of PAGON (the Norwegian division of CIAM) and design collaborator, Korsmo wanted "to make people rich, not in worldly goods, but in everything that exists.... Korsmo's point of departure was the site with its properties of space, form, material, color and light, everything man must come to terms with in order to be able to dwell in the true sense of the word. For this was Korsmo's ultimate goal: to help people to dwell." (KTO)

この住宅は、時代に合った「新しい住宅」を生み出すことに積極的だった事業家のアクセル・ダマンのために1930年に設計され1932年に完成した。アルネ・コルスモは、この住宅の設計を通して、住生活のプログラムに必要不可欠なものを球体、立方体、タワーといったシンボリックな形態からなる構成に翻訳することを目指した。この建物は、コルスモが彼のパートナーであるスヴェール・アースランドとともにデザインしたアブナ・アレという15軒からなる住宅開発地の一番奥に位置している。コルスモのダイアグラムに示されているように、この住宅には北東方向からアプローチする。庭から長いパーゴラによって塔のような入口へと導かれ、さらに入口の階段をあがると丘の上に横たわる交差軸上に位置するリヴィング・スペースへと導かれる。この住宅の平面計画は、敷地と人間の生命の論理に深く根差しており、パブリック・スペース（ワン・ルームのリヴィング・ダイニング、半円形の書斎、テラス）はフィヨルドに向かって南西に面している。コルスモは、ダマンが所有する美術コレクションの照明を考慮して、リヴィング・ダイニング・ルームの南西ファサードに沿って連続した高窓をデザインした。かつてこの住宅のオーナーだったコルスモの弟子のスヴェール・フェーンは、家が巨大な日時計のように機能するため、太陽の光が空間構成を活気づけると述べている。

この住宅において、建築家は構造の論理的なシークエンスを通して建築的経験をより高めることを目指した。リートフェルトやデュドックの作品によって展開されたコンポジションの思想にもとづき、コルスモは、大小、高低、開閉といった対比から生まれる緊張感を利用しながら、独自のまとまりのあるフリー・プランをつくりだした。暖炉のダイナミックな構成は、ライトのロビー邸と同じように、建物の中枢を形成している。ライト同様コルスモも、伝統的な住宅の静的でありきたりなデザインからこの住宅を開放している。この家の家具もほとんどデザインした彼は、後に同様の詩的かつ機能的な感性でガラス製品や食器類といった家庭用品をデザインした。PAGON（ノルウェーのCIAM支部）のメンバーであり、コルスモのデザイン協力者でもあったクリスチャン・ノルベルグ-シュルツによると、コルスモは「財産という意味ではなく、存在するすべてのものによって人々を豊かにしたかった。……コルスモの出発点は、敷地の空間的特性、形態、材料、色、そして光であり、それは人間が真の意味で居住することを可能にする上で折り合わねばならないすべてのものであった。コルスモの最終的な目標は、人が居住するのを助けることであったのだ」。 (KTO)

Above: Diagram of views by Arne Korsmo. Right: North facade with pergola to the leading entry. Opposite: View from Havna allé of entry passage.

上：コルスモによる視界のダイアグラム。右：北側のファサード。エントランスへとつづくパーゴラ。右頁：アヴナ・アレ通りからみる。

Above: View of the east facade.
Right: View of the east and north facades.

上：東側のファサードをみる。右：東側および北側のファサードをみる。

Above: South facade. Left: North and west facades.

上：南側のファサード。左：北側および西側のファサードをみる。

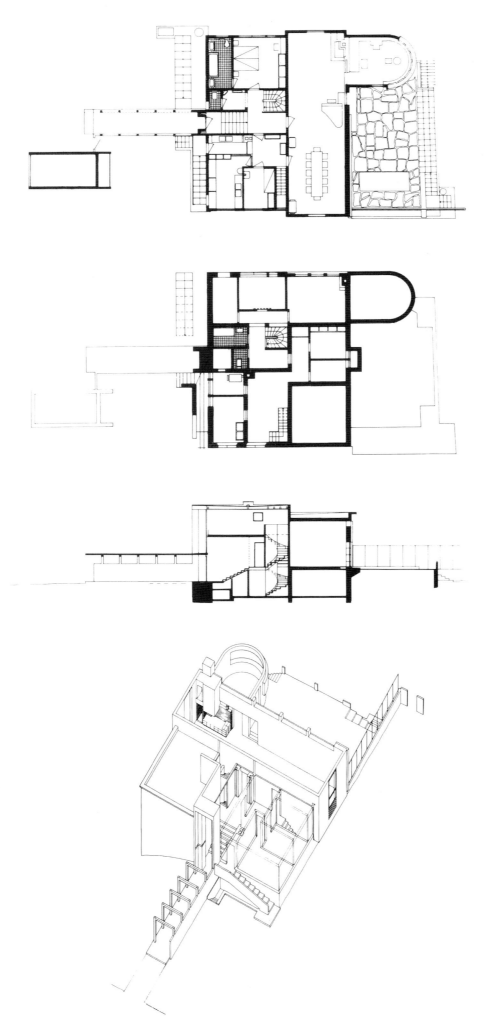

From top: Ground floor plan, basement plan, north-south section, axonometric drawing of the interior. Opposite: Exterior view of the half-cylindrical study from the south.

上から：１階平面図。地階平面図。南北断面図。内部空間のアクソノメトリック図。右頁：半円形の書斎の外観を南側からみる。

pp. 184-185: Dining area, looking toward the west. Above: View of living area from the dining area.

184〜185頁：食堂。西側をみる。上：
食堂から居間をみる。

Above: Study.   上：書斎。

Opposite: View of the study and garden to the south from the living area. Above: Entrance hall.

左頁：居間から書斎および南側の庭をみる。上：エントランス・ホール。

Schminke House
Löbau, Saxony, Germany 1933
Hans Scharoun

シュミンク邸
ドイツ、ザクソニー、ルーバウ　1933
ハンス・シャロウン

Built for Fritz Schminke, a wealthy industrialist with adventurous tastes, this house expresses the freedom of architect Hans Scharoun's spatial conception and his close responsiveness to site, function, and orientation. The house is located on the south end of a site near Schminke's noodle factory. The plan of this basically one-room-wide home is based on two axes determined by the site. The long axis of the house (from west to east) effectively serves as a screen between the road and main part of the garden. The diagonal axis from southwest to northeast follows the view towards the garden. Scharoun designed the main living space to have windows both to the south to bring in sun and located the main sofa towards the view to the north and east. Following a practice of organic functionalism, Scharoun twisted the "head of the house" containing the dining area and master bedroom area above as cantilevered flying forms extending towards the vista. Within its steel frame construction with plastered hollow block walls, Scharoun completed the living space with integral light fixtures and wire mesh tubular steel serving as light modulators to evoke a luminous feel.

The movement of the occupant, weaving the separate parts into a spatial continuum, becomes the overall organizing principle. Living space is divided only by movable partitions, as Scharoun abandoned the idea of stable entities of closed rooms and rigid walls. Dynamic spatial links are established through movement around the curve of the piano or stairs, naturally changing one's viewpoint. Scharoun conceived of such a particular choreography by observing daily routines and various passages from one space to another. Rather than being simply a formal composition of space designed from plan, this house thus organizes space from the fluctuating viewpoint of the inhabitant.

While the Schminke house was Scharoun's own favorite house design, it continues to stand witness to both external and internal change. As Scharoun's last building before the Nazi clamp-down, the building's continued existence through the twenty-first century in and of itself is remarkable. The house is presently owned by the City of Löbau and through its restoration from 1999-2000, the character of its original dynamic spirit will be reborn.　　　　　(KTO)

裕福な工場経営者で、冒険的な嗜好の持ち主であったフリッツ・シュミンクのために建てられたこの住宅は、建築家、ハンス・シャロウンの空間概念の自由さと、彼の敷地、機能、方位に対する緻密な対応を表現している。この住宅は、隣接するシュミンクのパスタ工場に近い、敷地の南端に位置している。基本的にワン・ルームとなっているこの住宅の平面計画は、敷地によって決定された二つの軸線にもとづいている。東西に伸びる長い軸線は、道路および工場と庭の間に横たわるスクリーンとして効果的に機能している。道路と平行に南西から北東に伸びる軸線は、庭の眺望を考慮している。シャロウンは、南からの採光のために、中心となる1階の居室の南側に窓を設け、また北と東方向の眺望を考慮して南側にソファを置いた。有機的機能主義を探求していたシャロウンは、片持ちの浮いた形態が前方の景色に向かって伸びていくように、ダイニング・スペースと主寝室がある「住宅の頭」の部分をひねった。鉄骨構造にプラスター仕上げの中空ブロック壁という構造の内部で、シャロウンは光り輝く印象を喚起させるために、造り付けの照明器具および照明の変調器として機能している金網でできた筒状のスティールで居室を完成させた。

部分と部分を空間の連続としてつなぎあわせることによって、居住者の動きが全体を組織化する原理となる。シャロウンは閉じられた部屋の堅固さと融通の利かない壁を放棄し、居室を可動式の間仕切りで分割した。ピアノや階段の曲線の周りを動き、自然に視線を変えることによって、ダイナミックな空間のつながりが生み出される。シャロウンは、日々の生活における日課や一つの空間から他の空間への様々な移動を観察することによってこのような特定の動線や動作を理解した。このように単なる平面から立ち上げられた空間の形態的構成ではなく、この住宅は居住者の視線の動きによって空間を組織化している。

シャロウンはシュミンク邸を非常に気に入っていたが、この住宅はその後様々な変化を経験しつづけた。ナチの弾圧が始まる前の最後の建物であることを考えると、この住宅が21世紀に向けて存在しつづけるという事実は驚くに値する。現在ルーバウ市が所有するこの住宅は、1999年から2000年にかけて行われる修復を経て、当時の力強い精神を取り戻すことだろう。　　　(KTO)

Left: View from northeast, c. 1933.
Opposite: View of the east end with the winter garden balcony on the ground floor and master bed room balcony on the 2nd floor.

左：北東からみる、1933年頃。右頁：東側の端部をみる。1階ウインター・ガーデン前のバルコニー、2階主寝室前のバルコニーをみる。

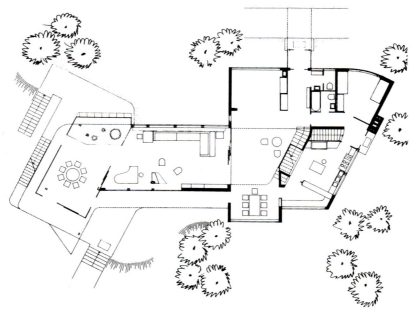

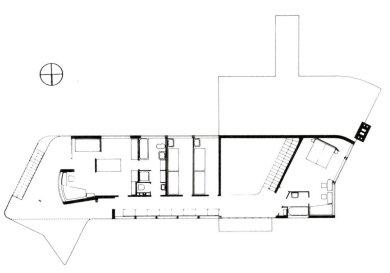

Opposite bottom: 1st floor plan. Above: North facade. Left: 2nd floor plan.

左頁、下：1階平面図。上：北側ファサード。左：2階平面図。

Above: Entrance canopy on the north side. Opposite: View of the exterior of the winter garden from the southeast.

上：北側のキャノピーのあるエントランス。右頁：南東側からみたウインター・ガーデンの外部構成。

Above: View of the living room looking toward the winter garden, c. 1933. Below: View toward the living room from the winter garden, c.1933.

上：居間。ウインター・ガーデン側をみる、1933年頃。下：ウインター・ガーデンから居間をみる、1933年頃。

*Above: View of the winter garden
from the living room.*

上：居間からウインター・ガーデンをみる。

On Color Restoration of the Villa Savoye

Arthur Rüegg

Translation by Lynnette Widder

サヴォア邸における色の修復について
アルトゥール・リュエッグ
木下壽子訳

Because of its status as "Grande Dame," the Villa Savoye is given a new dress every few years — on account of her fragile construction, or so it is said. In 1996-97, that garment was tailored in accordance with the dictates of historic preservation, and with the greatest amount of effort possible. Why, then, is the result so unconvincing in reality? Is it the fact that the villa and its guardhouse look like oversized models which — with the use of sharp chiaroscuro both inside and out in the same blinding, immaculate white — seem simultaneously dematerialized and scaleless?

Although the Villa Savoye may be considered the representative of a "white architecture," I am convinced that it never had that appearance. That suspicion is based upon three factors above all others: first of all, the quantity and character of the white paint; secondly, the incomplete logic in using color in an only fragmentary manner; and thirdly, the play amongst, and tactile quality of, the colored planes on the interior.

There will, however, never be absolute certainty about Le Corbusier and Pierre Jeanneret's intentions, and about the ensemble's original condition.[1] The large-format color transparencies by Lucien Hervé, which were not studied during the restoration, show the enormous quantity of stuccowork completed as part of the first renovation in 1966-67. Thus, the work which was finally done to determine the original colors used could only, at least on the exterior, produce isolated results.

Documents dating to the construction period,[2] preserved in the Fondation Le Corbusier, are more decisive. Initially, in Spring, 1929, it was apparently assumed that the entire exterior of the house would be painted by the site foreman using lime-based whitewash, whereas the painter would apply a distemper paint on the interior walls. In the course of construction, the quality of the painted finishes was progressively raised, as was the quality of many of the details. As early as July, 1929, a correspondence, still preserved in the Fondation, was initiated. Its subject was the rather high price of a "Jurasit" natural stucco[3] which was to be applied to the 316 sq. m. of the four primary exterior facades. One of the architect's few explicitly stated color concepts is documented in this correspondence: the stucco should be "parfaitement dressé, grèsé, de teinte pierre très claire (légèrement crème)." Thus, it should be the color of that very light stone which, in combination with the white and light blue of the sky, helps to produce the incomparably delicate coloristic atmosphere of the city of Paris.

Much speaks for the assumption that this solution was in fact realized: first, the fact that the records and "mémoires" of the painter Celio as well as Pierre Jeanneret's correspondence from 1930-31 never mention the primary facades when describing the exterior paint work. Second, the fact that a cloudy surface structure is clearly visible in the original prints of the contemporary photographs. They may have been painted at a later date, yet the 33 color slides I have studied from 1958[4] show no traces of paint on these facades, in contrast to the immediately adjacent *piloti* and almost every other part of the building but this may be due to the intense weathering of these unprotected surfaces.

For the remaining exterior paint work, the lime-based whitewash was to be replaced, on the emphatic recommendation of Pierre Jeanneret, by several coats of "Cimentol," a special oil paint (in lieu of the equally expensive use of oil paint on the interior that had been proposed in a second phase). Whatever was actually used on the relatively small exterior area, it was certainly paint with relatively great "body." Because it was applied with brushes, it gave the walls a

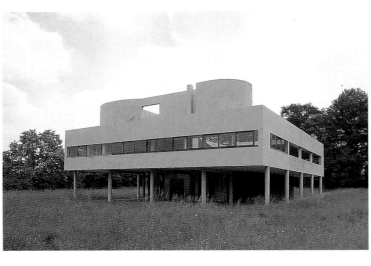

Above: Exterior view of the Villa Savoye, Poissy, 1929-31.

上：サヴォア邸外観、ポアジー、1929〜31年。

texture with an entirely different, evocative qualitative than the thinly painted, roller-applied, saturated white paint used today. Moreover, there were quite likely colored portions of the exterior which underpinned the architectural concept.

At least in the case of the guardhouse, a color scheme, drawn up by Jeanneret in May, 1930, for the painter Cerlio, is still preserved.[5] The base was denoted as dark green (correctly rendered today in pure Vert anglais). The columns, side walls and stair were dark gray, the longitudinal facade, however, in light "Vert anglais no. 2," the same color used on the rear wall of the semi-attached house at the Weißenhof Siedlung. Today, all this is white, despite the fact that all the elements of Le Corbusier's color strategy were realized in this small building: volumetric hierarchy was clarified by the dark base and piloti; the house's integration into the "atmosphere" of its context was accomplished by means of colors which relate the house to the vegetation; and the down-playing of sculptural effect was accomplished by the "Camouflage architectural," the change of color on the edges of the prismatic volume. This color concept enhances the differences between the planimetrically rectangular service building, embedded in the trees, and the almost square, free-standing — in the spirit of Palladio — "ideal villa," which has the same surface quality on all four sides. Moreover, the guardhouse embodies the Purist approach already developed in 1925, which dictated a polychrome but dematerialized building; whereas the villa's natural stucco marks the beginning of the post-Purist affection for materials which characterizes the architect's future.

Even in the case of this smaller building, the only original photograph (which was probably retouched for publication) very likely indicates that the color concept described above was executed: the piloti appear to be considerably darker than the longitudinal facade of the primary volume, and this dark shade is even more definitively legible because of some bright patches where the paint had been repaired with a lighter hue. Unfortunately, no comparable color schemes exist for the primary building. Tim Benton, who has studied the villa in the greatest detail,[6] had already noted in 1984 that documentation preserved refers to "burnt umber, gray and black for some of the concrete fitments and blue for the salon walls." He also pointed out the interesting detail that the painter Celio had first painted the curved walls on the ground floor "red" (certainly a pure burnt sienna, as in the base of the semi-attached house in Stuttgart), and then, "on the basis of new instructions, green," probably to assume the mood of the landscape. This green appears to be adequately supported by evidence (even if the green in today's version seems too pure); in an early publication from October, 1930, in the German magazine *Baumeister*, it is explicitly described as "dark green."

The same article also indicates that the structures on the roof were painted "light blue and ochre." This accords with a tenaciously held assumption which is supported by a model made in 1931 for Hitchcock and Johnson's famous 1932 exhibition at the Museum of Modern Art: there, the roof structures are intense blue and red in color.[7] On closer inspection of old photographs, it becomes apparent that the model was only colored this way at a later date. If the villa's primary volume was in fact stucco'd with "Jurasit," then presumably at least part of the roof structures was kept ocher/pink or light blue. In 1958, only a few, barely identifiable traces of color are left on these structures' exterior, whereas the color slides of the interior suggest that here, on the side of the solarium, several walls were in fact colored light pink or ochre. It is easier to support the supposition that the architectural

concept was also supported by the use of color on the piano nobile. The exterior space of the terrace and the interior space of the salon are joined seamlessly; the functional relationship and the exploitation of southern light are also expressed spatially. Thus, the pink trimmed rear wall, now painted as dictated by newly-uncovered evidence (as opposed to the light blue shade it was given in 1966), seems entirely isolated. In fact, it was probably part of a color scheme that also included the terrace's exterior wall (including the roofed portion) and thus emphasized the spatial unity of terrace and salon. The color photographs from 1958 show very well maintained shades of pink on the parapet and headers; even the pink of the columns in the horizontal slot. It is a color scheme which seems to be also identifiable in certain black and white original photographs from 1931, evidenced by the fact that the white wooden garden chairs by Pierre Dariel are clearly lighter than the background. It is possible to speculate in a similar vein on the details of the interior polychroming. The scholarly correct method of painting white those areas in which no evidence of color is found, probably contributes here as well to weakening of the original expression. Examples of this effect are the area around the high built-in closets whose niches more or less cry out for differentiation by means of color (especially palpable in the large bathroom; here René Burri's black and white photograph from 1959 shows in fact a very clear color hierarchy)[8]. The method of painting used is especially disorienting in that metal and wood, even handrails, have the same matte finish. This all contributes to the fact that the house, both inside and out, seems like an architectural model.

One would also have to ask questions about the exact nature of the various pink tones. Were they mixed according to evidence found in the house, or according to the "Salubra" wallpaper collection of 1931?[9] If chosen from that collection, then from which of the different pink series? In any case, it would have been correct to have used the standard powdered pigments which were common at that time. This practice would have insured that the various light tones were related.

Even such apparently secondary details as the futuristic form of the security cameras mounted on their brackets or the omission of curtains contribute to the inauthenticity of the overall impression made by the building. In this context, even the perfectly reconstructed, newly chromed lighting fixtures and door hardware [10] seem too assertive.

With all due respect for the immense effort invested in the reconstruction, one would still wish for a purist building which could evoke the domestic culture of Modernism with the same urgency as, for example, the Rietveld Schröder house in Utrecht, Chareau's Maison de Verre in Paris or Aalto's Villa Mairea in Noormarkku. An international group of specialists, as recently planned for consultation on Mies' Tugendhat house in Brno, might perhaps have been able to contribute to that goal. An even more promising approach would have been an appeal addressed to all those architects who, prior to 1959, were able to scale the fences around the Villa Savoye with their cameras in hand....

「近代建築の女王」というステイタスゆえに、構造がもろい（あるいは、もろいといわれている）サヴォア邸は数年ごとに装いが改められる。1996年から97年にかけて、この住宅の外装は、歴史的建築物保存の要請に従って、可能な限りの力を注いで仕立てられた。それにもかかわらず、なぜ現実的に、これほどまでにその成果が剥き出しなのだろうか。それは、サヴォア邸とその管理棟が、非物質的でスケール感のない巨大な模型（同じ建物の内部も外部も真っ白に塗られ、白と黒の陰影によってくっきりと調子をつけた）のようにみえるという事実によるものだろうか。

サヴォア邸は「白い建築」の代表と考えられているかもしれないが、実際には決してそうではなかったと私は確信している。この疑念は、主に三つの根拠にもとづいている。まず第一に、白い塗料の量と性質。第二に、断片的な方法で色彩を用いる論理が不完全であること。第三に、色が塗られた内部の面と面との関係にみられる遊びとその材質感である。

しかしながら、ル・コルビュジエとピエール・ジャンヌレの意図、そして全体のオリジナルの状態がはっきりとわかることはないだろう。[1] 修復の際に研究されなかったルシエン・エルヴェイによる大判のカラー・ポジからは、1966年から67年にかけて行われた最初の修復の際に、かなりの量のスタッコ仕上げが施されたことがわかる。そのため、建設当時に用いられたオリジナルの色を決定する最終的な作業は、少なくとも外観ついては、十分な成果を得ることはできなかった。

ル・コルビュジエ財団に保管されている建設時の記録[2]は決定的に重要である。それによると、当初、つまり1929年春の段階では、現場監督は、内部の壁に水性塗料を用いるのにたいし、この住宅の外観全体には石灰をベースとした水性白色塗料を塗ろうと考えていたようである。建設の過程で、ディテールの質同様、塗り仕上げの質も徐々に向上した。1929年7月の段階で、すでに手紙のやり取り（この資料は、財団に保管されている）が始まっている。手紙の内容は、四つの主要なファサード、合計316㎡の壁に塗る予定だった「ジュラシット」[3]天然スタッコは、やや高いというものだった。ル・コルビュジエが色に関して明確に述べた数少ないコンセプトが、このやりとりのなかに記録されている。それによると、スタッコは、空の白と明るい青と組み合わさって、パリ市の比類なくデリケートな色彩をもった雰囲気を生み出すことができる、非常に明るい石の色であるべきだった。

この案が実行されたという憶測には様々な根拠がある。まず第一に、塗装工のセルリオの記録と「記憶」、そして1930〜31年のピエール・ジャンヌレの手紙を読むと、外観の塗装作業についての説明のなかに、メインのファサードについて触れた部分がまったくないからである。第二に、くすんだ外観の構造体が、当時撮られた写真のオリジナル・プリントからはっきりと見てとれるということだ。私が検証した1958年に撮られた33枚のカラー・スライド[4]には、すぐ近くのピロティや建物の他の部分とは対照的に、これらのファサードが塗られたことを示す痕跡が見当たらないが、もしかしたらそれはもう少し後で塗られたのかもしれない。あるいは、剥き出しのファサードの表面が雨風の影響を激しく受けたためとも考えられる。それ以外の外壁の塗装作業には、石灰ベースの天然スタッコのかわりに、ピエール・ジャンヌレの強いすすめによって、「シメントール」という特別な油性塗料の膜（第2段階で提案された、内部に使用された同じくらい高価な油性塗料のかわりに）が用いられた。比較的狭い範囲の外壁に実際にどのようなものが使われたにしろ、それはまちがいなく、堂々とした「重厚さ」が出るように塗られた。これはブラシを使って塗られたため、今日使われているローラーで薄く塗った鮮明な水性白色塗料とはまったく異なった材質感を壁に与えた。さらに、建築的コンセプトを支持するように、外壁に色が塗られた部分がいくつかあった可能性は高い。

少なくとも管理棟に関しては、1930年5月にジャンヌレが塗装工のセルリオのためにつくった色彩に関する案が現在も残っている。[5] 1階の基礎部分は濃い緑（今日、正確に純粋な「ヴェール・アングレ（英国風の緑）」で再現された）と記されている。円柱、側壁、そして階段は濃いグレー、縦方向のファサードは、ヴァイゼンホーフ・ジードルンクの2戸建て住宅の裏壁で用いられたのと同じ明るい「ヴェール・アングレ No.2」と記されている。ル・コルビュジエの色彩戦略に関するすべての要素がこの小さな建物で実現されたにもかかわらず、今日、これらは皆、白色に塗られている。ヴォリュームの秩序は、暗いベース部分とピロティによって明確化され、この住宅がたっている文脈の「雰囲気」と住宅の統合は、住宅を周囲の植物と関連づける色彩によって成し遂げられている。また、彫刻的な効果は、多面的なヴォリュームの角の色を変えるという「建築的カモフラージュ」によって生み出されている。この色彩コンセプトが、木々に埋め込まれた方形のサーヴィス棟と、四面すべてが同じ質の外壁をもつ真四角に近い（パラディオの精神で）自立した構造の「理想的ヴィラ」の違いをより強調している。さらに管理棟は、1925年にル・コルビュジエがすでに展開していた、多彩色だが非物質化された建物というピューリスト的アプローチを具体化している。それにたいし、ヴィラの天然スタッコは、その後のル・コルビュジエを特徴づけることになる、材料にたいするポスト・ピューリスト的な態度を示している。

この小さいほうの建物ですら、唯一のオリジナル写真（これはおそらく出版のために修正された）は、先に説明した色彩コンセプトが実行されたことを示唆している。ピロティは主要なヴォリュームの縦方向のファサードよりもかなり暗く、明るい色合いの塗料を用いて修復されたいくつかの部分との対比によって、その暗い色調はよりいっそう決定的なものとなっている。

残念ながら、ヴィラのほうにはこれに匹敵する色彩計画は存在しない。この建物を詳細に研究したティム・ベントンは、[6]1984年の時点ですでに、「コンクリート造作の一部は、こげ茶色、グレー、黒。サロンの壁は青」と、保存された記録のなかで言及されていると書いている。ベントンはまた、塗装工のセルリオが最初、地上階のカーヴした壁を「赤」（シュトゥットガルトの2戸建て住宅のベース部分と同様に、まちがいなく純粋な赤こげ茶色）に塗り、その後おそらくランドスケープの雰囲気を考慮して、「新しい指示に従い、緑」に塗り直したと指摘している。この緑は、（今日塗られているものが純粋すぎるようにみえたとしても）証拠によってまちがいないことが立証されている。また、1930年10月発行のドイツの雑誌『Baumeister』には、それははっきりと「濃い緑」と描写されている。

さらにこの記事は、屋上の構造物が「明るい青と黄土色」に塗られたことを示唆している。これは、1932年にMoMAで行われたヒッチコックとジョンソンの有名な展覧会のために1931年につくられた模型が重要な根拠となって根強く維持されてきた仮定と一致する。屋上の構造物は、濃い青と赤で塗られている。[7] 古い写真をより詳しく診断すると、模型は後になってこのように塗られたことがわかる。もしヴィラの主要なヴォリュームが『ジュラシット』スタッコ仕上げであったとしたら、おそらく少なくとも屋根の構造の一部は黄土色/ピンク、あるいは明るい青のまま保たれたであろう。内部のカラー・スライドは、サンルームの脇のいくつかの壁が明るいピンクか黄土色だったことを示唆しているのにたいし、1958年、わずかに色を確認できる痕跡がいくつかこの構造の外壁に残された。

建築的コンセプトは、色を使うことによって、上の主階においても表現されたと推測するほうが自然である。テラスの外部空間とサロンの内部空間は、継ぎ目なく連結され、機能的な関係性と南方向からの採光の活用もまた、空間的に表現されている。このように、現在、新たに見つかった証拠（1966年に施された明るい青の色調に反して）に従って塗られたピンク色の幅木がついた裏壁は、まったく孤立しているようにみえる。実際、それはおそらくテラスの外壁（屋根が架かった部分を含む）を含む色彩計画の一部であり、そうすることによって、テラスとサロンの空間的統一感を強調したのだろう。1958年のカラー写真からは、非常によく維持されたパラペットとヘッダーのピンクの色合いが見てとれる。垂直スロットの円柱のピンクさえもみえる。また、1931年に撮られた

オリジナルのモノクロ写真のなかで、ピエール・ダリエルの白い木製ガーデン・チェアが明らかに背景よりも明るいという事実からも、この色彩計画が鑑定できる。内部の多彩色のディテールについても、同じ調子で推測することができる。色を裏づける証拠が見出せなかったため、学術的には正しい判断で白く塗られた部分は、ここではおそらくオリジナルの表現を弱めてしまっている。これはたとえば、背の高い造り付けのクローゼットの周辺に見出せる。ここでは、ニッチが色による区別を要求しているようにみえる(とりわけ大きな浴室をみればわかる。レネ・ブリが1959年に撮影したモノクロ写真は、実際、きわめて明快な色彩の秩序をみせている)。⁸ 使用された塗装法が、メタルも木も、手摺さえも同じマット仕上げとなっている点は、とくに混乱を招いている。その結果、この住宅は外部も内部も建築模型のようにみえてしまうからだ。

何種類かあるピンクの色調の性質についても検討する必要がある。これらは、この住宅から見つかった証拠をもとに混ぜられたのか、あるいは1931年の「サルブラ」壁紙コレクションによるものか。もしこのコレクションから選ばれたのだとすれば、どのピンク・シリーズから選ばれたのか。⁹ どちらにしろ、当時一般的だった標準的な粉末色素を用いたのは正解であった。この作業は、様々な明るい色調が同系のものであることを保証するだろう。

ブラケットに備え付けられた未来的な形態のセキュリティ・カメラや、カーテンの除去といった明らかに二次的なディテールですら、この建物がかもしだす不確かな印象をつくりだす要素となっている。この意味において、クローム・メッキが施された照明器具やドアのハードウェア¹⁰といった新たに再建された部分さえも、独断的すぎるように思える。再建につぎ込まれた不断の努力に当然の敬意を払いつつ、一人のピューリストの建物が、たとえばユトレヒトのリートフェルト設計によるシュレーダー邸、パリのピエール・シャロウ設計によるガラスの家、あるいはノールマルックのアアルト設計によるマイレア邸と同様の力強さで、モダニズムの住生活文化を生き生きと再現しうることを私は願う。最近、ミースが設計したブルノのトゥーゲントハット邸の調査が計画されているように、国際的な専門家グループによって、もしかするとこの目標が達成されるかもしれない。しかし、よりいっそう有望な方法は、1959年以前にサヴォア邸の周りのフェンスをカメラをもってよじ登った建築家たちに協力を求めることであろう。

Notes:

1. The villa (not including the guard-house) was already photographable in the summer of 1930. However, all of the painting was not completed until the date on which the clients finally moved in, in 1931.
2. Fondation Le Corbusier (FLC), Dossier H 1-12. Many thanks to Evelyne Tréhin for permitting the study of these documents.
3. The Terazzo- und Jurasit-Werke AG in Bärschwil (Switzerland) offered the high-quality stucco "Jurasit" in ca 400 soft, natural shades. The documents in the FLC mention the name "M. Affolter, Bärschwil."
4. I thank Alexander Henz, ETH Zurich, for permitting me access to his well-preserved collection of slides from 1958.
5. FLC 31871, formerly Boite H 1-12, Document 124.
6. See Tim Benton, "Villa Savoye and the Architects' Practice," in: H. Allen Brooks, ed., *The Le Corbusier Archive* Vol. VII, 1984, pp. IX-XXXI; Tim Benton, "Le Corbusier propos architectural," in: *Le Corbusier, Le ricerca paziente*, Calalogue Lugano, 1980, pp. 23-44; and Tim Benton, *Les villas de Le Corbusier 1920-1930*, Paris, 1984, pp. 190-207.
7. See the letter H 1-12, Document 144, sent from Berlin to Claude Pissaro on July 7, 1931. It stipulates that the model correspond precisely to reality. A color exploration of this model would be of great interest. For a short time (between the first and second renovation), the roof structures of the villa were painted in accordance with the painted New York model.
8. See Arthur Rüegg, ed., *Le Corbusier*. Photographs by René Burri/Magnum, Basel, Boston, Berlin, 1999, p. 32.
9. In the new guide to the Villa Savoye, published in July, 1997 by the "Editions du patrimoine," Le Corbusier's 1931 "Salubra" collection is noted as the source of the color restoration.
10. The painstakingly restored door handles "béquilles à boules" correspond to one of the standard models used on occasion by Le Corbusier, but are not apparent in early photographs of the Villa Savoye. Prior to 1928/29, such metal fittings were always nickel-planted (a yellowish finish).

原註

1-ヴィラ(管理棟は除く)は、1930年夏にすでに撮影された。しかし、1931年に施主が移り住む日まで、塗装は完成していなかった。
2-ル・コルビュジエ財団(FLC)、Dossier H1-12。これらの資料の研究を許可してくださったエヴェリーヌ・トレヒンさんに感謝の意を表する。
3-ベルシュヴィル(スイス)のTerazzo- und Jurasit- Werke AGが、ca400 soft、自然な色調の質の高いスタッコ、「ジュラシット」を提供してくれた。
4-1958年に撮影された、保存状態のよいスライド・コレクションを見ることを許可してくださったチューリッヒ連邦工科大学のアレキサンダー・ヘンツ氏に感謝の意を表する。
5- FLC 31871, 以前のBoite H 1-12, Document 124。
6-ティム・ベントンのH. Allen Brooks 編、『The Le Corbusier Archive』Vol.VII、1984、pp. IX-XXXIの「Villa Savoya and the Architects' Practice」およびカタログ『Le Corbusier, Le ricerca paziente』、ルガーノ、1980年、23~44頁の「Le Corbusier propos architectural」さらに『Les villas de Le Corbusier 1920-1930』パリ、1984年、190~207頁を参照。
7-ベルリンからクロード・ピサロに宛てて1931年7月7日に送られた手紙、H 1-12、Document 144参照。この手紙には、模型が現実と正確に一致することが明記されている。この模型の色に関する調査は、きわめて関心が高いであろう。短期間(1回目と2回目の修復の間)に、ヴィラの屋根の構造体はニューヨークの模型に従って塗装された。
8-アルトゥール・リュエッグ編著の『Le Corbusier』写真:レネ・ブリ/マグナム、バーゼル、ボストン、ベルリン、1999年、32頁参照。
9-1997年7月にEditions du patrimoineから出版されたサヴォア邸の新しいガイドには、ル・コルビュジエの1931年「Salubra」コレクションが、色彩修復の資料と明記されている。
10-苦心の末に修復されたドア・ハンドル「béquilles á boules」は、ル・コルビュジエが用いた標準モデルの一つと一致するが、サヴォア邸の初期の写真にはみられない。1928/29年以前、このようなメタルの取り付け部品は、つねにニッケル・プランティッド(黄色っぽい仕上げ)であった。

Summer House
Stennäs, Sweden 1937
Erik Gunnar Asplund

夏の家
スウェーデン、ステナス　1937
エリック・グンナー・アスプルンド

Built by Erik Gunnar Asplund for his family in 1937, this small summer house bridged the gap between modern and traditional architecture, a recurrent goal of this architect's later years. Asplund had established himself as the leading modern movement architect in Scandinavia with his 1930 Stockholm exhibition hall design. He then abandoned the functionalism of the mid-thirties in search of a humanistic and regionally-appropriate architecture. Asplund firmly believed these qualities inhered in *both* modern and traditional architecture. This house skillfully incorporated elements of the Swedish vernacular along with the rationalism of modern architecture. It shows just how diverse modern architecture in the 1930s could be.

Looking onto the small inlet and the village of Stennäs, 40 miles southwest of Stockholm, this single-story house is almost hidden at the foot of a great granite bluff, an apparently unremarkable house in the countryside. Upon closer examination, however, the house reveals its meticulous conception, from site planning down to window details. The entry foyer is located at the south end of the terrace. From it, one stair leads to the kitchen at the north end (towards the bluff), while another descends to the south, into the living space with its stunning view. Asplund avoided the monotony of many single-level houses by skillfully following the gentle slope from the granite bluff to the inlet with four different levels. A long 6.2 m-wide "tail" then opens out onto the "head": a 7.5 m-wide living room. Asplund cranked the peaceful space 8 degrees, thereby optimizing the view and introducing a dynamic diagonal axis at the hearth. The strong influence of farmhouse architecture appears in the organically-shaped fireplace, the most symbolic element of this house. Similarly, wood, brick, and stone were used according to an original consideration of their function and tactile effect. Asplund's use of central heating, functionally-designed built-in furniture, and rationally-conceived windows all express the spirit of modern architecture.

According to his Finnish contemporary Alvar Aalto, who was also trying to humanize modern architecture, Asplund gave birth to an architecture "that continues to employ the tools of the social sciences, but also includes the study of psychological problems – 'the unknown human' – in his totality." For Aalto, Asplund's work proved that "the art of architecture continues to have inexhaustible resources and means which flow directly from nature and the inexplicable reactions of human emotions." Today, even though 60 years have passed, the Asplund family continues to care lovingly for the house, maintaining both its original freshness and heartwarming character.

(TK)

アスプルンドが1937年に彼と家族のために建てたこの小さな夏の家は、近代建築と伝統の橋渡しという晩年におけるアスプルンドの取り組みが到達した一つの答えである。アスプルンドは、1930年に行われたストックホルム博覧会の会場デザインによって、北欧における近代建築運動の指導的建築家としての地位を確立するが、30年代の半ば頃から、純粋な機能主義的デザインを離れ、近代的精神と伝統的な建築が有する地域性や人間味を合わせもった建築のあり方を模索した。近代建築の合理的思考と、スウェーデンの農家の伝統が巧みに融合されたこの住宅は、30年代の近代建築がいかに多様であったかを物語っている。

ストックホルムの南西60kmに位置する人里離れた「ステナス」の小さな入り江に面し、剥き出しの花崗岩の崖に隠れるようにたつこの平屋の家は、一見、何の変哲もない地方の民家にしかみえない。しかし注意深くみるならば、配置計画から窓のディテールにいたるまで、きわめて綿密なスタディがなされていることがわかる。西側に面したテラスの南端に位置する玄関から中に入ると、北側（崖側）に台所へとつながる階段があり、南側には素晴らしい入り江の眺めが見渡せるリヴィング・スペースがある。アスプルンドは、崖から入り江に向かって緩やかに傾斜する敷地の性質を巧みに利用し、四つの微妙に異なる床レヴェルを設けることで、平屋の空間的単調さを回避した。基準となる台所のレヴェルから1.5m下がった位置にあるこのリヴィング・スペースは、残りの幅6.2mの細長い空間から西側にずれ、微妙に角度がつけられ、また幅が7.5mに拡張されている。その結果、窓から最も好ましい景色が望めると同時に、空間に広がりと独自の性格を与えている。この建物の最もシンボリックな要素である有機的な形態の白く塗られた石造の暖炉、あるいは木、煉瓦、石といった在来の素材の用い方は、伝統的な農家の影響を強く感じさせるが、その応用の仕方は機能性と人間の感覚を考慮したアスプルンド独自のものである。また、セントラル・ヒーティングの使用、機能的にデザインされた造り付け家具、合理的にデザインされた窓のディテールなどに、近代建築の精神が息づいている。

同じ頃、フィンランドで近代建築に地域性と人間らしさを回復しようと試みていたアルヴァ・アアルトは、「社会科学を引きつづき道具として用いながらも、全体として、精神的問題（知られざる人間）の研究も考慮した」より進んだ近代建築を生み出し、「建築芸術が、自然およびいまだ不可解な人間の感情という、潤沢な資源と方法を有しつづけることを証明した」として、アスプルンドの業績を高く評価した。60年以上経った現在も、この夏の家は、アスプルンドの家族が深い愛情をもって住みつづけ、建てられた当時の懐かしさと新鮮さを保ちつづけている。

(TK)

Opposite: View of the house and the open inlet from the top of the granite bluff, c. 1937. Above: View of the inlet through the southern living room window.

左頁：敷地北側の切り立つ花崗岩の上から、夏の家と広々とした入り江をみる、1937年頃。上：居間の南側の窓から入り江をみる。

pp. 204-205: Western view from the garden. Left top: View toward the south of descending gable roofs. Left bottom: East facade with steps to the upper living room. Opposite: Garden-side terrace and approach to entry foyer.

204～205頁：庭からみた西側全景。左上：北から南に降りてゆく切妻屋根。左下：エントランス・レヴェルの小さな居間への階段がある東側ファサード。右頁：庭側のテラスとメイン・エントランス。

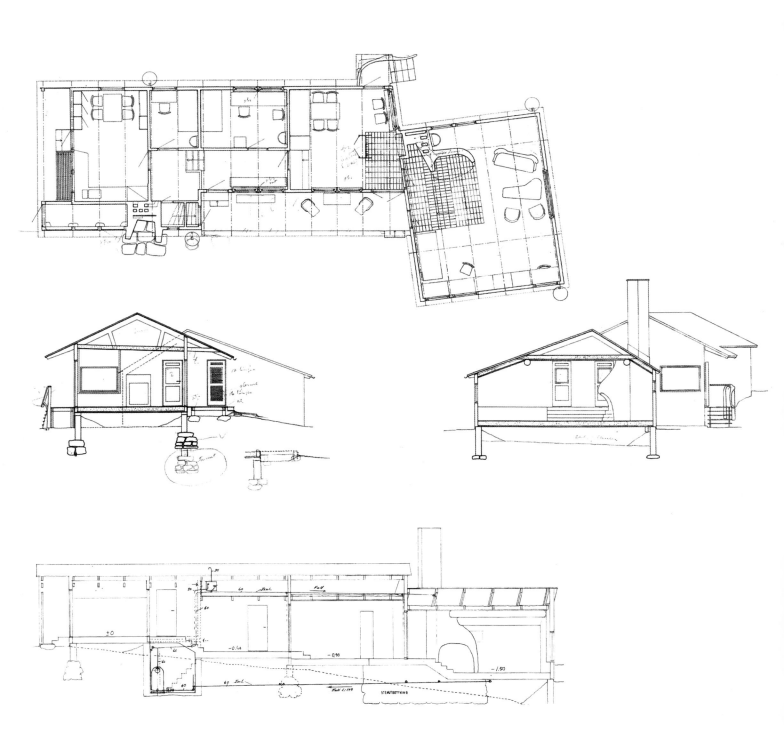

Top to bottom: Floor plan, cross
sections and longitudinal section.
Opposite: View of the east access
and the fireplace chimney in the
living space.

上から：平面図、短辺方向断面図、長辺
方向断面図。右頁：東側の出入り口。リ
ヴィング・スペースの暖炉の煙突がみえる。

Opposite: View of the terrace from
the living space. Above: View of the
west corner of the living space.
Below: Asplund and his wife in the
living space, 1937. pp. 212-213:
View of the living space with
fireplace.

左頁：リヴィング・スペースからテラス
をみる。上：リヴィング・スペース西側。
下：リヴィング・スペースでくつろぐア
スプルンド夫妻。1937年。212〜213
頁：リヴィング・スペース。暖炉のある
東側をみる。

*Left: Entry foyer and upper
living room. Opposite: Linked
passage toward the south along the
"tail."*

左：エントランス・ホールと小さな居間。
右頁：南側に向かって下る細長い空間に
沿う各室。

Gropius House
Lincoln, Massachusetts, USA 1938
Walter Gropius in collaboration with Marcel Breuer

グロピウス邸
米国、マサチューセッツ州、リンカーン　1938
ウォルター・グロピウス

Walter and Ise Gropius's home "was the first modern house to be built in the vicinity of Boston," according to longtime friend Sigfried Giedion. Gropius, director of the Bauhaus from 1919-1928, arrived in Boston in March 1937 to teach at the Harvard Graduate School of Design. He sought to create a home appropriate for his Bauhaus furniture and for the particular conditions of the New England context. Through the financial support of benefactor Mrs. James Storrow, the house was built to prove that modern architecture could take root on an idyllic New England country site: a hillock a half an hour from Harvard by car, within walking distance of Henry Thoreau's famous Walden Pond.

Gropius designed his home in collaboration with former Bauhaus student Marcel Breuer with the conviction that local New-England architecture was "entirely in (their Bauhaus) spirit in its simplicity, functionality, and uniformity." Gropius consequently used wood-frame construction, brick, and fieldstone to produce a version of the modern house based on traditional local practice. He assembled these materials into a compact home able to withstand harsh winters (record lows at minus 21°C) and hot summers. He sited the house at the top of a gentle slope surrounded by a large apple orchard for cooling summer breezes and a pleasant view of Mount Wachusett. Heeding the advice of Mrs. Storrow, Gropius sited the garage away from the house and closer to the main road, to reduce the need for snow removal. Trees were carefully selected for hardiness and to provide shade in the summer and color in the autumn. Further, stone retaining walls were built to create terraces preventing the invasion of weeds and insects from the surrounding fields.

Surprisingly livable, expansive spaces characterize this efficiently-designed four-bedroom house. The central entry hall ensures cross ventilation, with doors at both front and back, like many eighteenth-century homes in the region. Gropius reduced the number and length of corridors by using transitional space as living or workspace. His own study, for example, provided access to the living room, and the spiral stair leads directly to daughter Beate's bedroom. The freestanding angled glass block wall, a material rarely used in houses at the time, divides the study from the dining area, transmitting light through the house. The overhang on the south side was calculated to exclude the summer sun entirely, letting hot air rise through an opening between the overhang and the house wall. Further, Gropius used off-the-shelf standardized products such as industrial window and door hardware, chrome banisters, and commercial steel-plated wall sconces, all of which complemented Breuer's tubular steel Bauhaus furniture. Upstairs, ribbon windows admit morning sun and provide a spectacular view. The dimensions of the master bedroom suite precisely accommodate a king-size bed between two Breuer night tables. A transparent glass wall separates this space from the dressing room, allowing the Gropiuses to sleep in a cold environment and dress in a warmer one. Today, the house remains as the Gropiuses lived in it up until Walter's death in 1969. Ise Gropius bequeathed the home to the Society for the Preservation of New England Antiquities (SPNEA) and it was opened to the public in 1985 after her death in 1983. As she specified, the house now serves as an example of Gropius's contribution to modern architecture and its entire contents illustrate their modern, practical way of life.　　　　(KTO)

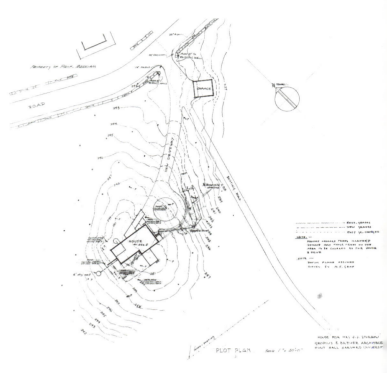

Top: Site plan. Above: Approach from the northeast. Opposite: View of the south facade with pergola eaves. Screened porch on the right in the back.

上：配置図。下：北東側のアプローチ。右頁：南側のファサード。手前上部にパーゴラのある庇が、右手奥に金網で囲われたポーチがみえる。

ウォルター・グロピウスとその妻イセの自邸は、彼らの長年の友人であったジークフリート・ギーディオンによれば、「ボストン近郊に建てられた最初のモダン・ハウス」であった。1919年から1928年までバウハウスの校長を務めたグロピウスは、ハーヴァード・グラデュエイト・スクール・オヴ・アートで教鞭をとるため、1937年3月にボストンへと移り住んだ。グロピウスはここで、彼が所有するバウハウス家具とニューイングランドの地域的文脈に適した住宅をつくろうと試みた。敷地はハーヴァードから車で30分のところにある小さな丘で、ヘンリー・ソローの著書を通して有名になったウォールデン・ポンドという名の池から歩いてすぐのところにあった。彼の後援者であるジェイムズ・ストロウ夫人の経済的支援を受けて建てられたこの住宅は、このような牧歌的なニューイングランドの田園地帯にも近代建築が根づくことを証明することとなった。

グロピウスは、地元のニューイングランドの建築は「その簡素さ、機能性、一貫性において、まったく（バウハウスの）精神をもっている」という確信にもとづいて、バウハウスで彼の教え子だったマルセル・ブロイヤーと共同で、この住宅をデザインした。伝統的な地元の施工技術にもとづいた近代住宅のモデルをつくろうと考えた彼は、白い下見板、バルーン構造と軽量木構造、煉瓦、粗石を用いた。そして、グロピウスはこれらの材料を、きびしい冬の過酷さ（摂氏マイナス21度まで下がる）と夏の暑さに耐えうるコンパクトな住宅にまとめあげた。この住宅の敷地は、夏の涼しいそよ風とワチュセット山の心休まる景色を考慮して、大きなりんごの果汁園に囲まれた緩やかな坂の頂部に定められた。ストロウ夫人のアドヴァイスに従い、雪かきの手間を減らすために、グロピウスはガレージを住宅から離れた道路の近くに置いた。樹木は、木の耐力、夏の日陰、秋の紅葉を念頭に注意深く選ばれた。さらに、高原のまわりの野原から侵入する雑草や昆虫を阻止するために、石造の擁壁が設けられた。

驚くほどに住みやすく広々とした空間が、この巧みにデザインされた4ベッド・ルームの住宅を特徴づけている。正面と裏手の両方にドアが設けられた中央の玄関ホールは、この地域に見られる18世紀の住宅と同じく、換気という点できわめて実用的である。また、移動空間を居室あるいは作業室として効果的に使うことによって、廊下の数と長さを削減している。たとえばグロピウスの書斎は、居間への通路でもあり、螺旋状の階段は、娘ベアットの寝室に直接的にアクセスしている。自立した構造のガラス・ブロック（当時住宅にはほとんど使われていなかった材料）の壁は、空間的には書斎とダイニングを仕切っているが、光は自由に通過することができる。南側の張り出しは、夏には日射を完全に部屋から遮断し、熱い空気が張り出しと住宅の壁の間を通って上昇するよう計算されている。さらにグロピウスは、ブロイヤーがデザインした鉄パイプのバウハウス家具に合わせて、工業用の窓とドア、入口に取り付けられたクロムめっきを施した手摺、市販の鋼板の障壁といった既製の規格化された製品を用いた。2階は、リボン窓から朝の日の光が入り、壮大な眺めが望める。主寝室の寸法は、ちょうどブロイヤーがデザインした二つのナイト・テーブルの間にキング・サイズのベッドに合うように計画され、またグロピウス夫妻が、寒い環境で就寝し、暖かい環境で着替えられるように、透明のガラスの壁がドレッシング・ルームと寝室を仕切っている。今日、この住宅は、グロピウスが1969年に亡くなるまで過ごしたそのままの状態で保存されている。イセ・グロピウスはこの家をニューイングランド古物保存協会（SPNEA）に遺贈し、1983年に彼女が亡くなった後、1985年から一般に公開されている。彼女が条件として明記したとおり、この住宅は現在、近代建築にたいするグロピウスの貢献を示す実例としての役割を果たし、この住宅が含むすべてのものから、彼らのモダンで実用的な生活を窺い知ることができる。　　　　　(KTO)

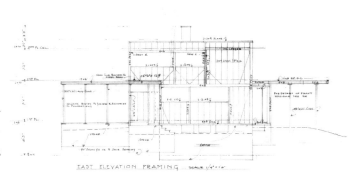

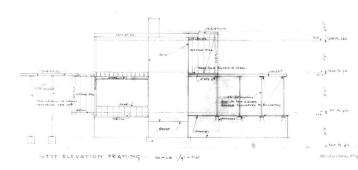

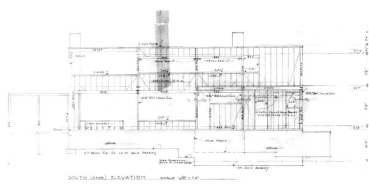

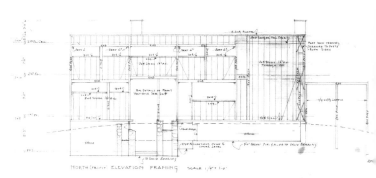

Above: Framing elevations. (top to bottom) East side, west side, south side, and north side. Opposite top: Ise Gropius on the roof deck, 1948. Opposite bottom: Walter and Ise Gropius in the screened porch, 1948.

上：軸組図。上から、東側、西側、南側、北側。右頁、上：ルーフ・デッキのイセ・グロピウス、1948年。下：金網で囲まれたポーチで憩う、グロピウスとイセ、1948年。

Above: North facade with canopied glass-block entry. Right: 1st floor plan. Opposite top: General view from the south. Opposite bottom: 2nd floor plan.

Legend of the 1st floor plan:
1) Entrance hall, 2) Coats,
3) Study, 4) Living room,
5) Dining room, 6) Toilet,
7) Maid's bath, 8) Maid's room,
9) Kitchen, 10) Pantry,
11) Screened porch, 12) Service porch

Legend of the 2nd floor plan:
1) Hall, 2) Bath, 3) Bath,
4) Dressing room, 5) Master bedroom, 6) Guest room,
7) Child's room, 8) Bed alcove,
9) Roof deck, 10) Sewing room.

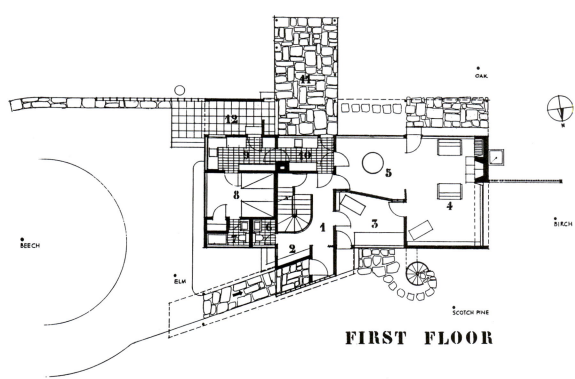

FIRST FLOOR

左頁、上：北側全景。庇のあるガラス・ブ
ロックを用いたエントランスがみえる。
左頁、下：1階平面図。上：南側全景。
左：2階平面図。
1階平面図凡例： 1）エントランス・ホ
ール、2）コート掛け、3）書斎、4）居
間、5）食堂、6）洗面室、7）使用人浴室、
8）使用人寝室、9）台所、10）配膳室、
11）金網で囲われたポーチ、12）勝手口
2階平面図凡例：1）階段ホール、2）浴
室、3）浴室、4）ドレッシング・ルーム、
5）主寝室、6）客室、7）子ども室、8）
子ども室寝室コーナー、9）ルーフ・デッ
キ、10）裁縫室

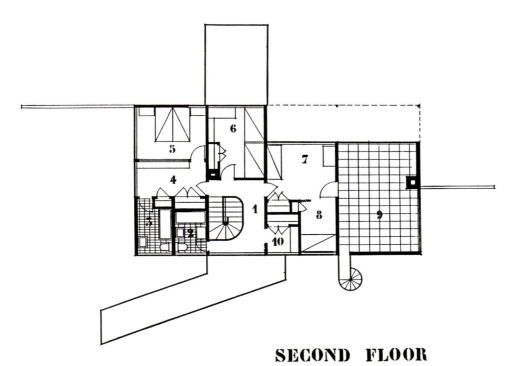

SECOND FLOOR

Above: Roof deck with the opening to the exterior spiral staircase on the north. Opposite: Detail of the western elevation with living room window.

上：ルーフ・デッキ。右手に北側の庭への螺旋階段の出入り口がみえる。右頁：居間西側のファサード構成。

*Above: Window on the west side of
the living room. Opposite top: View
of the living room toward the south
with screened porch beyond.
Opposite bottom: View of the living
room toward the southwest.*

上：居間西側の窓。右頁、上：居間南側。
窓から金網で囲われたポーチがみえる。
右頁、下：居間南西側をみる。

Above: View of the study looking toward the living room. Below: Dining room looking toward the living room. Opposite left: Glass block wall with glass counter in the dining room. Opposite right: Handle of the glazed living room door to the south garden.

上：書斎、居間側をみる。下：食堂。居間側をみる。右頁、左：食堂のガラス・ブロック壁とガラスの棚。右頁、右：居間から南側の庭へのガラス張りの扉の取っ手。

227

Opposite: Entrance hall staircase.
Above: Master bedroom and
dressing room. Below: Child's room
with access to the roof deck.

左頁：エントランス・ホールの階段室。
上：主寝室とドレッシング・ルーム。
下：子ども室。右手はルーフ・デッキへ
の出入り口。

House over the Brook
Mar del Plata, Argentina 1945
Amancio Williams

小川に架かる家
アルゼンチン、マル・デル・プラタ　1945
アマンシオ・ウィリアムズ

This bridge house, built over an existing brook in the verdure of the Argentinian landscape, embodies Williams' lifelong vision to create a floating architecture. As architect Emilio Ambasz has noted, "Amancio was always attracted by the idea of escaping from the force of gravity, first as a young aviator in the 1930s, and then as an inventor of architectural prototypes resembling flowers barely anchored to the ground by slender stems, with roots below ground in the memory of the past and the buildings themselves blossoming up above the ground." Designed for Williams' father, noted composer and musician Alberto Williams, this house consists of an elevated volume divided longitudinally in two parallel zones. The public zone—an open studio—faces north and wraps around the western end to include a piano area (the spiritual center of the house). The second zone contains a series of bedrooms facing south. Both sides of the building float within a forest of treetops.

This house creates both a synthetic and an abstract living unit. The reinforced-concrete structure includes a flat slab at the main level supported by a curved slab underneath. These two are connected by thin transverse walls. Two piers on the sides of the brook support the cantilevered ends of the upper slab and absorb part of the structure's horizontal thrust. Williams himself, his wife Delfina Gálvez, and two engineers constructed the house to precise tolerances. An error of under 1/2 cm in the structure and under 2 mm in most details resulted from more than 400 drawings, 430 days and nights of site supervision, and 120 trips to Mar del Plata.

Williams carefully planned the entry sequence to this structure, which functions literally as both bridge and house. As one proceeds from a dark entry and climbs the archway towards the light airy space of the main level, the "bridge" gradually disappears while the "house" comes into view. The living space seems especially high, with views of the treetops provided through careful use of the natural site. The parabolic shape of the lower slab almost mirrors the natural depression of the banks of the brook such that the distance from the living space to the brook is almost double the height actually climbed. Williams corresponded enthusiastically with Le Corbusier following the 1946 completion of this house, which recalls Le Corbusier's 1938 plan for Buenos Aires, in which artificial platforms were suspended above the ground. A relationship of mutual admiration developed between the two architects. Williams visited Le Corbusier in Paris in 1947 and subsequently served as the first site architect for Le Corbusier's Maison Curutchet. As critic Fernando Álvarez has concluded, "Doubtlessly, the bridge is what best reveals the ethical and practical dimension of engineering that Le Corbusier admired so much: it implies loyal, organic competence and solidarity between materials, forms and men, referring back to the origins of Humankind and its monuments without requiring confirmation from symbolic or even from abstract art." (KTO)

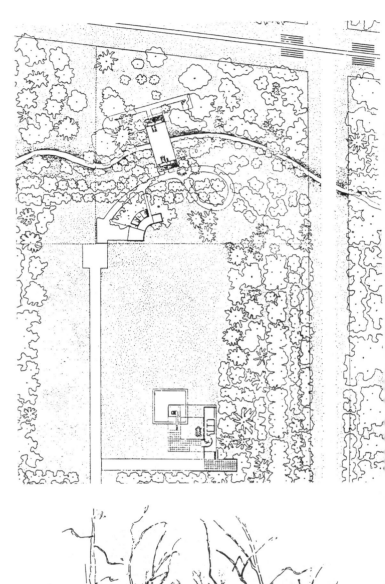

Above: Site plan. Below: Sketch by Amancio Williams. Opposite: Exterior view.

上：配置図。下：スケッチ。右頁：外観部分。

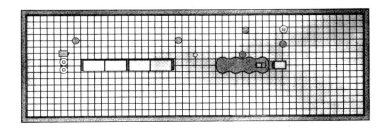

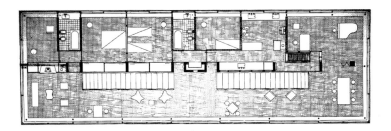

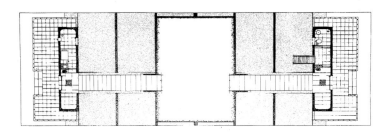

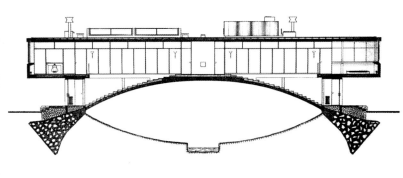

0   1   2   MTN.

pp. 232-233: General view. Above, top to bottom: Roof plan, 2nd floor plan, ground floor plan, and longitudinal section.

232〜233頁：全景。上から：屋根伏図、2階平面図、1階平面図、長辺方向断面図。

アマンシオ・ウィリアムズは、緑豊かなアルゼンチンのランドスケープのなかにある既存の小川を横断するように建てられたこの「橋の家」において、宙に浮いた建築を創造するという、生涯抱きつづけたヴィジョンを具現化した。建築家のエミリオ・アンバーツが述べているように、「アマンシオ・ウィリアムズは、常に、重力から逃れるという考えに魅了されていた。まずは1930年代に若い飛行家として、つづいて、過去の記憶とつながった地中の根と細い茎によってわずかに地面に固定され、地面から持ち上げられて開花するという、花に類似した建築プロトタイプの発明者として」。著名な作曲家であり演奏家でもあったウィリアムズの父、アルベルト・ウィリアムズのためにデザインされたこの住宅の居室は、地面から持ち上げられ、二つの平行する細長いゾーンに分割されている。パブリック・ゾーン（オープン・スタジオ）は北に面し、西端を包み込むことによってピアノが置かれた領域（この住宅の精神的中心）をこのゾーンのなかに組み込んでいる。もう一つのゾーンは、南に面した一連の寝室から構成される。そして北側も南側も、居室は森林の木々の梢に囲まれている。

この住宅は、総合的かつ抽象的な生活ユニットを生み出している。鉄筋コンクリート構造は、主要階のフラット・スラブとその下でこれを支えている放射状に曲げられたスラブから構成されている。この二つのスラブは、薄い隔壁によって連結されている。小川の脇にある二つの柱が片持ち梁のフラット・スラブの端を支え、水平方向の圧力の一部を吸収している。ウィリアムズ、妻のデルフィナ・ガルヴェス、そして二人のエンジニアは、きわめて精巧にこの住宅を施工した。誤差が構造部分で1/2cm以下、ほとんどのディテールで2mm以下という施工精度は、400以上におよぶ図面、430日間におよぶ日夜を通しての現場管理、120回におよぶマル・デル・プラタとの往復を通して達成された。

ウィリアムズは、文字どおり橋および住宅として機能するこの建物へのアプローチの仕方を注意深く計画した。薄暗い入口から、主要階の宙にふわりと浮いた開放的な空間に向かってアーチ状の階段を上ると、「橋」が次第に消えて「家」が視界にあらわれる。豊かな自然に囲まれた敷地を巧みに利用し、木々の梢が見渡せるように計画された居室は、とりわけ高い位置にあるように感じさせる。放射線状のスラブの形態は、小川の土手の自然な窪みをほぼ反射したような形であるため、居室から小川までの距離は、実際に上った高さのほぼ倍となっている。

この住宅は、ル・コルビュジエが1938年につくったブエノスアイレスのための計画のなかで彼が好んで用いた、地面から持ち上げられた人工的なプラットフォームを思い起こさせるが、この住宅が1946年に完成した後、ウィリアムズはル・コルビュジエと積極的に連絡をとりあった。次第に、二人の建築家はたがいに敬意を抱く間柄になり、ウィリアムズは1947年にパリのル・コルビュジエを訪れ、その後、ル・コルビュジエが設計したクルチェット邸の主任現場建築家を務めた。批評家のフェルナンド・アルヴァレスが述べているように、「ル・コルビュジエがかくも賞賛したように、橋は、まちがいなく工学技術の倫理的、実用的特質を最もよく表わしている。それは、象徴的な、あるいは抽象的な芸術によって確認するまでもなく、人類の源とそのモニュメントに照らし合わせれば、複数の材料、形態、そして人間の間の忠実さ、有機的な能力、そしてその結束を暗示している」。

（KTO）

Above: Western entrance porch.
Cantilevered dining area above.

上：西側のエントランス・ポーチ。上部
は片持ち梁で支えられた食堂。

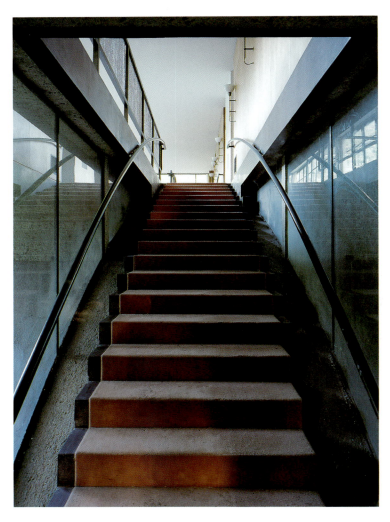

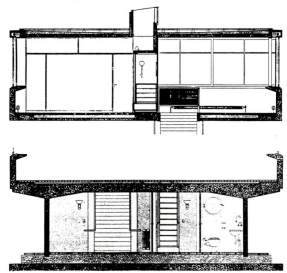

Right above: Staircase to the main floor from the west entrance. Right middle: Cross section through the main floor. Right below: Cross section through a pillar. Opposite: Open studio floor and stair to east entrance.

右上：西側のエントランスから主階への階段室。右中：主階短辺方向断面図。右下：柱を通る断面図。右頁：主階のスタジオと東側のエントランスへの階段をみる。

Above: View of living space/studio looking east. Right: Fireplace/section in the living space.

上：主階の居間とスタジオ。東側をみる。
右：居間の暖炉とその断面図。

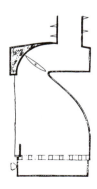

Above left: Bedroom corridor. Above right: Ladder access to the roof terrace. Left: West end piano area.

左上：寝室前の廊下。右上：屋上テラスへの梯子。左：西端のピアノ室。

Kaufmann Desert House
Palm Springs, California, USA 1946
Richard Neutra

カウフマン・デザート・ハウス
米国、カリフォルニア州、パーム・スプリングス　1946
リチャード・ノイトラ

Built for Pittsburgh department store owner Edgar J. Kaufmann just after WW II, this house was designed as a man-made pavilion for observing and living in close proximity to the desert. Kaufmann had also commissioned Frank Lloyd Wright to design "Fallingwater" (1936) as his home at Bear Run, Pennsylvania, but now "sought a greater feeling of lightness and openness" from Neutra for his winter vacation house for his family and up to four guests. Neutra designed a "four-quarter plan" formed by intersecting axes radiating from the central living/dining space. The four spokes of the resulting pinwheel contained the owner's private wing, a guest wing connected by an outdoor terrace, a service wing, and a garage. Here he pushed the limits of interior space by expanding centrifugally to the landscape and through the use of floor-to-ceiling glass openings. Neutra designed overhangs to provide shade and reduce glare, enhancing the view from the interior. The pool, not only a recreational asset, also intensified the view from the interior through its constantly changing reflections of the sky and clouds.

Using the latest industrial materials of the time, Neutra also thought of this house "as a forerunner of Man's approach to a design solution for a rocket station on the moon." Climbing the exterior stair adjacent to the living room, one reaches the "Gloriette," a raised deck with a 360-degree view of the rugged mountains and desert surrounding Palm Springs. This space was equipped with a fireplace and attached dumbwaiter, banquettes, hand-rubbed redwood slatted floors, and an adjustable aluminum louvered screen wall, providing the feeling of both an open porch and a snug, enclosed shelter. It can also evoke the feeling of floating, described by an early critic as "a ship riding on rocks and sand."

While Neutra's original vision of this landmark house was permanently captured in the legendary photographs of Julius Schulman, the house underwent tragic changes in subsequent decades, before being recently reborn. The successive owners enclosed integral open spaces, covered the roof with bulky air conditioners, and replaced the original polished white concrete floor with terrazzo. The previous owners had also decorated the house in themes ranging from a faux French Regency living room to an English garden bedroom. Through the painstaking efforts of the current owners Brent Harris, his architectural historian wife Beth Harris, and the design-build architectural firm of Marmol and Radziner, the house has been restored to its original conception. Using the restoration philosophy devised by the Harris', the restoration architects removed cumulative changes and replaced them with original finishes, including hand-applied mica glaze on plaster walls and birch-veneer cabinets, in a process that took more than five years. Still a retreat for its current owners and their children, Neutra's masterwork is now livable year round, through more felicitous changes such as a concealed heating and cooling system.

(KTO)

ピッツバーグのデパートのオーナー、エドガー・J・カウフマンのために第二次世界大戦直後に建てられたこの住宅は、砂漠に接近して生活し、観察するための人工的なパヴィリオンとしてデザインされた。カウフマンは、ペンシルヴェニア州ベア・ランの自宅として「落水荘」(1936)の設計をフランク・ロイド・ライトに依頼したが、今度は、彼の家族とゲストが四人まで冬の休暇を過ごせる別荘として、ノイトラに「よりいっそうの明るさと開放性を感じさせるものを求めた」。ノイトラは、中央のダイニング/リヴィング・スペースから四方に広がる二つの軸線の交差によって形成される「4/4プラン」を考案した。風車の形をした平面から生じた四つのスポークは、オーナー棟、外部のテラスと連結したゲスト棟、サーヴィス棟、そしてガレージから構成されている。ノイトラは、床から天井までの高さをもつガラス張りの開口を使うことによって、中心から外部のランドスケープへと内部空間の境界を押し広げた。また彼は、日陰をつくり、光の照り返しを少なくするための庇を設け、内部から見たランドスケープの眺めの素晴らしさをよりいっそう強調した。さらに、プールは単にレクリエーションのためだけでなく、空と雲の絶え間ない移り変わりを反射することによって内部からの眺めをより劇的なものとする役割も果たした。

当時の最先端の工業材料を使い、ノイトラはこの住宅を「月面のロケット・ステーションのデザインを考え出す人類の取り組みにおける先駆的仕事」と考えた。居間に隣接した外部階段を上ると、まわりを取り巻くパーム・スプリングスのでこぼこした山と砂漠の景色を360度見渡すことができる宙にもちあげられたデッキ、「グロリエッテ」へと導かれる。暖炉と食器用の小型エレヴェータ、アメリカスギの小割板張りの床、調節可能なアルミニウムのルーヴァー・スクリーンの壁といった設備が整ったこの空間は、屋外ポーチのようにも、心地よい閉じられたシェルターのようにも感じられる。さらに、批評家が「岩と砂の上を走る船」と描写したように、このデッキは宙に浮いているような感覚を起こさせた。

ノイトラがこの画期的な住宅にたいして抱いていたヴィジョンは、ジュリアス・シュールマンの伝説的な写真によってとらえられているが、この住宅は最近再生されるまでの数十年の間に悲劇的な変化を経験した。この住宅を引き継いだオーナーたちは、重要なオープン・スペースの多くを塞ぎ、屋根を巨大な空調機械で覆い、磨き上げられた白いコンクリートの床をテラゾーで覆った。彼らはまた、この家をフランス帝政風の居間から英国庭園風のベッドルームまで、あらゆるスタイルで装飾した。しかしながら、現在のオーナーであるブレント・ハリスと建築史家である妻のベス、そしてマーモルとラジナーが主宰する建築事務所の不断の努力によって、ハリス夫妻の修復哲学にもとづきながら、この住宅はオリジナルのコンセプトが意図した状態に修復された。設計・施工を担当した修復建築家は、5年の歳月をかけて増改築された部分を取り除き、マイカでつや出ししたプラスターの壁、樺合板のキャビネットなど、オリジナルと同様の仕上げを施した。現在のオーナーとその子どもたちの別荘として機能しながら、外から見えないように工夫された冷暖房システムをはじめとするより適切な改良によって、ノイトラの名作は、今では一年を通して住むことができる。

(KTO)

*Above: View of the entrance from
the south.*

上：エントランスへのアプローチ。南側
からみる。

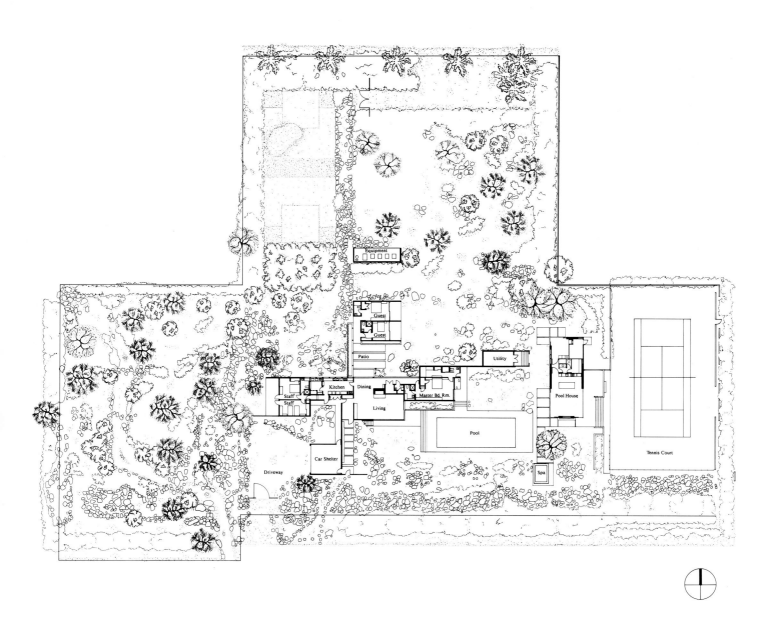

Equipment

Guest

Guest

Patio

Utility

Pool House

Staff

Staff

Kitchen

Dining

Master Bd. Rm.

Living

Tennis Court

Car Shelter

Driveway

Pool

Spa

Opposite: Site plan. Above: View of house and 2nd level "Gloriette" (observation deck) from southeast.

左頁：配置図。上：主棟。南東側からプール越しにみる。左手に 2 階の展望デッキ「グロリエッテ」がみえる。

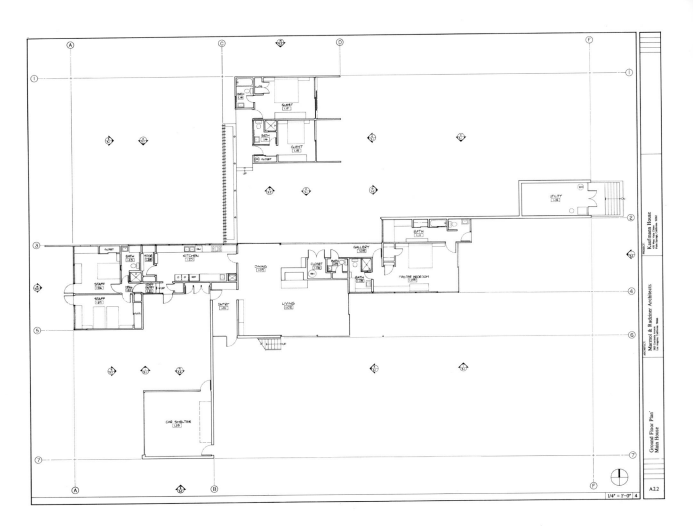

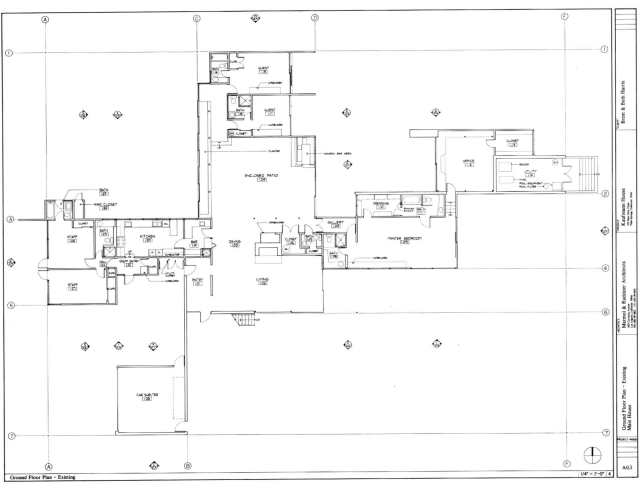

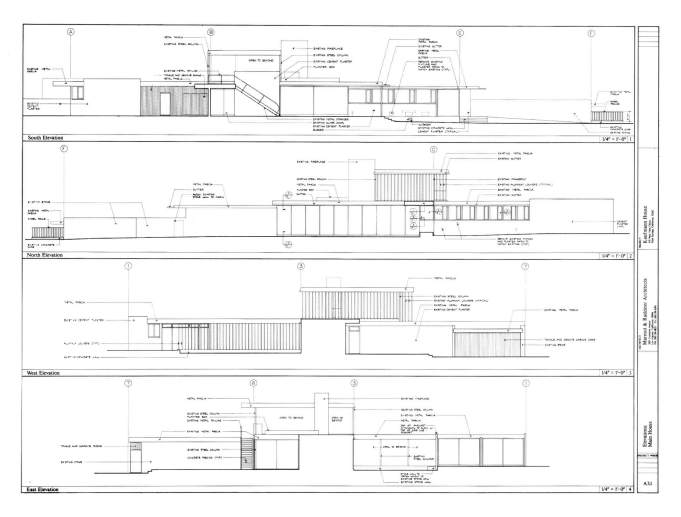

South Elevation   1/4" = 1'-0"   1

North Elevation   1/4" = 1'-0"   2

West Elevation   1/4" = 1'-0"   3

East Elevation   1/4" = 1'-0"   4

Kaufmann House

Marmol & Radziner Architects

Elevations
Main House

A3.1

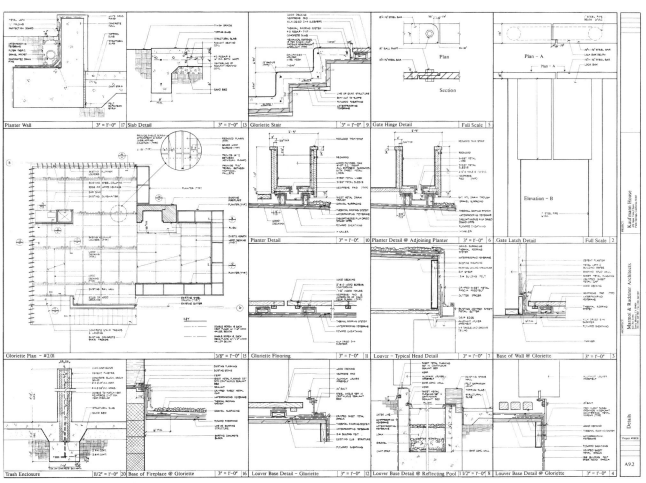

Planter Wall   3" = 1'-0"   17   Slab Detail   3" = 1'-0"   13   Gloriette Stair   3" = 1'-0"   9   Gate Hinge Detail   Full Scale   5

Gloriette Plan - #2.01   3/8" = 1'-0"   15   Planter Detail   3" = 1'-0"   10   Planter Detail @ Adjoining Planter   3" = 1'-0"   6   Gate Latch Detail   Full Scale   2

Trash Enclosure   11/2" = 1'-0"   20   Gloriette Flooring   3" = 1'-0"   11   Louver - Typical Head Detail   3" = 1'-0"   7   Base of Wall @ Gloriette   3" = 1'-0"   3

Base of Fireplace @ Gloriette   16   Louver Base Detail - Gloriette   3" = 1'-0"   12   Louver Base Detail @ Reflecting Pool   11/2" = 1'-0"   8   Louver Base Detail @ Gloriette   3" = 1'-0"   4

Kaufmann House

Marmol & Radziner Architects

Details

A9.2

p. 244, top: Ground floor plan after restoration. p. 244, bottom: ground floor plan before restoration. p. 245, top: Elevations of restored design. (from top) South elevation, north elevation, west elevation, east elevation. p. 245, bottom: Details. Left: Exterior view of the southeast corner of the master bedroom with desert mountains in the background. Opposite top: Covered passage of entry on the left. "Gloriette" observation deck is seen above the entrance. Opposite bottom: Night view of the living room.

244頁、上：修復後の平面図。244頁、下：修復前の平面図。245頁、上：修復後の立面図。（上から）南側立面図、北側立面図、西側立面図、東側立面図。245頁、下：修復のための詳細図。左：主寝室の東南側のコーナーと背後に砂漠の山並み。右頁、上：エントランスへの屋根で覆われた通路。エントランスの上に展望デッキ「グロリエッテ」がみえる。右頁、下：居間夜景。

Above: View toward the swimming pool from the living room. Opposite: Night view from the poolside of the master bedroom on the right and living room on the left.

上：居間からプールをみる。正面はプール・ハウス。右頁：プールサイド夜景。右手が主寝室、左手が居間。

pp. 250-251: "Gloriette" observation deck. View toward the west of the desert landscape through aluminum louvers. Above: Living room with the dining on the left. Right: View toward the guest wing beyond the patio.

250〜251頁：展望デッキ「グロリエッテ」。アルミニウム製のルーヴァーを通して砂漠の風景をみる。上：居間。左手は食堂。右：食堂からパティオを越えて客室棟をみる。

Above: View of the living room from the east. Left: View of the mountain landscape from the master bedroom.

上：東側からみた居間。左：主寝室の窓
から山々をみる。

Maison Curutchet
La Plata, Argentina 1949
Le Corbusier

クルチェット邸
アルゼンチン、ラ・プラタ　1949
ル・コルビュジエ

In designing this four-level house and clinic for Dr. Pedro Curutchet and his family, Le Corbusier took particular note of the sun orientation of this panoramic site facing a verdant park and boulevard in La Plata, a nineteenth-century planned town. Although he never visited the site, Le Corbusier had been to Argentina in 1929 to deliver a series of lectures on everything from city planning to furniture design, lectures later published as *Précisions*. During this visit, he noted that the Argentinean sky "is unlimited, as sparkling by day as by night with a transparent blue light or with myriads of stars, it spreads to all four horizons." While representing only a small commission, this urban dwelling allowed Le Corbusier to address the South American context in a design project that could potentially promote his urban proposals for Buenos Aires. Built on a site surrounded by party walls on three sides and cut at a 60-degree angle by its boulevard, this house contrasted with the surrounding Neo-classical buildings, creating a framework for enjoying the landscape.

Planned twenty years after the Villa Savoye, Maison Curutchet was designed during Le Corbusier's reflective period, when he integrated old and new architectural postulates from previous work. Using characteristic elements—*pilotis*, free-plan, free facade, strip windows, roof garden, and ramps ingeniously providing individual access to the residence and clinic—he placed the clinic in the lower front quadrant of the site, with the residence and "suspended garden" on the third and fourth evels. Like Maison Cook, his "cubic house" of 1925, the Maison Curutchet is based on a four-square plan with a fireplace at its center. The facade was laid out using regulating lines, but with the mathematical precision of the "*Modulor*" proportions he developed during World War II. In contrast to his Parisian villas from the 1920s, Le Corbusier here incorporated reinforced-concrete sunscreens (*brise-soleils*) and an elevated parasol roof

to modulate the South American sun and breeze. These screens not only reduce the amount of direct sunlight hitting the fully glazed "*pan de verre*" facades, but also manipulate the perception of frontal depth through multiple layers of built form.

Le Corbusier's architecture of the promenade lies behind the solid front door, set in a facade simply defined by a wire mesh fence. The poetic power of his design unfolds as one ascends the ramp, encountering contrasting spaces of light and shade, interior and exterior. While the ramped passage provides access to both the clinic and residence, the family's activities above were kept completely private by means of translucent glass, and by the depth of the *brise-soleil* frame. Entering the residence by a rear stair (which was reconfigured by site architect Amancio Williams, with Le Corbusier's approval), one enters a 2.26 m high living space that opens out to a double height interior and a 4.7 m high canopy roof, framing the green view. In fact, dining, bedrooms, and lower clinic were all ingeniously oriented toward the modulated sun and green. Despite being one of the most beautiful, poetic, and spatially dramatic houses designed by Le Corbusier, Maison Curutchet has until recently been one of his least known. While designed in 1949, construction under site architect Amancio Williams did not begin until 1951, and was not completed until 1954, due to a number of personal difficulties. After six arduous years of construction, Maison Curutchet was inhabited by its owners for little more than a decade due to unfortunate family circumstances. It was left virtually abandoned until 1987, and in 1988 underwent a major renovation.

However, more than half a century after its original design, its complex power can now be appreciated worldwide to provide lessons for dwelling in the 21st century.　　　　　(KTO)

Opposite: North street facade.

右頁：北側の通り側全景。

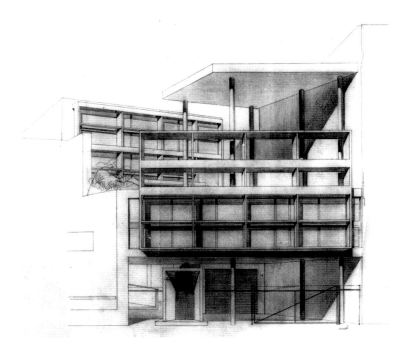

医師のペドロ・クルチェットと彼の家族のために建てられた、この4階建ての住宅および診療所をデザインするなかで、ル・コルビュジエは、緑に覆われた公園と19世紀に計画されたラ・プラタの大通りに面したこのパノラミックな敷地にたいする、太陽の動きにとりわけ注目した。ル・コルビュジエがこの敷地を訪れることは一度もなかったが、1929年にアルゼンチンを訪れ、都市計画から家具のデザインに至るまで幅広く語った一連のレクチュアを行っている。このレクチュアは、後に『プレシジョン』という表題で出版された。この訪問中、彼は、アルゼンチンの空は「際限なく、夜と同じくらい日中も、透明な青い光あるいは無数の星によってきらめき、四方の地平に広がる」と記している。規模の小さい仕事ではあったが、この住宅は彼が南米の文脈と実際に取り組む機会を与え、ル・コルビュジエがブエノスアイレスのために考案した都市計画案を実現する望みを与えた。三方を共有の壁で囲われ、大通りによって正面が60度に切り取られた敷地に建てられたこの住宅は、周囲の新古典主義様式の建物と対比をなし、ランドスケープを楽しむためのフレームワークとなった。

サヴォア邸の20年後に計画されたこのクルチェット邸は、ル・コルビュジエが新旧の建築的アイディアを統合しようと熟考していた時期にデザインされた。ピロティ、自由な平面、自由なファサード、水平連続窓、屋上庭園、そして住宅と診療所への個別のアクセスとなっている斜路、といったコルビュジエ特有の特徴的な要素を使いながら、診療所を建物の前方1/4の下半分に、住宅と「吊り庭園」を3階と4階に配置した。1925年に建てられたル・コルビュジエの「立方体の家」、クック邸のように、住宅は暖炉を中心とする四つの正方形平面から構成されている。ファサードは、幾何学的比例を用いてデザインされたが、ここではさらに、第二次世界大戦中に彼がつくりあげた「モデュロール」の数学的正確さが加わった。1920年代から彼がデザインしたパリのヴィラと異なり、南米の日射とそよ風を調節するために、彼は鉄筋コンクリート造の日除け（ブリーズ・ソレイユ）と、背の高いパラソル屋根を用いた。日除けの格子は、「パン・ド・ヴェーレ」、すなわちガラス張りのファサードへの直射日光を軽減するだけでなく、建物に複数の層を形成することによって奥行きにたいする認識を巧みに操作している。

ル・コルビュジエのプロムナード建築は、金網のフェンスによって簡単に形どられたファサードに設けられた堅固な正面ドアの背後に広がっている。斜路を上り、光と影、内部と外部が生み出す対比的な空間に足を踏み入れると、そこには彼のデザインがもつ詩的な力が満ちている。斜路は診療所と住宅双方へのアクセスとなっているが、半透明ガラスとブリーズ・ソレイユのフレームの奥行きによって、上階における家族の活動のプライヴァシーは完全に守られている。後部にある階段（ル・コルビュジエの許可を得て現場建築家のアマンシオ・ウィリアムズが変更した）を通って住宅に入ると、天井高2.26mのリヴィング・スペースがあり、そこからその2倍の天井高をもつ内部空間と、緑あふれる景色を縁どる高さ4.7mのキャノピーへと空間が開ける。ダイニング、ベッドルーム、そして下階の診療所はすべて、太陽の向きと緑あふれる景色を考慮して巧みに方向が決定された。

コルビュジエのデザインのなかでも最も美しく、詩的で、空間的に劇的な作品の一つであるにもかかわらず、最近まで、クルチェット邸は彼の作品のなかでも最も知られていない建物の一つだった。デザインは1949年にできあがっていたが、個人的な事情により、現場建築家のアマンシオ・ウィリアムズは1951年まで建設を開始せず、完成は1954年を待たねばならなかった。6年間におよぶ根気強い建設期間を経た後、不運な家庭事情のために、施主はクルチェット邸に10年余りしか住むことができなかった。その後1987年まで実質的に空き家と化していたが、1988年に本格的に修復が行われた。

ル・コルビュジエがデザインしてから半世紀以上経った今、21世紀の住宅に向けた様々な教訓を示すものとして、その複雑さに満ちた魅力は、世界的に再認識されるであろう。

（KTO）

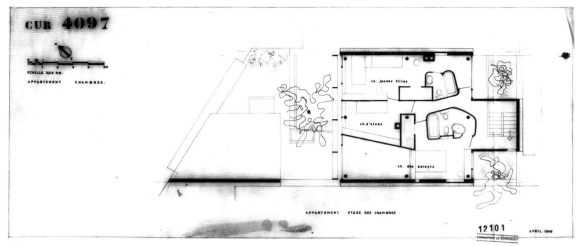

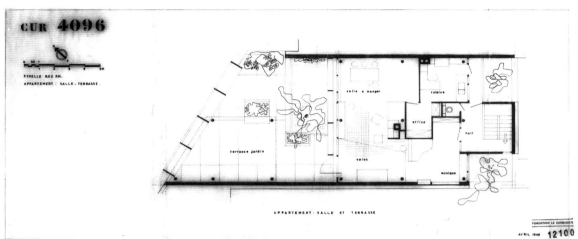

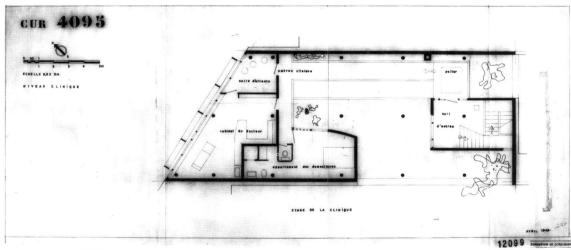

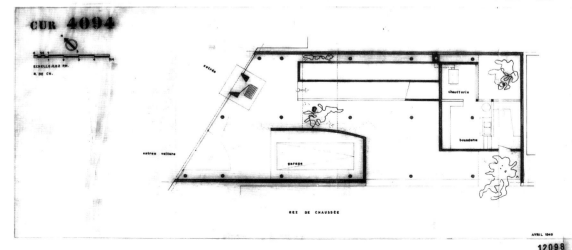

Opposite top: Perspective drawing from the street, 1949. Opposite, bottom left: Living room, c. late 1950s. Opposite, bottom right: Dr. Curutchet's consultation room, c. late 1950s. Right: Floor plans. (top to bottom) 3rd floor, 2nd floor, mezzanine floor, ground floor. [Note: Stairway not built as originally designed.]

左頁、上：北側の通りからみた透視図、1949年。左頁、左下：居間、1950年代後半。左頁、右下：医師クルチェット氏の診察室、1950年代後半。上から、3階平面図、2階平面図、中2階平面図、1階平面図。（階段室の設計はオリジナルとは異なる。）

Above left: Entrance. Above right:
Patio. View toward the entrance
from the southwest corner on the
ground level.

左上：通りからの入口。右上：パティオ。
１階南西の隅から入口方向をみる。

Above left: View of the ramp to the entrance of the residence. Above right: View of the ground-level patio and ramp to the clinic entrance from the entry vestibule of the residence.

左上：住居部分入口への斜路をみる。右上：住居部分入口ホールからパティオと診療所への斜路をみる。

pp. 260-261: View of the ramp toward ground-level entrance and 2nd-level entry to clinic. Opposite: View of the living room facade from suspended garden. Right: View toward the park and boulvard from the suspended garden with parasol roof. Bottom: Longitudinal sections along the ramps (left)/through the double-height suspended living room.

260〜261頁：パティオと斜路を見渡す。1階のエントランスと2階の診療所入口がみえる。左頁：吊り庭園から居間のファサードをみる。右：パラソル屋根で覆われた吊り庭園から北側の公園と大通り方向をみる。下：斜路沿いの長辺方向断面図（左）と居間の吹抜けを通る長辺方向断面図。

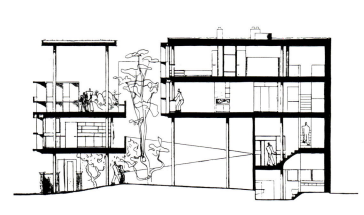

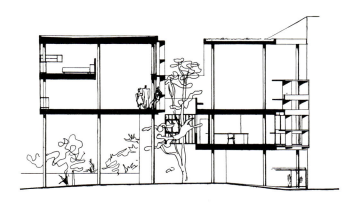

Opposite: View toward the suspended garden from the double-height living room. Above and below: Views of the living room with "pan de verre" facade.

左頁：2層分吹抜けの居間から吊り庭園をみる。上および下：パン・ド・ヴェーレのファサードをもつ居間。

Opposite: Double-height living room looking south. Above: View from the 3rd level master bedroom toward the park. The open study is on the right.

左頁：2層分吹抜けの居間。南側をみる。
上：3階主寝室から公園方向をみる。右手に居間上部の書斎がみえる。

Data /Credits
データ/クレジット

Hvitträsk

Design: 1901
Construction: 1901-1902
Original owners: Eliel Saarinen,
Herman Gesellius,
Armas Lindgren
Present owner:
Hvitträsk Museum
Address: Hvitträsk Museum,
Hvitträsk, 02440 Finland
Tel: 358.9.221.9230
Fax: 358.9.297-6293
Drawings (pp. 20-21) and
photograph (p. 26): Hvitträsk
Foundation, Museum of Finnish
Architecture
Portrait: Hvitträsk Museum
**Photographs except the
above**: Kenichi Suzuki,
Shinkenchiku-sha

Robie House

Design: 1908-1909
Construction: 1909-1910
Site: 60 feet x 210 feet
Original contractor:
Harrison Barnard
Owners: Frederick Carlton Robie
Subsequent owners: David Taylor
(1911-1912), Marshall Wilber
(1912-1926), Chicago Theological
Seminary(1926-1957); Webb and
Knapp, inc. (1957-1963);
University of Chicago(1963-).
Private residence until 1926.
Construction: load-bearing
brick and platform frame
modified by steel members;
limestone sills.
[wood-frame floors, and standard
balloon framing]
Restoration: 1992-2007
Restoration supervisor:
John Thorpe
Present owner:
University of Chicago
Present Occupant: University of
Chicago Alumni Association
Address: 5757 South Woodlawn
Avenue, Chicago, Illinois 60637
USA
Tel: 708-848-1976; http://www.
swcp.com/FLW
Drawings (pp. 34, 36, 40):
The drawings of Frank Lloyd
Wright are Copyright ©The Frank
Lloyd Wright Foundation,
Scottsdale, AZ, USA
Photographs: Shigeo Ogawa,
Shinkenchiku-sha

Scheu House

Design: 1912
Construction: 1912-1913
Original owner:
Dr. Gustav and Helen Scheu
Site area: 800 m²
Construction: Masonry-and-
wood-beam structure finished
with stucco; with steel and iron
reinforcing beams.
Renovation architects:
Heinz Neumann and Sepp Frank
Drawings (pp. 46, 48, 54):
Technische Universität Wien,
Institut für Hochbau
Martin Palmrich, Gustav
Pichelmann and Gerhard
Riedling, Vienna.
Photographs: Shigeo Ogawa,
Shinkenchiku-sha

Une Petite Maison

Design: 1923
Completion: 1924
Original owner: George and
Marie Jeanneret (Le Corbusier's
parents)
Total area: 60 m²
Site Area: 300 m²
Present owner:
Foundation Le Corbusier
Address: 21 route Lavaux,
Corseaux-Vevey, Lausanne
Open: Wednesday afternoon
from 2:00-6:00 except
December - February.
Tel: 52 78 61 to arrange for visits
during the winter months.
Drawings (p. 66): ©FLC 9376 and
9368: ©FLC L2 (4) 1-190/ADAGP,
Paris & SPDA, Tokyo, 2000
Photographs: Shigeo Ogawa,
Shinkenchiku-sha

Rietveld Schröder House

Design: 1923
Completion: 1924
Original owner: Truus Schröder
Renovation: Bertus Mulder
Address:
Prins Hendriklaan 50, Utrecht
Appointments:
31.(0)30 2362362
Drawings (pp. 96, 100-101):
Bertus Mulder/Michiel Oort,
Architects
Histrical photograph (p. 94):
Centraal Museum, Utrecht
**Photographs except the
above**: Kenichi Suzuki,
Shinkenchiku-sha

How House

Design: February-March 1925
Completion: September 1925
Area: 2772 f² (258 m²)
Construction:
Reinforced concrete; wood frame
Original owners: Dr. James and
Mrs. Eads How
Renovation: 1994
Restoration architect-builder:
Jeffrey Fink and Associates
Present owner:
Lionel March and Maureen Mary
Drawings (p. 114): Architectural
Drawing Collection, University
Art Museum, University of
California, Santa Barbara
Photographs: Shigeo Ogawa,
Shinkenchiku-sha

Melnikov House

Design: 1927
Completion:1929
Construction: Masonry with
stucco finish; two-way wooden
egg-crate lattice floors.
Site area: 720 m²
Total interior area: 236 m²
Original owner:
Konstantin Melnikov
Renovation: 1998
Present owner:
Viktor Konstantinovich Melnikov
and Lyudmila Konstantinovna
Melnikova
Address: 10 Krivoarbatski
Pereulok, Moscow
Drawings (pp. 122, 126),
photograph (p.126) and **portrait**:
Melnikov Family
**Photographs except the
above**: Kenichi Suzuki,
Shinkenchiku-sha

Tugendhat House

Design:
September-December 1928
Construction:
June 1929-November 1930
Building Company:
Maurice and Arthur Eisler.
Construction: Steel skeleton,
reinforced-concrete floors, steel
columns at 5 m centers. Internal
supports covered by chrome-
bronze shells; brick-panel walls;
loosely compressed peat slab
(Torfoleum) insulation. Yellow
travertine square slab-flooring,
white linoleum in living room.
Hot-air heating in main living
room, hot water heating pipes in
other rooms. "Tenesta" steel
windows.
Original owner: Fritz
Tugendhat (1895-) Grete Weiss
(1903-)
Renovation: 1969-1985
Present owner:
Museum of the City of Brno
Address: Cerno polni 45, Brno,
66224, Czech Republic
Open: Wednesday-Sunday,
10:00-18:00
Drawings (p. 152) :
Upper level plan [ink on tracing
paper, 22 1/4 x 34 1/2 inch (56.6
x 88 cm)]; Lower level plan [ink,
pencil on tracing paper, 24 1/2 x
38 1/2 inch (62.8 x 98 cm)].
The Mies van der Rohe Archive,
The Museum of Modern Art, New
York. Gift of the architect. ©1999
Photographs: Shigeo Ogawa,
Shinkenchiku-sha

Maison de Verre

Design/construction: 1928-1932
Design: Pierre Chareau with Bernard Bijvoît and Louis Dalvet.
Original owner: Doctor Jean and Madame Annie Dalsace
Restoration: 1985-1993
Restoration architect: Bernard Bauchet
Address: 31 Rue St. Guillaume, Paris, France
Drawings (pp. 171-172, 174-175): Courtesy of Kenneth Frampton
Photographs (pp. 170, 173-177): Centre Georges Pompidou Musée National d'Art Moderne Centre de Création Industrielle.
Photographs except the above: *Shinkenchiku-sha*

Dammann House

Design: 1930.
Completion: 1932
Design: Arne Korsmo with Sverre Aasland
Original owner: Axel Dammann
Present owner: Erling Kagge
Drawings (p. 182): Runé Sør-Reime, Copyright©1982-1999 Runé Sør-Reime. All rights reserved. Publication: *Byggekunst*
Portrait: NAM(Norsk Arkitekturmuseum)
Photographs: Makoto Yamamori, *Shinkenchiku-sha*

Schminke House

Design: 1932
Completion: 1933
Original owner: Fritz Schminke
Renovation: 1999 - 2000
Present owner: City of Löbau
Address: Kirshallee 1b, 02708 Löbau, Saxony, Germany
Drawings (pp. 192-193), **photographs** (pp. 190, 196) and **portrait**:
Stiftung Archiv der Akademie de Künst, Berlin/Hans Sharoun Archive
Photographs except the above: Shigeo Ogawa, *Shinkenchiku-sha*

Summer House

Completion: 1937
Original owner: Gunner Asplund
Present owner: Mr. Per Wahlman
Photographs, drawings (pp. 202, 208, 211) and **portrait**: ©Swedish Museum of Architecture
Photograph (p. 202), **drawings of the plan, cross section** (p. 208) and **portrait** : Unknown in Swedish Museum of Architecture
Drawing of the longitudinal section (p. 208):Hjertén, Thomas, Swedish Museum of Architecture
Photograph (p. 211): Feininger, Swedish Museum of Architecture
Photographs except the above: Makoto Yamamori, *Shinkenchiku-sha*

Gropius House

Design: 1937-1938
Completion: 1938
Design: Walter Gropius in collaboration with Marcel Breuer
Total square footage: 2,300
Original owner:
Walter and Ise Gropius
Builder: Casper J. Jenney
Construction: Fieldstone and mortar foundation walls; diagonally-braced wood frame floors, walls, ceilings.
Renovation: 1974, 1988-
Present owner: Society for New England Antiquities (SPNEA)
Address: 68 Baker Bridge Road, Lincoln, Massachusetts 01773 USA
Tel: 781.259.8098
Drawings (pp. 216, 218, 220-221): Courtesy of the Busch-Reisinger Museum, Harvard University Art Museums, Gift of Walter Gropius ©President and Fellows of Harvard College, Harvard University; First and second floor plans courtesy of the Society for New England Antiquities (SPNEA).
Photographs:
pp. 216, 220: Ken Tadashi Oshima; p. 219: Robert Damora, Courtesy of the Busch-Reisinger Museum, Harvard University Art Museums, Gift of Walter Gropius ©President and Fellows of Harvard College, Harvard University.
Photographs except the above: Seiichi Osawa, *Shinkenchiku-sha*

House over the Brook

Design: 1943
Completion: 1945
Original owner: Alberto Williams
Present owner: Juan Jose Lago
Address:
Mar del Plata, Argentina
Drawings (pp. 230, 234, 236, 238), **photograph** (p. 239) and **portrait**:
Amancio Williams Archives
Photographs except the above: Masao Nishikawa, *Shinkenchiku-sha*

Kaufmann Desert House

Design: 1946
Completion: 1946
Original owner:
Edgar J. Kaufmann
Interior area: 3200 f² (297 m²)
Restoration: 1992-1998
Restoration architect: Marmol & Radziner Architects, Santa Monica (Leo Marmol, Ron Radziner, principals; Chrisopher Shanley, project manager; Tim Day, Andrew Kraetzer, Spike Wolff, project architects); interior design: Marmol & Radziner Architects; landscape design: Eric Lamers, William Kopelk; general contractor: Marmol & Radziner Construction.
Present owner:
Brent & Beth Harris
Drawings (pp. 242, 244-245): Marmol & Radziner
Photographs: Shigeo Ogawa, *Shinkenchiku-sha*

Maison Curutchet

Design: 1949
Construction: 1949, 1951-55.
Collaborators:
Bernard Hoesli, Roger Aujame,
Site architects:
Amancio Williams (1st stage), Simon Ungers (2nd Stage), Engineer Alberto Valdes (3rd Stage)
Site: 9 m x 20 m.
Hot.: (168.5 m²) 180 m²
Covered area: 345 m²
Original owner:
Dr. Pedro Domingo Curutchet
Renovation: 1986-1987, Louis and Julio Grossman.
Present occupant: Superior Council of the Architects Association of the Province of Buenos Aires.
Address: Boulevard 53 No. 320-(1900) La Plata, Provincia de Buenos Aires, Argentina
Tel: (021)218032 fax: (021)822631; HYPERLINK mail-to:arq@capba.org.ar arq@capba.org.ar http://www.capba.org.ar
Drawings: ©FLC 12111 (p. 256), 12098-12101 (p. 257), and sections (p. 263) /ADAGP, Paris & SPDA, Tokyo, 2000
Photographs (p. 256) and **portrait**:
The Curutchet Collection, Frances Loeb Library, Harvard Design School
Photographs except the above: Masao Nishikawa, *Shinkenchiku-sha*

Born in Rantasalmi, Finland. Prolific career in Finland and the US spanned half a century. Studied painting at the University of Helsinki and architecture at the Polytechnic Institute, Helsinki, 1893-97. Partner with Herman Gesellius and Armas Lindgren, 1896-1905; Saarinen/Gesellius, 1905-07. Independent practice, 1907-37, and with son Eero, 1937-41, with Eero and Robert Swanson, 1941-47. Won second place in the Chicago Tribune Tower competition, 1922. Emigrated to the US, 1923. Director, 1925-32, President, 1932-50, and Director of the Graduate Department of Architecture and City Planning, 1948-50, Cranbrook Academy of Art, Bloomfield Hills, Michigan. Received numerous awards including Gold Medal, A.I.A. 1947 and Honorary Doctorates from the Karlsruhe Technical University, University of Michigan, Harvard, and Drake University. Major works include the Finnish National Museum, 1904-10 with Gesellius and Lindgren; Helsinki Railway Station, 1905-14; Cranbrook School for Boys, 1926-30; Cranbrook Academy of Art, 1926-41; Saarinen House, 1928-29; General Motors Technical Center, Warren, Michigan (with Eero and Smith, Hinchman and Grylls), 1945-1955. Publications include *The City: Its Growth, Its Decay, Its Future*, 1943.

Born in Richland Center, Wisconsin, USA, Wright sought to create an "organic architecture," and designed about one thousand structures, some four hundred of them built, through seventy years of practice. Entered the engineering school of the University of Wisconsin in 1884, leaving two years later for Chicago to briefly work for architect J. Lyman Silsbee and then the firm Adler and Sullivan from 1888-93. Private practice in Oak Park, IL, 1896-97; Chicago, 1897-1909; Spring Green, Wisconsin, 1911, Chicago, 1912; Taliesin II, 1914; Tokyo, 1915-20; La Jolla, California, 1928; Chandler, Arizona, 1928-29, 1933-38; Taliesin West, Scottsdale, Arizona, 1938-54. Masterworks include the Larkin Building, 1904; Unity Temple, 1907; Imperial Hotel, 1916; Fallingwater, 1936-46; Johnson Administration Building, 1937; Solomon R. Guggenheim Museum, 1957-66; and Marin County Civic Center, 1957-66. Major publications include *An Organic Architecture*, 1939; *The Natural House*, 1954: *The Living City*, 1958.

Born in Brno, Czech Republic (formerly Bruenn, Moravia) as the son of a stonemason. Educated at the Royal and Imperial State Technical College, Reichenberg, Bohemia, 1887-88; College of Technology, Dresden, 1890-93. Works little known outside of Austria during the Modern movement's formative years. Lived in the US working as a mason, floor-layer and dishwasher, 1893-96. Criticized the excesses of decoration in both traditional Viennese design and in the more recent products of the Vienna Secession and the Wiener Werkstätte; journalist for the *Neue Freie Presse*, Vienna, 1896-97. Founding director of Free School of Architecture, Vienna. Lived in Paris, 1922-28; Lecturer at the Sorbonne, 1926. Major works include Villa Karma, Clarens, Switzerland, 1906; Kärntner Bar, Vienna, 1906; Goldman Building, Vienna, 1910; Chicago Tribune Tower competition entry of a skyscraper in the form of a Doric column, 1922; Müller house, Prague, 1930. Seminal essays include "Ornament und Verbrechen (Ornament and Crime)," 1908; "Architektur," 1910.

Gottleib Eliel Saarinen
1873-1950

Frank Lloyd Wright
1867-1959

Adolf Loos
1870-1933

Architects
建築家略歴

ゴットレイブ・エリエル・サーリネン
1873〜1950

フランク・ロイド・ライト
1867〜1959

アドルフ・ロース
1870〜1933

フィンランドのランタサルミに生まれる。フィンランドおよび米国で展開した多彩な設計活動は半世紀に及ぶ。1893〜97年、ヘルシンキ大学で絵画を、ヘルシンキの工芸学校で建築を学ぶ。1896〜1905年にはH・ゲゼリウスおよびA・リンドグレンと、1905〜07年にはゲゼリウスとパートナーシップを組む。1907年に独立し、その後1937〜41年には息子のエーロと、1941〜47年にはエーロおよびロバート・スワンソンと協働する。1922年にシカゴ・トリビューン設計競技2位に入賞し、1923年に米国に移住。ミシガン州にあるクランブルック芸術アカデミーにおいて、1925〜32年にディレクター、1932〜50年に学長、1948〜50年にふたたびディレクターを務めた。1947年にAIAゴールド・メダルを受賞。また、カールスルーエ工科大学、ミシガン大学、ハーヴァード大学、ドレーク大学から名誉博士号を受けたほか、受賞多数。主な作品に、フィンランド国立博物館（ゲゼリウス、リンドグレンと共作、1904〜10）、ヘルシンキ中央駅（1905〜14）、クランブルック男子学校（1926〜30）、クランブルック芸術アカデミー（1926〜41）、サーリネン邸（1928〜29）、ジェネラル・モーター技術センター（エーロ、スミス、ヒンチマン、グリルスと共作、1945〜55）などがある。著書に『The City: Its Growth, Its Decay, Its Future』（1943）などがある。

米国ウィスコンシン州リッチランド・センターに生まれたライトは、70年に及ぶ活動を通して（およそ1000の建造物をデザインし、うち約400が実現）、「有機的建築」を創出しようと試みた。1884年、ウィスコンシン大学の工科学校に入学し、その2年後、1888年から1893年にかけてJ・ライマン・シルスビーおよびアドラー・アンド・サリヴァンの設計事務所で働くためにシカゴへ赴いた。1896〜97年にイリノイ州オーク・パーク、1897〜1909年にシカゴ、1911年にウィスコンシン州スプリング・グリーン、1912年にシカゴ、1914年にタリアセンII、1915〜20年に東京、1928年にカリフォルニア州ラ・ホーヤ、1928〜29年および1933〜38年にアリゾナ州チャンドラー、1938〜54年にアリゾナ州スコッツデールのタリアセン・ウエストで設計活動を行った。主な代表作に、ラーキン・ビルディング（1904）、ユニティ教会（1907）、帝国ホテル（1916）、落水荘（1936〜46）、ジョンソン・ワックス本社ビル（1937）グッゲンハイム美術館（1957〜66）、マリン郡庁舎（1957〜66）がある。著書に『An Organic Architecture』（1939）、『ライトの住宅：人間、自然、建築』（1954）、『ライトの都市論』（1958）がある。

石工の息子として、チェコ共和国ブルノ（かつてのモラヴィア、ブルーエン）に生まれる。1887〜88年、ボヘミア、ライフェンベルクの帝国工科大学、1890〜93年、ドレスデン工科大学で教育を受ける。彼の建築は、近代運動の形成期にはオーストリア国外ではほとんど知られていなかった。1893〜96年、米国に滞在し石工、床材積み、皿洗いとして働く。ロースは、伝統的なウィーンのデザインおよび、同時代のウィーン・ゼツェッションやウィンナー・ヴェルクシュタットによる装飾過多な作品を批判した。1896〜97年、『ノイエ・フライエ・プレッセ』紙の記者を務める。ウィーンの建築自由学校の初代校長。1922〜28年、パリに滞在。1926年にはソルボンヌで講師を務めた。代表作に、ヴィラ・カルマ（スイス、クラレンス、1906）、ケルントナー・バー（ウィーン、1906）、ゴールドマン・ビルディング（ウィーン、1910）、シカゴ・トリビューン・タワー設計競技案（ドリス式の円柱をかたちづくったスカイスクレーパー、1922）、ミュラー邸（プラハ、1930）などがある。論文に「装飾と罪悪」（1908）、「建築」（1910）などがある。

Born in La Chaux de Fonds, Switzerland, Charles-Edouard Jeanneret-Gris was a tremendously prolific modern master as an architect, urbanist, designer, painter, sculptor and writer. Studied engraving at the School of Applied Arts, La Chaux-de-Fonds, 1900-05. Worked under Josef Hoffman, 1907; August Perret and Peter Behrens, 1910. Emigrated to France in 1917 and adopted the name Le Corbusier in 1920. Through his private practice from 1917-65, he produced more than 32,000 architectural and urbanistic drawings and plans with almost 400 projects, 300 paintings, and more than 70,000 drawings and other designs. Worked in partnership with his cousin Pierre Jeanneret, 1922-40 and collaborated with architect/designer Charlotte Perriand, 1927-29. Founder-Editor with Amédée Ozenfant and Paul Dermée, *L'Esprit Nouveau*, 1919-25. Founder Member, CIAM, 1928. Major projects include Villa Savoye, 1929-31; Unité d'habitation, Marseille, 1946-52; Notre-Dame-du Haut Chapel, Ronchamp, 1950-55. Profoundly influential publications include *Vers une architecture*, 1923; *Urbanisme*, 1925; *L'Art décoratif d'aujourd'hui*, 1925, and *Précisions sur un etat présent de l'architecture et de l'urbanisme*, 1930.

Born and died in Utrecht. Worked in his father's cabinet-making business, 1899-1906. Studied architectural drawing with architect P. Houtzagers, Utrecht, 1908-11; architecture with P.J. Klaarhamer, 1911-15. In private practice as a cabinet-maker, 1911-19; architect 1919-60. Collaborated on architectural and interior projects with Mrs. Truus Schröder-Schrader, 1921-64. Teaching posts include instructor at Academie voor Baukunst, Amsterdam 1942-58. Member with Van Doesburg, Huszar, Oud, and Wils, de Stijl Group, 1919-31; Founder-Member, CIAM, 1926-28. Major works include his Red-Blue Chair, 1918; Rietveld Schröder house, 1924; Garage and Chauffeur's Quarters (1927-28); Low-cost housing, Werkbund Sidlung, Vienna, 1930-32. Received an honorary doctorate from the Technical College, Delft, 1964.

Born in Vienna. Studied at the Imperial Technical Institute, 1906-11; graduated from the Academy of Arts in 1913 with degrees in architecture and engineering. Inspired to go to America in part through Otto Wagner, Adolf Loos, and the Wasmuth Portfolio of F.L. Wright. Worked for Wright, 1918-21, and appointed superintendent of his Chicago Office in 1919. Moved to Los Angeles in 1920 to supervise construction of the Barnsdall "Hollyhock" House and established his own practice in 1921. Through a vast 40-year career of 330 buildings and projects, Schindler pioneered the use of tilt-up concrete slab construction and "Schindler frame" wood construction. Seminal works include his own King's Road house, 1921-22, and the Lovell Beach house, 1926, Newport Beach, California.

Born in Moscow, Konstantin Stepanovich Melnikov was one of the major innovators of early Soviet architecture. Initially studied painting at the Moscow School of Painting, Sculpture and Architecture in 1905 and then architecture, 1912-17. Developed a new city plan for Moscow after the 1917 Revolution. Taught at the first faculty of architecture at Vkhutemas, the Soviet parallel to the Bauhaus, 1921-23. Colleague with Vladimir Tatlin. Received international acclaim for his design of the Soviet Pavilion at the 1925 Paris Exposition des Arts Décoratifs. A majority of his architectural projects were workers clubs including Rusakov factory workers' club, Moscow, 1927; Svoboda (now Gorkii) factory workers' club, 1927-29. In 1937, he was banned from practicing architecture and subsequently independently pursued art in his own studio-home until his death.

Le Corbusier
1887-1965

Gerrit Thomas Rietveld
1888-1964

Rudolph Michael Schindler
1887-1953

Konstantin Stepanovich Melnikov
1890-1974

ル・コルビュジエ
1887〜1965

ヘリット・トマス・リートフェルト
1888〜1964

ルドルフ・ミハエル・シンドラー
1887〜1953

コンスタンティン・S・メルニコフ
1890〜1974

スイスのラ・ショー・ド・フォンに生まれた ル・コルビュジエ（本名、シャルル・エドゥ アール・ジャンヌレ・グリス）は、建築家、 都市計画家、デザイナー、画家、彫刻家、著 述家として、圧倒的な数の作品を創出した近 代の巨匠であった。1900〜05年、ラ・ショー・ ド・フォンの応用芸術学校で彫刻を学ぶ。 1907年にヨセフ・ホフマンのもとで、1910年にオ ーギュスト・ペレおよびペーター・ベーレンス のもとで働く。1917年にフランスに移住し、1920 年にル・コルビュジエを名のる。1917年から 1965年に及ぶ活動のなかで、32,000以上の建 築および都市の図面、約400のプロジェクト、 300点の絵画、そして7万点のその他のデザイ ンを描いた。1922〜40年、従弟のピエール・ ジャンヌレとパートナーシップを組み、1927 〜29年、建築家でありデザイナーであった シャルロット・ペリアンと共同でデザインを行 う。『レスプリ・ヌーヴォー』誌（1919〜25） をアメデ・オザンファンおよびパウル・デルメ とともに発行。1928年に設立されたCIAMの 創設メンバー。代表作に、サヴォア邸(1929〜 31)、ユニテ・ダビタシオン（マルセイユ、1946 〜52）、ロンシャンの教会（1950〜55）などが ある。著作には、『建築をめざして』（1923）、 『ユルバニズム』（1925）、『今日の装飾芸術』 (1925)、『プレシジョン』（1930）などがある。

ユトレヒトに生まれ、ユトレヒトで亡くなる。 1899〜1906年、父親の家具製作作業を手伝う。 1908〜11年、ユトレヒトの建築家、P・ホウツザ ガースのもとで建築製図を学び、1911〜15年、 P・J・クラールハマーのもとで建築を学ぶ。 1911〜19年、家具師として、1919〜60年、建 築家として働く。1921〜64年、建築および イ ンテリアのプロジェクトをトゥルース・シュ レーダー・シュラーダー夫人と共同で行う。 1942〜58年、アムステルダムのアカデミー・ フォール・バウクンストでインストラクター を務めるなど、建築教育にも携わった。1919 〜31年、ファン・ドゥースブルフ、アウト、ウィ ルスらとともにデ・スティル・グループのメン バーで、CIAMの創設メンバーでもあった。 主な作品に、レッド・ブルー・チェア（1918）、 リートフェルト・シュレーダー邸（1924）、シ ョーファーの家を含むガレージの改装（1927 〜28）、ヴェルクブント・ジードルングにお けるローコスト・ハウジング（ウィーン、1930 〜32）。 1964年、デルフト工科大学から名誉 博士号を授与される。

ウィーンに生まれる。1906〜11年、帝国工科 大学で学ぶ。1913年に芸術アカデミーを卒業 し、建築とエンジニアリングの学位を受ける。 オットー・ワグナー、アドルフ・ロース、ヴァ スムート社が出版したフランク・ロイド・ラ イトの作品集などから影響を受け、米国に渡 る。1918〜21年、ライトのもとで働き、1919 年にライトのシカゴ事務所長に任命される。 1920年、バーンズドール「ホリーホック」邸 の現場監理のためロサンゼルスに移り、1921 年に独立し同地で事務所を設立する。40年に 及ぶ活動を通じて330の建物とプロジェクト を手がけたシンドラーは、ティルトアップ・ コンクリート・スラブ工法および「シンドラ ー・フレーム」木造の先駆者となった。主な 作品に、自邸のキングス・ロードの家（1921 〜22）、ロヴェル・ビーチ・ハウス（1926）、 ニューポート・ビーチなどがある。

モスクワに生まれる。コンスタンティン・ステ パーノヴィッチ・メルニコフは、初期のソヴィ エトにおける最も革新的な建築家の一人だっ た。1905年にまずはモスクワの絵画・彫刻・ 建築学校で絵画を学び、つづいて1912〜17年 に建築を学んだ。1917年の革命の後、モスクワ の新しい都市計画をつくった。1921〜23年、 ウラディミール・タトリンらとともにソヴィ エトのバウハウスに相当するヴクテマスの建 築学科で教える。1925年のパリ装飾芸術博の ためにデザインしたソヴィエト館で国際的な 称賛を受ける。メルニコフの建築作品のほと んどは労働者クラブで、ルサコフ工場労働者 クラブ（モスクワ、1927）、スヴォボダ（現ゴ ルキ）工場労働者クラブ（1927〜29）。1937年 に建築活動を禁止された彼は、死ぬまで、自 宅のスタジオで芸術活動を行った。

Born in Aachen, Germany, Mies was one of the most influential architect/designer/educators in the twentieth century with works spanning two continents. Worked in the family stone-carving business, 1900-02. Apprenticed to architect and furniture designer Bruno Paul, 1905-07; Peter Behrens, 1908-11. Director of the Bauhaus 1930-33. Private practice, Berlin, 1911-14, 1919-37; Chicago, 1938-69. Director of Architecture, Illinois Institute of Technology, 1938-59. Co-founder, *G (Gestaltung)* magazine, 1921, First Vice-President, Deutscher Werkbund, Berlin, 1926-32 and director of the Werkbund exhibition *Weissenhofsiedlung*, Stuttgart, 1927 and the Werkbund section, "The Dwelling," at the Berlin Building Exhibition, 1931. Emigrated to the United States, 1938 and became a naturalized American citizen. Major projects include the German Pavilion, International Exposition, Barcelona, 1929; Lake Shore Drive Apartments, 1951, Farnsworth house, 1950; Crown Hall, IIT, 1956; Seagram Building, 1958, Nationalgalerie, 1968. Major publications include *Der moderne Zweckbau*, 1926 and *Mies van der Rohe* by Philip Johnson, 1947. Recipient of the American Institute of Architects Gold Medal, 1960.

Born in Bordeaux, France into a family of shipowners from Le Havre. Studied painting, music, architecture from 1900-08 at the Paris Ecole des Beaux Arts. Apprentice in furniture design at Waring and Gillow (1908-14). Established his own practice after the war in 1918. First commissioned for the remodeling of the apartment of Dr. and Mrs. Dalsace, which included the design of a set of original furniture exhibited the following year at the Salon d'Automne. Noted for innovative use of materials such as plywood, ebony, palm, and metal tubes. Associate with Bernard Bijvoet (1925-35). Commissioned to design the Maison de Verre in 1928. As one of the founders of the Union des Artistes Moderne (UAM) Chareau was noted for his nonacademic, uncompromising attitude. Moved to New York in 1940 where he designed a house for the painter Robert Motherwell.

Born in Oslo, Norway, Korsmo is remembered as one of the first functionalist Scandinavian architects. Educated at the Technical University, Trondheim, 1920-26. First established his practice with Sverre Aasland, 1929. His designs included architecture, furniture, stage sets, and industrial design. Instructor and subsequently Head of the Department of Interior Design, Oslo National College of Art, Crafts and Design from 1936-41, 1945-56. Designed the Norwegian Pavilion at the 1937 Paris exhibition for which he was made a knight of the French Legion of Honor. Collaborated with Jørn Utzon on several Norwegian competitions including the Oslo Central Railway Station, 1947. Headed the group of Norwegian architects – PAGON – at the CIAM congress in 1950. Collaborated with Christian Norberg-Schulz on projects including Atrium Houses, 1951, and urban plan for central Oslo, 1952-53. Won the Grand Prix at the 1954 Milan Triennale. Professor of Architecture, Technical University of Trendheim, 1956-68.

Born in Bremen, Germany. Noted for his ability to integrate principles of orthodox modernism, Expressionism, and the tenets of *das Neue Bauen* (new building), a design philosophy articulated by Hugo Häring. Studied architecture at the Technical University in Berlin-Charlottenburg. Committed to an organic ideal according to which form becomes an expression of programmatic function. Professor of Architecture, Academy of Arts, Breslau (now Wroclaw, Poland) (1925-32). Participated in re-establishing the architectural faculty of the Berlin Technical University, where he was a senior professor in the town-planning department, 1946-58. Major works include the Berlin Philharmonic Hall (1959-63) and the Senate Library, Berlin, completed after his death (1967-78).

Ludwig Mies van der Rohe
1886-1969

Pierre Chareau
1883-1950

Arne Korsmo
1900-1968

Hans Scharoun
1893-1972

ルードヴィッヒ・ミース・ファン・デル・ローエ
1886～1969

ピエール・シャロウ
1883～1950

アルネ・コルスモ
1900～1968

ハンス・シャロウン
1893～1972

ドイツのアーヘンに生まれたミースは、二つの大陸（ヨーロッパとアメリカ）で20世紀における最も影響力の大きい建築家、デザイナー、教育者の一人であった。1900～02年、家業であった石材業に従事し、1905～07年に建築家のブルーノ・パウル、1908～11年にペーター・ベーレンスのもとで修業を積む。1930年から1933年までバウハウスの校長を務める。1911～14年／1919～37年にベルリン、1938～69年にシカゴで設計活動を行う。1938～59年、イリノイ工科大学建築学科のディレクターを務める。1921年に創刊された『G（Gestaltung）』誌の創立者の一人。1926～32年、ドイツ工作連盟の初代副会長、1927年にシュトゥットガルトのヴァイゼンホーフ・ジードルングで行われた工作連盟展および1931年のベルリン・ビルディング展における「住宅」部門のディレクターを務める。1938年に米国に移住し、帰化する。主な作品に、バルセロナ万博ドイツ館（1929）、レイク・ショア・ドライヴ・アパートメンツ（1951）、ファンズワース邸（1950）、IITクラウン・ホール（1956）、シーグラム・ビル（1958）、ナショナルギャラリー（ベルリン、1968）などがある。著書に、『Der moderne Zweckbau』（1926）。ミースに関する出版物に『Mies van der Rohe』（フィリップ・ジョンソン著、1947）などがある。1960年、A.I.A.ゴールドメダル受賞。

ル・アブレの船主の息子として、フランス、ボルドーに生まれる。1900～08年、パリのエコール・デ・ボザールで絵画、音楽、建築を学ぶ。1908～14年、高級家具店のウェアリング・アンド・ギローで家具デザインの修業を積む。第一次世界大戦後の1918年に自らの事務所を設立。最初の仕事は、医師のダグラス夫妻のアパートメントの改装、およびオリジナル家具（翌年、サロン・ドートンヌで展示された）のデザインだった。合板、黒檀、パーム、金属管といった材料の革新的な使用で知られている。ベルナルド・ベイフォートと協働（1925～35）。1928年にガラスの家のデザインを依頼される。ユニオン・デ・アーティステ・モダーン（UAM）の創設者の一人であったシャロウは、アカデミズムにとらわれず、妥協を許さない態度で知られていた。1940年にニューヨークへ移り、画家のロバート・マザウェルの住宅をデザインした。

ノルウェー、オスロに生まれる。コルスモは、スカンジナヴィアで最初の機能主義者の一人として記憶されている。1920～26年、トロントハイムの工科大学で教育を受ける。スヴェール・アースランドとともに1929年に事務所を設立。建築、家具、舞台セット、工業デザインなど幅広くデザイン活動を行う。1936～41年、オスロ美術・工芸・デザイン国立大学のインテリア・デザイン学科インストラクター、1945～56年に同学科長を務める。1937年のパリ博でノルウェー館を設計し、フランスのレジョン・ド・ヌール勲章を受けた。オスロ中央駅舎（1947）をはじめとするいくつかのノルウェーの設計競技でデンマーク人建築家のヨルン・ウッツォンと協働。1950年のCIAM会議においてノルウェー建築家のグループ（PAGON）の代表を務めた。アトリウム・ハウス（1951）、オスロ中心部の都市計画（1952～53）などのプロジェクトでクリスチャン・ノルベルグーシュルツと協働。1954年、ミラノ・トリエンナーレでグランプリを受賞。1956～68年、トロントハイム工科大学建築学科教授。

ドイツ、ブレーメンに生まれる。正統的なモダニズム、表現主義の原則、およびフーゴ・ヘーリンクによって表現されたデザイン思想、ノイエ・バウエン（新建築）の教義を統合したことで知られる。ベルリンのシャルロッテンブルクの工科大学で建築を学ぶ。形態がプログラムの機能の表現となる有機的理想に傾倒した。1925～32年、ブレスラウ（現ポーランド、ヴロツワフ）の芸術アカデミーにおいて建築学科の教授を務める。1946年から58年まで都市計画学科の助教授を務めたベルリン工科大学で、建築学科の再建に努めた。代表作に、ベルリン交響楽団ホール（1959～63）と彼の死後に完成したベルリンの国立図書館（1967～78）がある。

Born in Stockholm and generally considered Sweden's leading Interwar architect. Educated at the Royal Institute of Technology, Stockholm, 1905-09. Worked for architects Tengbom, Westman and Östberg, 1910-11. In private practice, Stockholm, 1911-40. His steel and glass Stockholm Exhibition design, 1928-30, was heralded as a revolution in Scandinavian modern architecture. Professor of Architecture at the Royal Institute of Technology, Stockholm, 1931-40. Editor, *Arkitektur*, 1917-20. Major projects include Snellman villa, 1918; Woodland Chapel, Stockholm South Cemetery, 1918-20; Pavilion, Paris Exposition of 1925, 1922-24, and Stockholm Public Library, 1920-28.

Born in Berlin. Educated at the Humanistisches Gymnasium, Berlin, 1903; Technical University, Munich, 1903-04; Technical University, Charlottenburg, Berlin, 1905-07. Apprenticed at the office of Peter Behrens, 1907-10. Early practice in association with Adolf Meyer and devotion to advocating the social needs and economic benefits of mass-produced housing. Founded the Bauhaus in 1919 to bring together all of the arts; director 1919-28. Founder-Member and President, 1928, and Vice-President, 1929-57, CIAM. Exiled to London in 1934 and collaborated with Maxwell Fry, 1934-36. Professor of Architecture, Harvard Graduate School of Design, 1937-52; Chairman of the Department of Architecture, 1938-52. Founder/Partner with seven associates, The Architects Collaborative (TAC), 1946-69. Visited Japan in 1954. Major works include Fagus Factory (with Adolf Meyer) Alfeld, Germany, 1912; Werkbund Exhibition (with Adolf Meyer) Cologne, Germany, 1914; Bauhaus, Dessau, Germany, 1926; Harvard Graduate Center, 1949; Pan American Building (with Pietro Belluschi) NY, 1957. Major publications include *Internationale Architektur*, 1925; *The New Architecture and the Bauhaus*, 1935, *The Scope of Total Architecture*, 1955.

Born in Buenos Aires. Studied engineering, navigation, and aviation at the School of Engineering, University of Buenos Aires, 1931-34; Faculty of Architecture, 1938-41. Represented the Argentine CIAM along with Bonet, Ferrari Hardoy and Kurchan. Major projects include Hall for Visual Spectacle and Sound in Space, 1943-1953, and Office Building for Buenos Aires, 1948. 1st site architect for Le Corbusier's Maison Curutchet, 1949. Received the Gold Medal, *World's Fair*, Brussels, 1958. Selected in 1968 to be the Argentine consultant to Walter Gropius in designing the new German Embassy for Buenos Aires.

Born in Vienna. Graduated in 1917 from the Technical University, Vienna, where he was taught by Adolf Loos and influenced by Otto Wagner. Worked for Erich Mendelsohn in 1921-22 and in 1923 emigrated to the US where he worked for Frank Lloyd Wright at Taliesin during the fall of 1924 and collaborated on several projects with Rudolf N. Schindler before establishing his own practice. Neutra created a modern regionalism for Southern California, which combined a light metal frame with a stucco finish to create a light effortless appearance. He specialized in extending architectural space into a carefully arranged landscape. The dramatic images of flat-surfaced, industrialized residential buildings contrasted against nature were popularized by the photography of Julius Shulman. Neutra's major works include the Lovell "Health" House (1929), Strathmore Apartments (1937), and the Tremaine House (1948). Publications include *Wie Baut Amerika?* (1927), *Survival Through Design* (1954), *Life and Shape* (1962).

Erik Gunnar Asplund
1885-1940

エリック・グンナー・アスプルンド
1885〜1940

Walter Gropius
1883-1969

ウォルター・グロピウス
1883〜1969

Amancio Williams
1913-1989

アマンシオ・ウィリアムズ
1913〜1989

Richard Neutra
1892-1970

リチャード・ノイトラ
1892〜1970

ストックホルムに生まれる。スウェーデンを代表する建築家。主に二つの大戦の間の時代に活躍した。1905〜09年、ストックホルムの王立工科大学で建築教育を受ける。1910〜11年、建築家のテングボム、ヴェストマン、エストベリのもとで働く。1911年から40年までストックホルムで設計活動を行う。鉄とガラスを巧みに用いた1930年のストックホルム博覧会の会場デザインを通して、スウェーデンにおけるモダニズムの幕開けを世界的に印象づけた。1931〜40年、王立工科大学建築学科教授を務める。1917〜20年、「Arkitektur」誌の編集者。主な作品に、スネルマン邸 (1918)、ウッドランド墓地 (1918〜20)、1925年パリ万博パヴィリオン (1922〜24)、ストックホルム市立図書館(1920〜28)などがある。

ベルリンに生まれる。1903年にベルリンのフマニスティシェス・ギムナジウムで、1903〜04年にミュンヘンの工科大学で、1905〜07年にベルリン、シャルロッテンブルクの工科大学で教育を受ける。1907〜10年、ペーター・ベーレンスの事務所で修業を積む。活動の初期において、アドルフ・マイヤーとともに量産住宅の社会的必要性と経済的恩恵を唱導する活動に取り組んだ。1919年、あらゆる芸術の統合を目指してバウハウスを創立。1919〜28年まで学長を務める。CIAMの創立メンバーで、1928年に総裁、1929〜57年に副総裁を務める。1934年にロンドンに亡命し、1934〜36年、マクスウェル・フライと協働。1937〜52年、ハーヴァード・グラデュエート・スクール・オヴ・デザインの建築学科教授。1938〜52年には建築学科チェアマンも務める。1946年に七人のアソシエイトとTACを創設しパートナーとなる。1954年に日本を訪れる。主な作品に、ファグス靴工場 (マイヤーと共作、アルフェルド、1912)、工作連盟展 (マイヤーと共作、1914)、バウハウス校舎 (デッサウ、1926)、ハーヴァード・グラデュエート・センター (1949)、パン・アメリカン・ビルディング (ピエトロ・ベルスキと共作、1957) など。主な著作に、『国際建築』(1925)、『New Architecture and the Bauhaus』(1935)、『生活空間の創造』(1955) などがある。

ブエノスアイレスに生まれる。1931〜34年、ブエノスアイレス大学工学部でエンジニアリング、航空学、飛行術を、1938〜41年、建築を学ぶ。ボネット、フェラリ・ハードイ、およびクーチャンとともにCIAMアルゼンチンを代表する。主な作品に、視覚スペクタクルと宇宙における音のホール(1943〜53)、ブエノスアイレスのオフィス・ビル (1948) などがある。1949年に、ル・コルビュジエが設計したクルチェット邸の主任現場建築家を務める。1958年、ブリュッセルのワールド・フェアでゴールド・メダルを受賞。1968年、ブエノスアイレスのドイツ大使館の設計において、ウォルター・グロピウスのコンサルタントを務める。

ウィーンに生まれる。1917年にウィーン工科大学を卒業。ノイトラは大学でアドルフ・ロースの教えを受け、オットー・ワグナーの影響を受けた。1921〜22年、エーリッヒ・メンデルゾーンのもとで働く。1923年に米国に移民し、1924年の秋にタリアセンのフランク・ロイド・ライトのもとで働き、独立する前にルドルフ・M・シンドラーと共同でいくつかのプロジェクトを手がけた。ノイトラは、軽やかな外観をつくりだすために軽いメタル・フレームをスタッコ仕上げと組み合わせ、南カリフォルニアの近代的なリージョナリズムを創出した。彼は、注意深くアレンジされたランドスケープに建築空間を拡張することを得意とした。自然と対照的な、平らな表面の工業化された住宅の劇的なイメージは、ジュリアス・シュールマンの写真を通して一般に普及した。ノイトラの代表作には、ロヴェル「健康」住宅 (1929)、ストラスモア・アパートメンツ (1937)、トレメイン邸 (1948) などがある。著書に『Wie Baut Amerika?』(1927)、『Survival Through Design』(1954)、『Life and Shape』(1962)などがある。

Selected Bibliography
文献目録

Álvarez, Fernando. "Amancio Williams: el hombre que fue puente."*Quaderns*, 1994, n. 204, p. 40-47.

Amberg, Anna-Lisa and Juhani Pallasmaa. *Hvitträsk: The Home as a Work of Art*. (1997)

Arts Council of Great Britain, *The Architecture of Adolf Loos: an Arts Council Exhibition*. (1985)

Banham, Reyner. *Theory and Design in the First Machine Age*. (1960-1995)

バンハム、レイナー、『第一機械時代の理論とデザイン』石原達二、増成隆士訳、鹿島出版会、1976年。

Benton, Tim. *The Villas of Le Corbusier* 1920-1930. (1987)

——, ed. *Form and Function : a source book for the history of architecture and design 1890-1939*. (1975)

Brown, E. *Casas Latinoamericanas: Latin American Houses*. (1994)

Büller, Lenneke, ed. *The Rietveld Schröder House*. (1992)

Caldenby, Claes and Olof, Hultin. *Asplund*, Arkitektur Forlag, (1985)

Colomina, Beatriz. *Privacy and Publicity: Modern Architecture as Mass Media*. (1996)

コロミーナ、ベアトリス、『マスメディアとしての近代建築：アドルフ・ロースとル・コルビュジェ』、松畑強 訳、鹿島出版会、1996年。

Conrads, Ulrich, ed. *Programs and Manifestoes on 20th-Century Architecture*. (1970)

Connors, Joseph. *The Robie House of Frank Lloyd Wright*. (1984)

Cruickshank, Dan, ed. *AJ Masters of Building* "Erik Gunnar Asplund" (1988)

Dunster, David. *Key Buildings of the 20th century 1&2*. (1985, 1990)

Ford, Edward R. *Details of Modern Architecture*. Vol. I [1879-1948]. (1990)

——. *Details of Modern Architecture*. Vol. II [1828-1988]. (1996)

フォード、エドワード・R、『巨匠たちのディテールVol.1』、八木幸二訳、丸善、 1999年。

Ford, James and Katherine Morrow Ford. *Classic Modern Homes of the Thirties*. (1940, 1989)

Frampton, Kenneth. "Maison de Verre," *Perspecta* (The Yale Architectural Journal), No. 12, 1969, pp.77-126.

——. *Modern Architecture: A Critical History*.(1980, 1985, 1992)

「現代建築への道程」中村敏男訳、『a+u』1985年1月号～1988年7月号。

Frieman, Ziva. "Back to Neutra," *Progressive Architecture*. 1995 Nov., v.76, n.11, pp.72-79.

Geist, Johann Friedrich. *Hans Scharoun, Chronik zu Leben und Werk*. (1993)

Gephard, David. *Rudolph Schindler*. (1972)

Gephard, David and Patricia; Marla C. Berns, ed. *The Furniture of R. M. Schindler*. (1996)

Giedion, Sigfried. *Walter Gropius: Work and Teamwork*. (1954)

——. *Space, Time and Architecture*. (1941, 1967)

ギーディオン、ジークフリート、『空間・時間・建築1・2 』大田実訳、丸善、1955年。

——. *Architecture You and Me* (1958)

『現代建築の発展』生田勉，樋口清　訳，みすず書房，1961年。

Gravagnuolo, Benedetto. *Adolf Loos, theory and works*. (1982)

Gropius, Walter. "Towards a Living Architecture," *American Architect*, January/February 1938.

Hay, David. "A Modernist Masterpiece in the Desert Is Reborn," *Architectural Record*. September 1999, pp. 92-98.

Heidegger, Martin. "Building, Dwelling, Thinking." in *Poetry, Language, Thought*. (1977)

Hines, Thomas S. *Richard Neutra and the Search for Modern Architecture*. (1982,1994)

Hitchcock, Henry-Russell Jr. *Architecture of the Nineteenth and Twentieth Centuries*. (1958, 1987)

Hitchcock, Henry-Russell Jr. and Philip Johnson. *The International Style*. (1932)
ヒッチコック、ヘンリー＝ラッセル、ジョンソン、フィリップ、『インターナショナルスタイル』、武澤秀一訳、鹿島出版会、1994年。

Hoffmann, Donald. *Frank Lloyd Wright's Robie House*. (1984)

Irace Fulvio, "Amancio Williams," *Abitare* 1995 July-Aug.,n.342, p.108-[111].

Jaffe, H.L.C. *De Stijl, 1917-1931*. (1956, 1986)

James, Warren A. "Preservation: Corb in context," *Progressive Architecture* 1989. April, v.70., no.4, p.22.

Kinoshita, Toshiko. "English modern houses in the 30's," *a+u: architecture and urbanism* 1997 July, n.7(322), pp.138-143; 1997 Sept., n.9(324), pp.[3]-9; 1998 Mar., n.3(330), pp.102-107.
「30年代イギリスのモダンハウス」『a+u』1997年7月号No.322、138〜143頁、1997年9月号No.324、3〜9頁、1998年3月号No.330、102〜107頁。

Lahiji, Nadir and D.S. Friedman, eds. *Plumbing: sounding modern architecture*. (1997)

Lapunzina, Alejandro. *Le Corbusier's Maison Curutchet*. (1997)

Le Corbusier. *Towards a New Architecture*. (1923, 1960)
ル・コルビュエ、『建築をめざして』、吉阪隆正 訳、鹿島出版会、1972年。

——. *Précisions*. (1930, 1991)
『プレシジョン』、井田安弘、芝優子 訳、鹿島出版会、1984年。

——. *Une Petite Maison*. (1954)
『小さな家』、森田一敏 訳、集文社、1980年。

Lizon, Peter. *Villa Tugendhat in Brno*. (1996)

——. "Mies Imperative: A Total Design- Villa Tugendhat in Bruno is Open to Public," *a+u* 1997 April, n.4 (319), pp.3-13.
「ミースの規範：トータルデザイン―ブルノのテューゲントハット邸の公開」『a+u』 1997年4月号No. 319、3〜13頁。

Luciani, Roberta. "Korsmo and Oslo," *Domus* 1998 Dec., n.810, p.[129-136]

March, Lionel and Judith Sheine eds. *RM Schindler: Composition and Construction*. (1993)

——(text), Yukio Futagawa (editor and photographer). *Rudolph M Schindler, Global Architecture 77*. (1999)
GAグローバル・アーキテクチュア No.77 ＜ルドルフ・シンドラー＞ シンドラー自邸 1921-22 ハウ邸 1925 文 マーチ、ライオネル。

Manson, Grant C. *Frank Lloyd Wright to 1910: the first golden age*. (1958)

McCoy, Esther. *Case Study Houses 1945-1962*. (1977)

——. *Five California Architects*. (1960)

Mock, Elizabeth. *Built in U.S.A: 1932-1944*. (1945)

——. *Tomorrow's Small House*. (1941)

Mulder, Bertus and Ida van Zijl. *Rietveld Schröder House*. (1997)

Münz, Ludwig. *Adolf Loos*. (1989)

Muthesius, Hermann. *The English House*. (1904, 1979)

——. *Style-Architecture and Building-Art: Transformations in the Nineteenth Century and its Present Condition*. (1902, 1994)

Niedenthal, Simon. "'Glamourized Houses': Neutra, Photography, and the Kaufmann House," *Journal of Architectural Education*, November 1993, pp. 101-112.

Nicolin, Pierluigi. ed. "Living in Architecture," *Lotus International* 60. (1989)

Nelson, Paul. "Maison de Verre," *L'Architectured'Aujourd'hui*, no. 9, November-December 1933.

Neumeyer, Fritz. *The Artless Word*. (1991)

Norberg-Schulz, Christian. *The Functionalist Arne Korsmo*. (1986)

Overy, Paul. *De Stijl*. (1991)

Pallasmaa, Juhani. *The Melnikov House, Moscow*. (1996)

Pfeiffer, Bruce B. and Gerald Nordland, ed. *Frank Lloyd Wright: In the Realm of Ideas*. (1987)

Doubilet, Susan. "Preservation: Tugendhat House" *Progressive Architecture* 1989 April, v.70. no.4, p.21, 26, 28.

Reichlin, Bruno. " 'Une petite maison' on Lake Léman," *Lotus International*. no. 60, 1988/4, p.58-77.

Riley, Terence. *The International Style: exhibition 15 and the Museum of Modern Art*. (1992)

——. *The Un-Private House*. (1999)

Risselada, Max, ed. *Raumplan versus Plan Libre: Adolf Loos and Le Corbusier*. (1988)

Rowe, Colin. *The Mathematics of the Ideal Villa and Other Essays*. (1977)
ロウ、コーリン、『マニエリスムと近代建築：コーリン・ロウ建築論選集』、伊東豊雄、松永安光訳、彰国社、1981年。

Rykwert, Joseph. "Adolf Loos: the new vision," *Studio International*. July/August. 1973, 17-21.

Scharoun, Hans. *Hans Scharoun : Bauten, Entwürfe, Texte*. (1974)

Silvetti, Jorge, ed. *Amancio Williams*. (1987)

Starr, S. Frederick. *Melnikov: solo architect in a mass society*. (1978)

Stirling, James. "From Garches to Jaoul. Le Corbusier as domestic architect in 1927 and in 1953," *Architectural Review*. September 1955.

Steele, James. *How House: RM Schindler*. (1996)

Tegethoff, Wolf. *Mies van der Rohe: The Villas and Country Houses*. (1985)

Treib, Mark "A Reconciliation with History: Gunnar Asplund and Architecture Past," *a+u, architecture and urbanism* 1991 April, n.4 (247), pp.38-65.
トライブ、マーク、「歴史との和解：グンナー・アスプルンドと建築の過去」『a+u』1994年4月号No.247、38〜65頁。

Vellay, Marc. *Pierre Chareau, architect and craftsman, 1883-1950*. (1985)

Vellay, Marc and Kenneth Frampton. *Pierre Chareau, Architect and Craftsman, 1883-1950*. (1986)

"Villa Damman," *Byggekunst*. 6/1985. p. 310-317.

von Vegesack, Alexander, ed. *Mies van der Rohe: architecture and design in Stuttgart, Barcelona, Brno*. (1998)

Wagner, Otto. *Modern Architecture*. (1896 & 1988)
ヴァーグナー、オットー『近代建築—学生に与える建築手引き』、樋口清、佐久間博訳、中央口論美術出版、1985年。

Williams, Amancio. *Amancio Williams*. (1987, 1990)

Wrede, Stuart. *The Architecture of Erik Gunnar Aspund*. (1980)
スチュアート、レーデ、『アスプルンドの建築：北欧近代建築の黎明』、樋口清、武藤章 訳、鹿島出版会、1982年。

Wright, Frank Lloyd. *Frank Lloyd Wright: Collected Writings*, 5 v. (1992-)

Wright, Gwendolyn. *Moralism and the Modern Home: 1870-1913*. (1980)

——. *Building the Dream: A Social History of Housing in America*. (1981)

Yorke, F.R.S. *The Modern House*. (1934)

Born in 1928 in UK. Professor Kenneth Frampton holds the position of Ware Professor of Architecture at Columbia University. He is an architect and architectural historian. He was educated at the Architectural Association at London and has worked as an architect in England, Israel and the United States. From1964 to 1972 he was a member of the faculty at the School of Architecture at Princeton University, and since 1972 he became a fellow of the Institute for Architecture and Urban Studies in New York and was a co-founding editor of its magazine Oppositions. In 1988 he served as a member of the jury for the Alvar Aalto Medal Committee and was President of the EEC Jury to Award a Prize to a Building built in the European Economic Community, Mies van der Rohe Foundation, Barcelona, Spain. He has written extensivery and contributed to numerous journals internationally. His publications include *Modern Architecture: A Critical History*, *Modern Architecture 1851 to 1945*, and *Studies in Tectonic Culture*. *Portrait by Dorothy Alexander.*

A recognised specialist on Le Corbusier, Bruno Reichlin is a practicing architect, critic and teacher based in Switzerland. He is Professor of Architecture at the École d'Architecture at the University of Geneva and is in architectural practice with Fabio Reinhart in Lugano since 1970. He has published widely on contemporary and modern architecture and curated a number of exhibitions, including "De Stijl et l'architecture en France" (1985) and "L'aventure Le Corbusier"in Paris (1987). *Portrait courtesy of the author.*

Born in 1953 in Königswinter, Nordrhein-Westfalen, Germany. 1974-78, studied history, economic history, and urban planning at the University of Bonn. Studied at Columbia University, New York on a Fulbright scholarship, 1978-79 and at University of Bonn, 1979-81. Received his Ph. D. in art history, University of Bonn, May 1981 . 1978-79, Research Assistant at the Mies van der Rohe Archive, The Museum of Modern Art, New York. 1981-87, Assistant Professor at the Department of Art History, University of Kiel, Germany. 1987-91, Vice-Director (1989-91 acting Director), Zentralinstitut für Kunstgeschichte, Munich. Since 1991 Director, Zentralinstitut für Kunstgeschichte, Munich. *Portrait courtesy of the author.*

Kenneth Frampton

Bruno Reichlin

Wolf Tegethoff

Authors
筆者略歴

ケネス・フランプトン

ブルーノ・ライヒリン

ヴォルフ・テゲトフ

1928年、英国に生まれる。コロンビア大学建築学科教授で、フランプトンは歴史家として知られているが、AAスクール出身の建築家であり、英国、イスラエル、米国で設計活動を行った。彼の書く歴史や評論に建物の具体的説明が多いのもこのためである。彼の立場はフランクフルト学派に与するもので、ポスト・ストラクチュアリズムの趨勢のなかでモダニズムの成熟を望んでいる。クリティカル・リージョナリズムすなわち批判としての地域主義はそのための段階の一つとみられる。アングロ・サクソンの批評家として言説過剰に陥ることなく、資本主義体制、消費社会機構、情報化社会にたいして批判的姿勢を崩さず、技術と労働と人間を視点としての執筆をしている。著書には『Modern Architecture: A Critical History（モダン・アーキテクチュア：ア・クリティカル・ヒストリー)』(「現代建築への道程」として本誌に翻訳連載された)、『Modern Architecture 1851 to1945（モダン・アーキテクチュア　1851～1945)』と『Studies in Tectonic Culture（技術文化の研究)』がある。

ル・コルビュジエの研究者として知られているブルーノ・ライヒリンは、建築家、評論家、そして教育者としてスイスで活躍している。彼はジュネーヴ大学建築学部の教授であり、また1970年以来、ルガーノでファビオ・ラインハルトとともに建築設計を行っている。ライヒリンには、デ・スティルとフランスについての論考（1985）、パリにおけるル・コルビュジエについての考察（1987）など現代建築、近代建築に関する著作がある。また、キュレーターとして展覧会の企画にも携わっている。

1953年、ドイツ、ノルト・ラインのケーニッヒスヴィンターに生まれる。1974～78年、ボン大学で歴史、経済史、都市計画を学ぶ。1978～79年、フルブライト奨学生として、ニューヨークのコロンビア大学に学ぶ。さらに1979～81年、ボン大学に学び、1981年、美術史の博士号を取得。1978～79年、ニューヨーク近代美術館のミース・ファン・デル・ローエ・アーカイヴの研究助手、1981～87年、ドイツのキール大学美術史学科の助教授、1987～91年、ミュンヘンの造形芸術中央研究所の副ディレクターを経て、1991年以来、同研究所でディレクターを勤めている。

Born in 1942. He is a partner of ARCOOP Architects Zurich. Professor at Federal Institute of Technology (ETH) in Zurich since 1971. He researches in the field of Design (Le Corbusier, Wohnbedart), and polychromy and construction in 20th century architecture.
Portrait courtesy of the author.

Born in Colorado, USA in 1965. Graduated from Harvard College with an A.B. degree, *magna cum laude* in 1988 and the University of California at Berkeley with a M. Arch degree in 1993. Fulbright scholar at the Tokyo Institute of Technology from 1994-95. Ph.D. candidate in Modern Architectural History and Theory under the direction of Kenneth Frampton and Gwendolyn Wright at Columbia University. Presently a visiting researcher at Tokyo University. Publications include the 9-part series, "The Modern House in the Postwar Period," *a+u*, [1997-2000] and essays on modern architecture and urbanism in *Japan Architect, Shinkenchiku, Kenchiku Bunka*, and *the Journal of the Society of Architectural Historians.*
Portrait courtesy of the author.

Born in Kobe, Japan in 1969. Graduated from Japan Women's University with a Bachelor of Science degree in 1993, Shibaura Institute of Technology with a Master of Science degree in 1995 and University of London with a Master of Arts degree in 1996. Rotary Foundation scholar at the Mackintosh School of Architecture from 1996-97. Lecturer in architectural history at Tokyo Science University. Publications include a 4-part series "English Modern Houses in the 30s," *a+u* (1997-98) and "The Heyday of the Modern House in Denmark," *Space Design* (1996.9).
Portrait courtesy of the author.

Arthur Rüegg

アルトゥール・リュエッグ

1942年生まれ。現在、チューリッヒの建築事務所ARCOOPのパートナー。1971年以降スイス連邦工科大学 (ETH) の教授を務める。コルビュジエやヴォーンベダルトを中心に建築デザインについて研究し、さらに20世紀の建築の多彩性や構造についても研究している。

Guest Editors
ゲスト・エディター略歴

Ken Tadashi Oshima

ケン・タダシ・オオシマ

1965年、米国コロラド州に生まれる。1988年にハーヴァード大学を2位の成績で卒業後、1993年にカリフォルニア大学バークレー校にて修士課程修了。1994～95年、フルブライト奨学生として東京工業大学で学ぶ。現在、コロンビア大学でケネス・フランプトンおよびグエンドリン・ライトの指導のもと、近代建築史および理論における博士号の取得に向けて研究を行う。また現在、東京大学研究員。『a+u』9回シリーズの「戦後の現代住宅」(1997～2000) をはじめ、近代建築と都市に関するエッセイを『JA』『新建築』『建築文化』『the Journal of the Society of Architectural Historians』などに多数執筆。

Toshiko Kinoshita

木下壽子

1969年、兵庫県神戸市に生まれる。1993年、日本女子大学家政学部住居学科卒業。1995年に芝浦工業大学大学院修士課程修了後、1996年にロンドン大学大学院修士課程を修了。1996～97年、ロータリー財団国際親善奨学生としてグラスゴー大学マッキントッシュ建築学校で研究を行う。現在、東京理科大学非常勤講師および『a+u』エディトリアル・アソシエイトを務める。『a+u』4回シリーズの「30年代イギリスのモダン・ハウス」(1997～98)、「デンマーク・モダンハウスの最盛期」(『SD』1996年9月号) など、近代建築に関するエッセイの執筆、翻訳を手がける。

Credits for Essay Photographs and Drawings
エッセイ図版クレジットおよび出典

Introduction: Towards a Vision of the Real

Photographs
p. 8: Toshiko Kinoshita.
p. 13, bottom: from *a+u*.
p. 15: from *Shinkentiku* January, 1935, volume 11.
All photographs except the above: *Shinkenchiku-sha*.

Manifestoes of the Modern House

p. 56
Left: From *Towards a New Architecture*, Le Corbusier, Praeger Publishers, New York-Washington, 1970 (4th printing), pp. 222-223.
Middle: From "Building," *G*, no.2 (September 1923).
Right: Poster for the Werkbund exhibition
"The Dwelling," Stuttgart, 1927.
Die Baumeister, Ludwig Mies van der Rohe, and Werner Gräff.

Stories of Windows

Essay originally published in *The Architecture of the Window*, Vittorio Magnago Lampugnani, ed. YKK Architectural Products Inc., 1995.
Photographs
p. 80: ©FLC L2 (4) 1-190/ADAGP, Paris & SPDA, Tokyo, 2000.
p. 89, top: ©FLC L2 (5) 19/ADAGP, Paris & SPDA, Tokyo, 2000.
All photographs except the above: *Shinkenchiku-sha*.
All drawings by the author.

Dialogue with Kenneth Frampton

Photographs
p. 139: John Nicolais.
p. 140, top: Hideyuki Takagi.
p. 140, bottom: Alo Zanetta.
p. 143, top: Balthasar Burkhard.
pp. 143, 145: Toshiko Kinoshita.
All photographs except the above: *Shinkenchiku-sha*.

Ludwig Mies van der Rohe's Tugendhat House: A Model Home of Its Time?

Photographs:
pp. 161, 163, 165 left: Fritz Tugendthat.
p. 165 right: de Sandalo.
p. 167: unknown photographer.
Photos on pp. 161, 163, 165, 167: ©Danela Hammer-Tugendhat, Wien/Zentralinstitut für Kunstgeschichte, München.
All photographs except the above: *Shinkenchiku-sha*.

On Color Restoration of the Villa Savoye

Photograph
p. 198: *Shinkenchiku-sha*.

Acknowledgements
謝辞

Our role as guest editors for this special issue initially emerged from our individual series of articles in the monthly edition of *a+u* from 1997 on modern houses. These articles reexamined houses from the 20th century, which while lesser known than iconic works such as Le Corbusier's Villa Savoye, expressed a vision for new living in their particular time. These houses were of both nostalgic interest to older readers and had a sense of newness to younger readers. Subsequently, plans arose to produce a special year 2000 issue of *a+u* on the theme "Modern Houses in the 20th Century" and to our great fortune, we were entrusted with the responsibility to oversee its assembly. Thus began what would become a nearly three-year attempt to reexamine the wealth of fine examples of existing modern houses from around the world. In order to grasp the wide-ranging geographical and chronological span of the 20th century house, we received advice and most generous guidance from many individuals. In particular, we are especially indebted to the invaluable editorial advice of Professors Kenneth Frampton and Gwendolyn Wright of Columbia University as well as Terence Riley, chief curator of architecture and design at the Museum of Modern Art. This project would not have been possible without the most gracious cooperation of the individual owners of these homes and organizations entrusted with the preservation of important drawings and documents. Our heartfelt appreciation goes to Evelyne Tréhin, Fondation Le Corbusier; Kurt Helfrich, University of California at Santa Barbara Archives; Ida van Zijl, Jaap Oosternhoff, Centraal Museum, Utrecht; Werkplaats voor Architectuur Utrecht; Mary Daniels, Special Collections Harvard Graduate School of Design; Elizabeth Gombosi, Harvard University Art Museums; Matilda McQuaid, Mies van der Rohe Archive, Museum of Modern Art; Society for the Preservation of New England Antiquities; Margo Stipe, FLLW Archives; FLW Home & Studio Foundation; Helena Vilímková, Muzeum Mêsta Brno; Arkitekturmuseet, Sweden; Timo Keinänen, Museum of Finnish Architecture; Pepita Ehrnrooth, Hvitträsk Museum; Claudio Williams, Archives Amancio Williams; Patricia Mendez, CEDODAL; Birgitte Sauge, Norsk Arkitekturmuseum; Bjørn Larsen, *Byggekunst*; Christine Sarin, Centre Georges Pompidou; Matthais Schirren, Stiftung Archiv der Akademie der Künste; YKK; Viktor Konstantinovich Melnikov; Sylvia Leodolter; Runé Sør-Reime; Martin Palmrich; Per Wahlman; City of Lobau; Lionel & Marueen March; Brent and Beth Harris, Marmol and Radziner. In addition, this project spanning the world would not have been possible without the generous assistance and insights of particular regions from Friedrich Achleitner, Sverre Fehn, Wolf Deitrich Heim, Christiana Hageneder, Ariela Katz, René Kural, Vittorio Magnago Lampugnani, Rishat Mullagildin, Tomoko Makita, Junichi Ishizaki, Juan Pablo Ordónes, Eeva Pelkenon, Ioanna Theocharopoulou, and Marc Treib. Furthermore, we would like to extend our profound appreciation to the following individuals who copy edited the texts and checked translations: Claire Zimmerman, Thomas Donahue, Sachiko Sugiura, Mark Brewer, Mark Oshima, Kerry Ross, Masaaki Nakada and Mari Nakahara. Together, all of the above and many more helped develop this project from initial vision to printed realization.

(TK, KTO)

私たちが今回ゲスト・エディターを務めるきっかけとなったのは、1997年からそれぞれ月刊『a+u』に執筆を開始した、モダン・ハウスに関する連載であった。ル・コルビュジエのサヴォア邸のようなイコン的存在の作品に比べると知名度は低いが、その時代の新しい生活にたいするヴィジョンを表現した優れた20世紀の住宅を取り上げたこの連載は、年配の読者には懐かしさをもって、若い読者には新鮮さをもって受けとられたようである。連載がスタートして間もなく、2000年を記念して、「20世紀のモダン・ハウス」をテーマとした『a+u』臨時増刊号の制作が企画され、幸運にも、その監修を私たち二人が担当させていただくことになった。こうして、世界各地に現存する貴重なモダン・ハウスを再検証するという、3年近くに及んだ私たちの試みが始まったのである。

20世紀のモダン・ハウスという、時間的にも地理的にも広範にわたるテーマに取り組むにあたって、実に多くの方々のご指導、ご協力を賜った。とりわけ、コロンビア大学のケネス・フランプトン教授とグウェンドリン・ライト教授、ならびにMoMAキュレーターのテレンス・ライリー氏には、大変貴重な編集上のアドヴァイスをいただいた。この場を借りて心から感謝の意を表したい。また、いうまでもなく、住宅の撮影および掲載を快く受け入れてくださった各住宅の所有者の方々、あるいは貴重な図面などの資料の調査・掲載を許可してくださった個人および機関の協力なくしては、我々の企画は実現しなかった。ル・コルビュジエ財団、カリフォルニア大学サンタ・バーバラ・アーカイヴ、ユトレヒト中央博物館、ヴェルクプラッツ・フォール・アルヒテクツール・ユトレヒト、ハーヴァード大学デザイン学部大学院特別コレクション、ハーヴァード大学美術館、MoMAミース・ファン・デル・ローエ・アーカイヴ、ニュー・イングランド古物保存協会、F.L.ライト・アーカイヴ、F.L.ライト住宅&スタジオ財団、ブルノ市立博物館、スウェーデン建築博物館、フィンランド建築博物館、ノルウェー建築博物館、ヴィトラスク博物館、CEDODAL、アマンシオ・ウィリアムズ・アーカイヴ、ルーバウ市、『Byggekunst』誌、ポンピドゥ・センター、シュティフツング・アルヒフ・デル・アカデミー・デル・キュンスト、YKK、ヴィクター・コンスタンチノヴィッチ・メルニコフ、シルヴィア・レオドルター、ルネ・ソーレイム、マーティン・パルムリッヒ、ペール・ワールマン、クラウディオ・ウイリアム、ライオネル&モウリーン・マーチ、ブレント&ベス・ハリス、以上の各氏および機関にこの場を借りて心からお礼申し上げる。加えて、世界各地の住宅を取材するにあたり、現地の方々の多大なるお力添えをいただいた。フリードリッヒ・アッハライトナー、スヴェール・フェーン、ヴォルフ・リードリッヒ・ハイム、クリスチャン・ハゲネダー、アリエラ・カッツ、レネ・クラール、ヴィットリオ・M・ランプニャーニ、リシャット・ムラギルディン、牧田知子、石崎順一、ホアン・パブロ・オルドネス、イーヴァ・ペルケノン、イオアナ・テオカロポウロ、マーク・トレイブ、以上の皆さんに感謝の意を表したい。さらに、多忙ななか、我々の原稿の校正および翻訳をお引き受けいただいた、クレア・ジマーマン、トマス・ドナヒュー、マーク・ブルーアー、マーク・オオシマ、ケリー・ロス、杉浦幸子、中田雅章、中原まり、以上の皆さんにも心からお礼申し上げる。

最後に、当初抱かれていたヴィジョンを臨時増刊号というかたちで実現させる上でお力添えをいただいた、その他の多くの方々にも、この場を借りて感謝の意を表したいと思う。

(TK、KTO)

a+u March 2000 Special Issue
Visions of the Real:
Modern Houses in the 20th Century I
Guest Editors: Ken Tadashi Oshima
and Toshiko Kinoshita

©2000 by a+u Publishing Co., Ltd.
Printed in Japan
Published by a+u Publishing Co., Ltd.
30-8 Yushima 2-chome, Bunkyo-ku,
Tokyo 113-0034, Japan
Tel: (03)3816-2935
Fax: (03)3816-2937
E-mail: au@japan-architect.co.jp
Internet:
http://www.japan-architect.co.jp/au

Publisher/Editor:
Nobuyuki Yoshida

Editorial Associates:
Erwin J.S.Viray
Marc I. Bretler

Design Consultant:
Massimo Vignelli

Advisers:
Tadao Ando, Osaka
Jacques Herzog, Basel
Toyo Ito, Tokyo
Rem Koolhaas, Rotterdam
Terence Riley, N.Y.
Bernard Tschumi, N.Y.
Michael Speaks, Los Angeles
Peter Allison, London

Editorial Staff:
Tadashi Yasuda

Planning & Advertising Dept.:
Yukinobu Takizawa

Distributor:
a+u = Architecture and Urbanism is
handled exclusively by
The Japan Architect Co., Ltd.:
Mina Watanabe
Ryugo Maru

31-2 Yushima 2-chome, Bunkyo-ku,
Tokyo 113-8501, Japan
Tel: (03)3816-2532
Fax: (03)3812-8229
E-mail:
ja-business@japan-architect.co.jp
Price Outside Japan
¥5,800 + ¥1,500 (Surface Mail)
U.S.Dollars, Sterling Pounds, German
Marks, Swiss Francs and French
Francs equivalent to the above
Japanese Yen prices are acceptable.
Payment should be converted at the
current exchange rate upon
remittance.

2000年3月臨時増刊号
20世紀のモダン・ハウス：
理想の実現I
ゲスト・エディター：
　ケン・タダシ・オオシマ／木下壽子

©建築と都市　2000年3月20日発行
定価4,800円（本体4,571円）

発行：株式会社エー・アンド・ユー
　　　東京都文京区湯島 2-30-8
　　　〒113-0034
電話：(03)3816-2935(代)
FAX：(03)3816-2937
E-mail：au@japan-architect.co.jp
Internet: http://www.japan-architect.co.jp/au
振替：00130-5-98119

発行者／編集者
吉田信之

エディトリアル・アソシエイツ
エルウィン・J・S・ビライ
マーク・I・ブレットラー

デザイン・コンサルタント
マッシモ・ヴィネリ

アドヴァイザー
安藤忠雄、大阪
ジャック・ヘルツォーグ、バーゼル
伊東豊雄、東京
レム・コールハース、ロッテルダム
テレンス・ライリー、ニューヨーク
バーナード・チュミ、ニューヨーク
マイケル・スピークス、ロサンゼルス
ピーター・アリソン、ロンドン

編集
安田董

企画・広告部
滝沢幸信

印刷：大日本印刷株式会社
取次店：トーハン・日販・大阪屋・中央社・
　　　　栗田出版・誠光堂

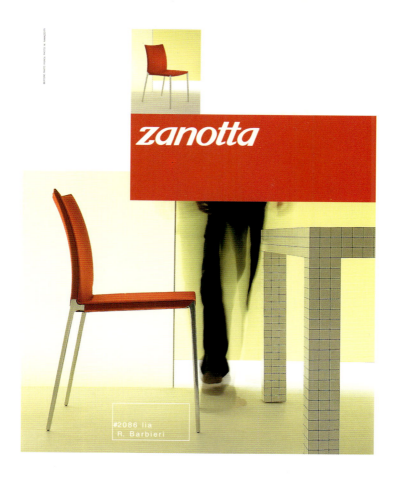

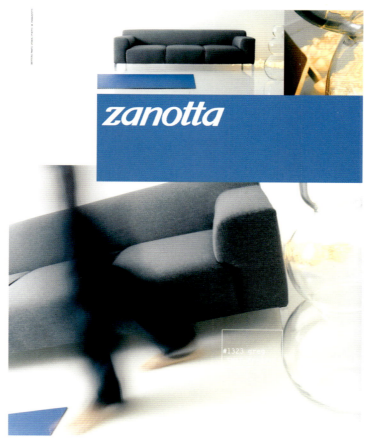

コメルツバンク［ドイツ］

クアラルンプール国際空港［マレーシア］

オフィスビルディング［オーストリア］

リーハウス［ロンドン］

世界の流れはリサイクル
天井材 シーリング

inter.office

Tel. 03-5420-4040 ［MC事業部］
http://www.interoffice.co.jp
当社では業務拡張にともない建築界からインテリア設計および営業担当の人材を求めています。
ご連絡は 03-3280-4341 人事部まで。

ヨーロッパ最大のメタルシーリングメーカー

●●●● gema